Praise for John Mills's Fiction

'... outrageous and often hilarious ...' *Ottawa Citizen*

'... intellectually taut and provocative ... ' *Toronto Star*

'... continuously funny and high-spirited ... ' *The Weekly* (Seattle)

'You cannot introduce it into a normal decent home, but if you get a taste of it, you cannot put it down ... filthy, full of four-letter words, sexual imagery, erotic extravaganza. Yes. *But*, assuming that doesn't put you off, assuming you can take it on its own terms – it is also a brilliant, blazing, rocket display of virtuosity.' *Sunday Times* (U.K.)

and now ...

Thank Your Mother for the Rabbits

The unconventional autobiography of the Canadian novelist who was a malingerer in Her Majesty's Armed Forces, a radar technician on the DEW-Line, a Gandy-dancer for the CPR, a maths crammer in an eccentric private school, friend and confidante of Irving Layton and Milton Acorn, the owner of a steam laundry in Montreal, professor of Chaucerian studies at Simon Fraser, and, after decades of atheism, a convert to Christianity.

' ... articulate mockery that suggests his uncompromising standards and complete individuality.'
Oxford Companion To Canadian Literature

Thank Your Mother for the Rabbits

JOHN MILLS

To Michael
with all my love — S.
Feb. 4/2001

The Porcupine's Quill, Inc.

CANADIAN CATALOGUING IN PUBLICATION DATA

Mills, John, 1930-
Thank your mother for the rabbits

ISBN 0-88984-160-8

1. Mills, John, 1930- - Biography. 2. Novelists, Canadian (English) – 20th century – Biography.*
I. Title.

PS8576.I57Z53 1993 C813′.54 C93-094426-7
PR9199.3.M55Z474 1993

Published by The Porcupine's Quill, Inc., 68 Main Street, Erin, Ontario N0B 1T0 with financial assistance from The Canada Council and the Ontario Arts Council. The support of the Government of Ontario through the Ministry of Culture, Tourism and Recreation is also gratefully acknowledged. Thanks to Simon Fraser University for a subvention towards publication.

Distributed by General Publishing Co. Ltd.,
30 Lesmill Road, Don Mills, Ontario M3B 2T6.

Readied for the press by John Metcalf.
Copy edited by Doris Cowan.

Cover is after the photograph 'The Potteries: Looking towards Burslem', courtesy of *The Times*.

Contents

To Elaina
and
La Vita Nuova

Foreword

THOUGH THE MATERIAL in this book is autobiographical, I have not tried to arrange it in any chronological order. This is because I can see no good reason why I should try to write a conventional autobiography. Without wanting to sound churlish about it, I am happy to leave such work to politicians, show business people, famous artists, sports celebrities, and important businessmen whose life stories, ghost-written or not, I can often read with pleasure. But in my case Fame is not the Spur. What fame I've acquired as a writer exists among a small group of Canadians interested in non-genre fiction and literary criticism – surely a minority in any country – and not enough to provoke a systematic life story. Nor do I claim that these essays deploy a strong and idiosyncratic style that would make them literature in their own right. Nevertheless, the personal essays I've published over the years have been generously enough received to encourage me to collect some of them here together with others that have so far not been in print. They deal with subjects my readers may find relevant to their own lives – jobs, travel, relationships between husbands and wives, parents and children. Concerning such matters each of us carries around his or her story – stories I am more than happy to hear. Thus and by extension I hope the reader will be happy to hear mine.

In case such a reader needs some chronological structure, let me briefly outline one here. I was born in London in 1930, educated at a grammar school in a London suburb, then won a scholarship to the University College of North Wales to study agriculture. I failed miserably at this subject, switched to 'arts', and failed that too. Mountain climbing and post-adolescent sexual explorations consumed my time and energy, as did trying to keep out of the British Army. I emigrated to Canada a year or so after my army service and worked at a variety of trades until I became a radar technician. This took me to the Mid-Canada and DEW Lines, later to Montreal where I tried to make my living as a tutor, laundryman, and financier. Much of this frenetic activity was unsuccessful until I finally solved my economic problems by getting married, escaping to Vancouver, and going back to university. By 1965 I had finished my graduate work at Stanford and got a job at the newly opened Simon Fraser University where I have been based ever since. The first few essays in this book deal with events selected from those years.

Compared to Sir Richard Burton's, or Lawrence of Arabia's, my life has not been particularly adventurous. I still get asked why I have elected to imprison myself in the 'ivory tower' of university life. When, these people ask me, am I going to get out into 'real life'? I answer that real life, even if you want to evade it (and I do not) has the habit of seeking you out. Thus the events I describe in the last part of the book – 'Unicorn Evils'. Here I struggle with a central and outwardly very minor adventure, a journey to England in 1966, whose ramifications have stayed in my mind and which I am still trying to understand. The narrative goes backwards and forwards in time and from it I have tried to grasp my own personal set of metaphors and symbols. When I wrote a first, second, third, and final version of 'Unicorn Evils' I attempted, while sticking to the facts, to employ the techniques of the novelist. I called the result, and call it now, a 'non-fiction,' a term borrowed from Truman Capote who invented it for his *In Cold Blood.* The tone of my narrative darkens as it proceeds, but I make no apologies for this. If the reader is concerned about 'real' as opposed to 'university' life here, in particular, is where he or she may find it.

Parts of 'Unicorn Evils' have already been published in *Queen's Quarterly* and in my book *Lizard in the Grass.* In both publications they appeared out of their context – indeed, I have been working on that context for a number of years. 'Memoirs of a Mud-Wrestler' was first published in *The Macmillan Anthology*, 'The Night of Lucia' in Keath Fraser's anthology *Bad Trips* (Vintage Books), 'Compassion Practicum' in *West Coast Review* and in *Best Canadian Essays of 1989*, and 'The Book of Jobs' in *The Georgia Straight.* I am most grateful to these sources for allowing me to reprint the essays in this present volume.

The Book of Jobs

THIS SUMMER (of 1975) I crept from my early forties to my middle forties – an event which, though painless, surely puts me in the ranks of the 'older generation'. My younger friends ask me what it is *like* to be so unimaginably old; is my body beginning to fail me? Do I spend my time meditating on Death, Judgement, Heaven, and Hell – the Four Last Things Ever to be Remembered? I answer that though my rock-climbing days are over, I still feel fairly spry and that I conducted my most intense exploration of the human condition – Death, the Void, the screaming fantods of *angst* – when I was about thirty. *Thirty* is the birthday to fear, I tell them, and after that one's existential agonies begin to taper off. Apart from general information of this sort there is very little about which I can advise them. Indeed, it seems to be a fact that one generation learns little from its predecessor; had it ever learned much, history would have presented a more positive image of the human lot. As it stands, however, my consciousness at, let's say, eighteen must have been very different from that of a modern teenager. For one thing my friends and I were convinced of an imminent atomic holocaust, that we would necessarily be involved in it, and that if we were to make it past twenty-two we would be lucky indeed. Every year I remain on this planet still seems to be an unexpected bonus.

Secondly, I'd been brought up in England, which since 1930, the year of my birth, had undergone a variety of sudden and dramatic changes. (I do not like the words 'progress' and 'regress' very much since, depending on the speaker, they have come to be associated with 'good' and 'bad'. So let us agree to use the verb 'gress' to denote the march of time.) By 1948, then, England had gressed in my lifetime from an economically depressed area into a country of violent political polarizations, then to a besieged, bombarded island, then to an American airstrip, then to what Arthur Koestler called 'a land of virtuous gloom' under its first post-war government. By 1948 it was a good place to get out of and much of my energy was expended in plotting a means of escape.

Thirdly, England was, as everybody knows, a class-obsessed nation and this means that depending on one's school and accent certain slots in the social system were opened up and others closed. I was working-class with a grammar school education and a strong London dialect so that I could have become a day-labourer, office worker, or bank teller, but not a plumber, electrician, diplomat, industrial tycoon, trade unionist, or Anglican clergyman. If I were willing to play my cards right I could just about have become an army officer, but of low rank, a doctor, though not a Harley Street specialist, a clerk in the civil service, but not a permanent under-secretary of state. There has been enough gress, since those days, to make such a structure look archaic, even in England, but I sense that other structures have replaced it which seem just as menacing and infrangible to young people of a particular temperament now as the future did to me. The following account of my own attempts to grapple with the World of Jobs and Careers may not, to such people, be entirely irrelevant.

I was sixteen when I first entered the job world. The exact place was London and the time a school vacation in the summer of 1946. The job involved scraping out, with cold chisels, the inside of an enormous chimney. My mentor was a wry, ancient cockney of the old regime who'd been scraping and chipping since the day he'd been invalided out of the army following the battle of the Somme.

Pointing upwards to the circle of light at the top of the chimney he said: 'That's yer wai aht, matey ... see them spikes? When yer ears an igh-pitched sort of a whistle yer wanna fuck orff up them spikes as quick as yer can. Don't look up ... you'll get a great gobba shit in the mince.'

We began to chip masses of hardened soot from the brick lining of the chimney. We hadn't been there for more than twenty minutes when a siren blew and the cockney, old enough to be my grandfather, scampered up the line of pitons with the agility of a marmoset. I shoved my chisel in my pocket and scuttled up behind him. At the top he ducked over the chimney's lip and onto a narrow, concentric roof. He beckoned me to hurry. Ten seconds after I joined him a great spout of yellow flame whooshed out of the chimney into the sky. It subsided with a bluish, monoxidey flicker while the old man counted out half a minute on an 1870 turnip watch.

'Sife ter go back,' he said. 'Remember, when that bleedin ooter goes, it pays yer to fuck orff up them spikes as quick as yer can.'

The pay for this job was fifteen bob a day – a fortune to a lad of frugal habits. It was pleasant at first because the chipping got interrupted almost every hour by the dramatic gush of the flame so that I could relax on the parapet, rest my arms, and enjoy a fine view of the factories and terrace slums of Lower Streatham, Hackbridge, and Thornton Heath. Scampering about punctured the job's monotony and fended off, for about a week, the inevitable boredom that attaches to repetitive tasks.

The cockney's pay was only slightly higher than mine, though he'd spent his manhood there, and it was obvious the job bored him as much as it did me.

'It's all fer a crust and a sleep wiv a woman,' he'd say.

He envied me my escape back into the non-job world.

I had to wait a year before I could make another experiment in bread-winning respectability. I'd smartened up a bit by then. The Game, as I saw it, was not to seek for work as such but *for status on somebody's payroll* – a very different matter. For example, I heard, while hanging around the Labour Exchange, that there was a job (known locally as a 'start') at a nearby power station where labourers were hired at the front office and sent over to one of several gangs. For a percentage of your salary a certain ganger would allow you to escape through a gap in the back fence. A man could, if he wished, walk over to a nearby construction site and work there – thus drawing two pay-cheques. My informant and I enrolled, bribed the ganger, went out the back, got starts across the street and clocked in at two jobs daily for nearly a month before the ganger was caught at his trade and fired, his men along with him. I had, however, as my mother would've put it, 'another job to fall back on'. A profitable summer.

I found that the world of casual labour thrives, fitfully, on such tricks. Most of my workmates were work-shy. There wasn't one of them who enjoyed his work, yet not one, in my experience, could be dismissed airily by the usual middle-class denunciation, 'Oh, if you gave those people leisure they wouldn't know what to do with it.' They would've known what to do with it, all right; booze, sex, dog-racing, and football pools occupied their dreams – pastimes that seem to me in no way inferior to the antique-hunting and lawn-watering practised by the white-collar worker. The fact is that to these men eight or nine hours' work was eight or nine hours gone forever with no satisfaction in it but the price of a beer.

The heart sinks right at the beginning. You approach a gate, yard, or punch-clock at some outrageous hour of the morning, located in a wasteland ravaged by the industrial revolution, with the knowledge that you will spend two-fifths of a precious day in discomfort and futility. At very few jobs of this sort have I actually *worked*. Instead there have been short, fierce bouts with intransigent matter followed by long periods of trying to avoid the ganger's eye. I admit that I have worked in jobs where I felt, for brief periods, meshed in with the activity itself – commercial fishing was one, farming was another, and such labour, though prolonged, is often strangely enjoyable. But it's industrial labour I'm complaining about – unskilled construction, ditch-digging, pick-and-shovel work for the corporation, coal-heaving, assembly-line labour – grim, hopeless non-tasks supervised by ex-provost corporals or by remote men bearing clipboards and blueprints where you spend the day wandering through acres of mud or through vast, reverberating factories, and where you used to be paid just enough to satisfy a landlord and a thirst. Prolonged association with it, among those who have neither the talent nor the ambition to escape it, leads to the boozer, the casual ward, the knacker's yard.

In my youth the non-job probably awaited eight young people out of ten – I have no idea what the figure is today. Possibly it is even gloomier; possibly there are few jobs, non or otherwise. But in 1948 it was the white-collar non-job that my friends and I worked and plotted to evade. We saw clearly enough that a job of some sort is pretty well inevitable at one stage or another in a person's life. It was the possibility that our lives would consist of a finite series of jobs, ending with death, that appalled us. What if one should discover that one lacks the talent, or the obsession, that changes a task into a vocation? What if one fails to make the big money that buys release? What, in other words, *if one is forced to become resigned – to grow up – to become 'mature?'* What if you must *learn to cut your coat according to your cloth?* All my friends of that period shared my longing for permanent work that would be socially useful, profitable, and – above all – enjoyable. I envied those amongst them who were narrow enough to have discovered, before they were twenty even, a sense of vocation – medical and engineering students and the like. All that the rest of us could see ahead was failure, or teaching, or some form of glorified clerical work.

I did an amateur sociological analysis of the 'mature' – friends and relatives of friends who were still in jobs after the age of forty. One thought seemed to keep them going – retirement. That was the goal. Until retirement they would keep busy 'adjusting' – developing hobbies like pigeon-fancying, whippet-racing, growing beans and Brussels sprouts, playing darts in pubs, and it was these hobbies that became their reality. Real life started when the five o'clock whistle blew, or it began on Friday night, ending on Monday morning. Forty years of this and then the old age pension – but by that time they were mostly too aged and knackered by a lifetime's futile expenditure of vital energy – on grappling with highways and public transport in rush hours; on paying taxes and making ends meet; on being frightened of the boss or of upstart and pushy underlings; on piecemealing out wages that remain static in times of rising costs; on mortgages and landlords – to do more than potter feebly in their backyards, vaguely aware that something was wrong, *something missing*. Like, or so I supposed, the newly released lifer on a road gang missing his ankle chain.

Naturally I asked them how they'd stood it all those years and whether they'd ever felt like making a neat pile of mortgage, insurance policy, wife and kids, and dunning letters and putting a match to it. They replied that of course they *had*, but they'd 'come to realize' that a job is an evil and inevitable feature of existence like cancer, thrombosis, vivisection, tempests, lawsuits, acts of God, napalm, central government, war, flood, aldermen, and automobiles. That a job wasn't exactly paradise, but it wasn't Buchenwald or Auschwitz either, though it runs those admittedly extreme forms of the Land of Jobs pretty close. But to a man they were resentful and embittered at the mysterious process by which they had relinquished control of their lives.

So shall it not be with us, we said. We began to make plans, many of them, in retrospect, demented. One of my first consisted of working on fishing boats for a few months and thereby saving enough money to start a sort of fishing and farming community in Norway. What in these days we call a commune. Two of us embarked on this project; we planned to set it up then send for our girl-friends later. Within a year I was back in England and in the British Army after a chain of farcical circumstances – a possibly entertaining story but irrelevant at this point. Two years passed and when I was sprung from the army I reconsidered the whole situation.

It seemed to me that Europe generally, and Britain in particular, was finished as far as penniless gentlemen of leisure were concerned. My family was far too poor to make a remittance man of me and a life dedicated to crime would have required a different kind of imagination from my own, together with a good deal more physical courage than I possess. Canada attracted me – there was a considerable amount of propaganda in its favour. It was said that a man could work in the northern part of the country and amass great sums of money he could then parlay, through legitimate business means, into a fortune. Nobody I knew altogether believed these stories, nor was anyone taken in by the assertions of the clerks at the Immigration office who told us there was full employment. Nevertheless we consulted statistics and decided that there was a genuine and even a generous margin between what the worker earned and what it cost him or her to live. Life itself, then, could not be so bleak, so slovenly, so desperate as it was in England. This I found to be true, on the whole, and I believe it remains true even now. Accordingly (and after a set of weird events from which I propose one day to carve a novel) a friend and I set foot on the Land God gave to Cain. We spent six weeks on the railroad gangs in the Algoma district of Ontario, then arrived in Toronto in the late fall of 1953 to mark time by becoming encyclopaedia salesmen.

For this job you need a white shirt, a florid tie, and an insincere smile. The books cost seven dollars to produce and we sold them door to door for two hundred. The mark-up was so huge because between consumer and producer there stretched a line of thirsty, white-collared throats. 'Smash and grab' or the 'badger game' would've been more honest. But the job had one attraction which was this: that the salesman thinks he sees an income that rises exponentially with the hours he puts in. It looks preferable, at first sight, to going straight and being thrown on the scrap-heap in middle age. The truth was, though, that it created little apart from a few dollars, high blood pressure, negativity, and enemies. One *learns about life*, of course, *one gets to know one's fellow man* and Salesmanship, as everybody knows, is the quintessence of Western culture. In those days it seemed to me that half the population of a city like Toronto existed by selling expensive-looking trash to the other half ... half the population, we said, engaged in this semi-delinquent activity! Why, it creates a pall of guilt you can smell even before the train slows through Scarborough. Half the population, and this does not include lawyers, racketeers, stock-market sharks, real-estate crooks, notaries public, dope-pushers, dentists, and others of like kidney. It was a depressing prospect.

My first crew manager, though he looked sixty, was in his middle forties. He'd sold cars, freezers, vacuum cleaners, pot-and-pan deals, and waterless cookware. He was already starting to degenerate. At the time I knew him he'd sunk to books, later it was to be magazines. And after that, of course, town relief, the United Way, finally the potter's field. What made this poor sod doubly pathetic was his ambition to become a door-to-door peddler of Bibles. He was finally taken off the job because of the shakes and I came under the control of a thin-lipped, vulpine hotshot whose specialty was selling Bibles to recent immigrants with a poor command of the language. To these he would say he was, 'from the government'.

'Oh, yah, yah,' they'd say. 'Vatever de Gov'ment vant us to buy, ve buy.' Later we were able to slough the crew managers and take off on our own through the Ontario northland, which was just then enjoying a uranium boom. There was a lot of money around and nothing to spend it on, and the pitch we used was the company's standard pitch. It appealed to our youthful cynicism (I included an account of it in my novel *The October Men*).

It took us a year to grow nauseated with this. We returned to Toronto to clean the place up. First rung of the ladder. We made plans ... to get into the bulldozer hire business ... the trucking industry. We created then abandoned a scheme for making and marketing doughnuts. And another that involved off-loading other people's inventions to manufacturers. My friend Jerome remembered that Orson Welles in *Citizen Kane* had said it might be fun to own a newspaper. We agreed; it would be fun and certainly we would own one, though it might have to wait awhile. None of these plans fructified and our money disappeared. And it came to pass that once again we found ourselves stranded in the bleak desert valleys of the World of Jobs.

Most young men and women have experienced jobs of the kind I have been describing, of that I'm certain. The difference between them and myself at their age is that then there was no youth culture. It was less easy to travel just after the war and the traveller, as I discovered to my cost on a few occasions, was usually regarded as a spy. There were few drugs. Marijuana was around, of course – it's been around for most of recorded history – but no marijuana cult. LSD was unknown and a life-style based on acid, or any other drug, did not manifest itself to me, nor would I have been much interested if it had. My friends and I were interested in beating the system on its own terms and it would never have occurred to us, as it seemed to occur to the next generation, the one before this, that you could beat it through drugs. The thoughts going through our heads at the time, though commonplace now, were alien then even to most of the people I knew of my own age. This intensified the feeling of isolation. The culture itself was a middle-aged culture and the people who rejected it were treated much as the first hippies were back in the sixties. I am not complaining about this. My encounters with the job world were nearly always abrasive but seldom heavy and usually instructive. But at this point I must come to the end of Part 1 of the Book of Jobs.

TWO

MY OWN CIRCLE of friends, all of us in our late teens, had decided as early as 1949 that the world of wage slavery so affirmed by our elders was not for us. Since we were young men and women without private means, most of us found ourselves forced, when wits failed, to revoke our own very reasonable hypotheses and go out punching clocks. I should like now to describe a white-collar experience that befell me. It was during a period in 1955 when my luck had temporarily vanished and I was at a low spiritual and economic ebb. The job yielded a meagre $290 a month and I could see that even by the standards of those days I was underpaid. I looked in vain for ways to escape. At the same time I felt that I was finished with trying to live differently ... that was all in the past. It was regular income I needed now ... no matter how paltry ... security ... sense of a job well done. I was getting too old to play about, that was what it was ... feet on the first rung of the ladder ... turn straight. I saw my future, if you can believe this, in electronics. I hated the job, naturally, but I thought it was because mine was a bad example of what jobs had to offer. Look around, I told myself, and something will turn up. I continued with my head down on the road to squaredom. It is a measure of how depressed I was that I conformed to the fifties courtship rituals (which I had previously rejected) and 'took girls out'. I even proposed to some of them. Wisely, they turned me down. It used to break me up. What's the matter with me, I thought.

The matter was that I worked as a technical writer for Canadair, an enormous aircraft plant in Montreal for, as I say, $290 a month. The word 'loser' must have been written all over me. It was, even by depressed standards, an odd place to work. The equipment, the manuals for which I was supposed to be writing, changed weekly so that what one wrote on a Monday was obsolete by the weekend. Each two weeks I drew my pay-cheque and thrust the work I had completed in the waste-paper basket. I spent most of the time trying to avoid the kapo's eye in much the same way as I had learned to grapple with hostile or over-conscientious gangers. The amount of work I did per week could have been compressed into twenty minutes – between eight and eight-twenty on a Monday morning. One day I got called in by the supervisor.

'Sit down, John,' he said. 'Just been looking at your card.' He waved my punch-card with an oily smile. 'Late twice last week,' he said. 'See – 8:02 and 8:06. Can't have that, you know.'

'Why not?' I said.

'Because our working arrangements say your hours are from eight to four-thirty with half an hour off for lunch.'

'You don't understand,' I said. 'Why should two, or even six minutes matter since things are so slack?'

'I'm not arguing with you,' he said. 'You know what the system is, or would do if you were some sort of an adult.'

'Tell you what I'll do with you,' I said. 'Whenever I get to work five minutes late I'll stay right here in the office until five o'clock. How's that?'

He rejected this on the face of it very reasonable offer and the interview ended in a shambles with him muttering something about honesty and the consequences of everybody taking such an attitude. A week later he complained about my wearing sports shirts.

'Can't have that,' he said. 'Sets a bad example. I want you to show up in a business shirt and tie.'

'What difference does it make what I wear?'

'You're meeting the public.'

'Public never comes in here.'

'The boss does, members of the board of directors do, and people see you coming in and going out. In any case, where do you think you are, Miami, Florida? I'm not arguing with you, you'll either come to work in a business shirt or go and collect your cards.'

I tried to tell him that since there was no business being conducted as far as I could see I might just as well come to work in a bathrobe or naked but for a jock-strap, but he kicked me out. I remember the faces of my co-workers when I emerged from the boss's office: stony and blank and silent, but the minds beneath them happy that one of their number had received a rocket – a little drama with someone else the victim makes the day dance more brightly and the hour of release seem closer to hand – I cursed the lot of them. Why did they not rise up and stone their oppressors? And why didn't I?

One had to sign a book every time one left the office to go to the toilet. No one knew what his neighbour earned for doing the same work. Wages were paid according to what kind of deal you could squeeze out of the personnel department. Everybody hated everybody else's guts and made up stories about one another. 'What makes you stay here?' I asked them individually. They said they didn't think things were too good on 'the outside' and in any case one job was just as lousy as another. 'I've got a wife and children,' some of them admitted. I bitched to them about working conditions. 'What's the matter with you?' they answered. 'You're getting two-ninety a month just to show up here at eight in a white shirt. No one ought to kick about that.' It was money for old rope, that was their attitude. I said it wasn't good enough. 'Things are the same everywhere,' they said. I said, 'Why $290? Why not $500? $1,000? $2,000?' They told me there were, in fact, jobs like that but you needed a degree, a brass neck, and lots and lots of bullshit. I told them I wanted work to be fun. They laughed at me. I said I thought I had an innate sense of adventure and zest for life that was going unsatisfied. They said I'd soon get over that. I was immature, that was my problem. That feeling you get that life is slipping past you, they said, you'll learn to live with it like the rest of us.

This was in the fifties and unions have made a difference to both working conditions and salaries. Nevertheless I believe that the structures of the job world remain very much the same. It is naive to question one's supervisor in the way that I tried to question mine. One starts work at an exact time and in certain types of clothing regarded as suitable not for reasons of efficiency but for reasons of law and order. It is for the job world that human beings are prepared at elementary and high school with their lists of rules, their orderly files of children marching 'neither too quickly or too slowly' (as one high school rule book I've seen puts it) into the classrooms.

Our upbringing and education are designed to cause us to internalize these structures in such a way that we can hardly do without them. This is a fact so well known, so well documented by people like Erich Fromm, Paul Goodman, and others, that it is useless to discuss it here. The question remains, why? Who benefits? At first I thought it was the supervisors who benefit, but I was clearly wrong. One's immediate boss is nearly always a fellow worker – one who has mastered the system and assimilated it well enough to function as a petty official. His salary is only slightly less trivial than one's own and he tends to work much harder. Observation convinced me that the directors, the chairmen of the board, do not benefit, for the ones I met worked sixteen hours a day and were either eaten alive with stomach ulcers or prone to keel over at fifty with coronaries. Perhaps, it occurred to me, the Marxist is right and it is the Capitalist, that Sinister Figure behind the scenes, who manipulates the rest of us. But the Marxist explanation never revealed to me why it is that those who are victims of the system acquiesce in it, and indeed, with his jargon concerning progress, means of production, proletariat, workers, etc., the Marxist seems to acquiesce in it as much as anybody.

There is but one conclusion to be drawn: *in this World of Jobs there are no winners.*

If I were more certain of my audience I would be tempted to account for the Job phenomenon as one of the consequences of the Fall – in terms of aboriginal catastrophe or Original Sin. Human nature, in other words, incorporates an inner dislocation (*vide* Dorothy L. Sayers) which forces us not only to enslave ourselves, but to turn our cities into a mixture of slums and skyscrapers and our landscapes into industrial deserts.

Though the way out, as I see it, depends on a re-invigoration of a sense of community, we are at the present time each forced to seek our own individual paths through this wilderness. Whilst at Canadair I was able to learn enough electronics and related matters to qualify as a technician. I spent the next three or four years in and out of the Arctic working on radar stations. At the beginning of 1959 I'd saved about seven thousand dollars; by the end of 1959 I was about six thousand dollars in debt. Fortune's wheel had turned, I was once more in need of money, and once again the job world yawned open before me like the jaws of a shark.

THREE

I WROTE the following account of a job experience shortly after the event and published the result in a magazine called *Edge*. It is not merely based on fact – it *is* fact, and it convinced me that I should stop taking the job world seriously and instead seek out a lightning-struck pine on a blasted heath and beneath it swear a solemn oath never to work (in the job sense) again – an oath I have been lucky enough, with the exception of a couple of minor lapses, to keep. I called the story 'The Colander'.

The posters in the subway said, I GOT MY JOB THROUGH THE NEW YORK TIMES and there was a comforting picture of a man in a white shirt and tie with a tiny smirk on his face against a dim background of electronic apparatus and water coolers. The man was warm, dry, and out of the rain. There was no mistaking the smirk – that of a man with good purchasing power and credit rating. In any case he was able to eat whereas I had a dollar fifty and a writful of debts. I bought a copy of the *New York Times*.

FLATIRON CORPORATION
Men wanted to wash apartment walls ...

and there was a Madison Avenue address. I walked with confidence across the park and down four blocks to 89th Street. In the office was a wooden barricade and two rows of chairs in front of it and behind it two rows of girls.

'I've come about the ad,' I told the nearest girl.

'Mr. Squid's out,' she said, 'but you can wait if you like.'

I sat down and looked around me. There was another wall-washer there; a man with red, aggressive hair and skinny hands, white and musty of face, tattered of clothes. On his lap was a copy of the *New York Times*, very dirty and pulpy. The man was crouched over it, mouthing; a finger ran like a spider over the magazine section. Every now and again he gave a vast epileptic twitch, which dislodged both hand and paper, the latter falling to the floor. With a curse he would get it all rearranged, mouth, etc., until the next tremor hit him, when the business would start afresh. I watched him, fascinated-Sisyphus.

Two black men came in, smiled happily and sat down without saying anything. Then another – this one rather stately – wearing a broad-brimmed hat. He said nothing either. We waited a long, dusty half-hour, the girls exchanging gossip in raucous Bronx whines, the zany twitching, the black men durable.

A man with a white shirt straight off a poster came in and beamed paternally. He was short and unctuous with benign horn rims.

'Well,' he said, 'I wonder you guys didn't start a crap game.'

We all grinned uneasily. The redhead began to sweat.

'It's a damn shame, fellers, but it's the truth that not everybody applying for a job gets it. If that were so we'd have no unemployment.'

'Thass no good to me,' the redhead hurriedly gabbled in an obscure accent. 'Thass no good to me at all ... I phone the girl an she say come on over she say job she said. I said you got jobs she said yes she ... '

'Now, just a minute, feller, just a minute ... '

'Said yes she said come right over. I come. I come by subway. Fifteen cents it cost me ... you got no right she got no right ... '

Squid raised a paternal eyebrow and frowned in mock anger at the receptionist.

'Mr. Squid, he's loyee-ing,' she spat. 'I juss wanyataknow I din say nuddin a de sort.'

I felt sorry for her. She was terrified of Mr. Squid. *When will it all end*, I thought.

'She tole me an I spend fifteen cents an I gotta go back is anudder fifteen ... '

'All right, all right,' Squid soothed. 'Take it easy. Now, fellers, we have a little business here and I always like to see the men who work for me in person. Are you married?' He pointed at the big black man who nodded. 'Are you?' I nodded. 'All right.' Squid lay low for one cunning moment. Then, very quickly, he said, 'I'll talk to you, you, and you.' He'd picked the big black, the redhead, and myself. 'I'm sorry fellers,' he told the others, 'but what can I do? I hate to send you away, but there it is. The three of you come into the office. I'm sorry, fellers.' He spread his arms, palms upwards, and a cherubic, wistful smile crept out and spread around him.

In the office he dropped thirty cents into the redhead's hand, saying:

'No hard feelings, hey? I can't give everybody a job and you and I wouldn't get along, would we?'

The redhead slithered away; he seemed moderately content. Perhaps I had underestimated him.

'Phew,' said Mr. Squid, settling like hot pitch into a chair. 'You see how it is? Happens every day – oddballs. I try to get along with them. Feller like that wouldn't be any use to me, now would he?'

The black man and I shook our heads wisely.

'Well now, a feller that works for me finds good, steady work,' Squid said. 'We clean out people's apartments all the year round. You won't get rich because I'm not. What have you done before?'

'Worked in a buildin,' the black man said. 'Worked in lotsa buildins. Cleanin an such.'

'What about you?'

'Worked in buildings,' I said, copying the black man for safety's sake. 'Worked in buildings, up and down the country.'

'Ever wash a wall before?'

'Some walls I washed,' I answered, still playing it by ear. 'Done a whole mess a windows.'

'We don't touch windows. Not in this here city. But you washed walls. Good enough. I got my ways of doing things. Feller likes to do things my way and I always find that he and I gets along. If we don't, what's the use of having bad feelings? He just goes his way and I go mine. I don't argue with fellers, what's the use of arguing? Now what I pay is good enough for some and not quite good enough for others ... There again, there's no bad feeling. Feller for whom it isn't quite enough just keeps on looking. I pay a dollar an hour, forty a week. Pays that little old landlady, doesn't it, fellers? But as I say, for some fellers it may not be suitable. How about you?'

'No, sir,' the black man said. 'That ain't quite enough.'

Squid shrugged. 'Well, just like I said, for some it's enough, for others it ain't quite enough. No hard feelings?'

'No, sir.'

That left me.

'How about you? Is forty enough for you?'

'So long as it's steady,' I said, saying what I thought he wanted, 'it's all right by me ... '

'Well, that's it. Can't please everybody and I ain't aiming to. If you and I get along and I like your work I give you an extra five dollars in a month's time. After another month I give you another five bringing you up to fifty. Start tomorrow?'

'Yes.'

'Well it may not be a fortune, but then I ain't got a fortune. Tomorrow at seven-thirty, then, and fill out this form.'

The form wanted name, address, social security number, army service, previous employment, and my signature to the statement that I would not wash walls for any other firm, or allow myself to be contracted out to anyone I came into contact with during my period of employment, or in any way give other firms information as to contracts within a region bounded by Park Avenue to the east, and between 50th Street to the south and 98th Street to the north, under penalty of immediate dismissal and severe fine.

I walked back across the park to my cheap hotel saying, joyfully:

'I got a job. *Moneys accrue*.'

'I don't understand,' my wife said. 'What kind of a job?'

I explained in tones of euphoria. Three days' work or so and we'd have the fare back to Canada. To get out – I gazed out of the window at the dog-turd-anointed sidewalks, the sneering, malevolent traffic, the sweating, scratching, three-quarters wild, and wholly depraved inhabitants clawing dollar bills out of one another's hands in the gutters ... this place was no more than an enormous, disharmonious and stenching fart; and what's more it was, as we used to say in the army, a fart in a colander.

Next morning Squid was waiting for me on the steps.

'Got the form?'

I had forgotten it. Squid looked angry and rather dangerous. No more was he the smooth, conciliatory Squid of the previous day. This was a Squid to be reckoned with.

'What's your social security number?' he asked, filling a new form in for me with his ball point.

'I don't have one.'

'Don't have one, ha? Who do you expect to keep you when you're old?'

'Why worry?' I answered, trying a 'wry jest'. 'You'll be dead before I'm old.'

'Law says you got to have a social security number. You better get one, buddy.'

In a little while some men came in carrying pails.

'Go with them,' Squid said.

Four of us climbed into a car and drove down Madison Avenue to 52nd Street. An elevator took us to a six-roomed apartment. The foreman said:

'Four hunnerd bucks a month dey pay fer dis little place.' He looked around slyly. 'Maid ain't here yet, neither's Squid. May as well have a cup a corffee. Plenny a time.'

Later he showed me how to wash walls. *See dis orange powder? Dat's detoigent. Ya fill de bucket wid water and stoy it up. You put de rag in an squeeze her dry. Don't let Squid catch ya geddin water on de floor ...*

A whole morning I rinsed a wall feeling very happy. Never had I earned my dollar more easily or pleasantly. Squid came in about noon.

'Put that cigarette out,' he told one of the men. 'Where do you think you are?'

'Yeah, who said you could smoke in here?' the foreman said.

Squid moseyed around and passed fingers along mouldings. Then he spotted me. Unluckily, I had taken my shoes off and was walking around in bare feet.

'Look, son, that we don't allow, walking around in bare feet.'

'Put ya shoes back on,' the foreman said. 'I never said you could take dem orff.'

'How would you feel if someone took his shoes off in your apartment?' Squid *ad hominem*ed. 'That's all very well for a beach. I know I don't pay no ten dollars an hour, but I don't expect you to walk around like a bum. What the hell's the matter with you?'

Exit muttering. I debated whether or not to tell him where he could stuff his walls. No point. That three days' work would pay our fare. It wasn't worth it. At four o'clock we went back to the office. The girl handed me another form.

'Income tax,' she snarled. 'Ya gotta fill it in.'

It was slightly easier than the other form. I was grappling with it when Squid interrupted me.

'I think I'm going to give you your money,' he said. 'I don't think you and I are going to get along. No hard feelings. I mean that stuff's all right at a beach. Here's a quarter. Get yourself a coffee downstairs and come back for your cheque.'

I found to my disgust I was shaking with rage. That this squirt should fire me! And to give me a tip as though I were a redheaded zany! I threw the quarter on the floor like a child with an irritating toy. 'Stuff it up your arse,' I said.

In the coffee shop the injustice of it all nearly made me weep. If only I had confronted him about those bloddy thongs that morning! In the everlasting, ubiquitous game of ego-manship I had lost out. Fired from a job like this for not wearing shoes! The absurdity of it struck me. It was impossible to hate Squid. It was also the End. I got my job through the *New York Times*. Never again. No more jobs. Not in that sense of the word, by God. Through the window I could see the edge of Central Park. It looked extraordinarily green and peaceful.

Poor Squid, I said to myself.

Upstairs the cheque was made out for fifty cents too much.

'I couldn't be bothered to work out your income tax,' Squid said, winning all over again.

'That's OK.'

'No hard feelings?'

'No feelings of any kind.'

'Bye then.'

'Best of luck with your walls.'

And I was off, out into the arrogant street and across the park.

The Night of Lucia

ÖSTERSUND, SWEDEN – about the middle of December, 1949. Our first day out was bleak but relatively mild. The landscape lay under a frigid grey mist through which the outlines of the trees showed blurred and dark grey. The sky was dark, for thick clouds had grown slowly during the night and fused with the mist on the low hills. I never knew whether the road itself was paved or not. Perhaps by now it has become a concrete super-highway – Sundsval to Trondheim with exits for Hammerstrand, Brecke, Östersund and Åre – but then it was covered with a layer of snow and gravel which had frozen together to produce a dense substance whose surface seemed as hard as diamond. I could feel every ice-embedded pebble in it through the thin soles of my rubber boots – Wellington boots: the kind a man wears in England for a quiet day's weeding in the garden. The warmer weather rendered the ice slippery – a boot would skate on the heavier gravel and I'd totter wildly, trying to regain balance, plunging the other boot around for a foothold, but it would slip, in its turn, and I'd land with a bone-shaking crash on the steel-hard road. So from time to time I'd give up and walk on the heaps of packed, brownish snow on the road's shoulder, but this had become almost as treacherous, to my useless boots, as the gravel itself and it was like slithering over *verglas*-coated screes. Beyond the shoulder was a drainage ditch filled with light, powdery snow under a brittle crust – a boot whacked into the ditch would sink straight down with a crunching sound and fill with this finer snow, which would melt, then freeze into thick transparent icicles in the tops of my socks. My rucksack was too heavy and too cumbersome, for I'd strapped a small valise to the top of it . The arrangement did its best to pull me out of the vertical and would swing heavily to complete the job of throwing me to the ground whenever I started to topple off balance. I improved its stability when we stopped to eat by jettisoning some of the rucksack's contents and stuffing the valise inside.

We had seen no building of any sort so at noon we stumbled through the unstained, shallow snow of a disused loop road – a resting place for maintenance vehicles. We found some logs and, placing them side by side, built a twig fire in the space between and started the long job of melting snow for coffee. Sam poked at the fire, singing under his breath a song popular in those dark, post-war days: *Evening shadows make me blue*, he muttered but without much conviction, *when each weary day is through* ... he'd not had too bad a time of it, for his boots were of the solid, Vibram-soled type and, what's more, they fitted him. He'd fallen a couple of times but he was by no means the bruised, numbed, and useless object he was trying to encourage. Apart from this, however, he had the invaluable knack of accurate focus. For example, I was a man trying to get to Norway against time and under the pressure of future hunger; he, on the other hand, was a man walking along the road, who had stopped for lunch and who, dressed in warm clothing, was also solving the problem of keeping on his feet. I wished to act in such a way that my movements were planned, meaningful, and patterned; Sam knew, without even thinking about it, that coherence lies only in the present moment and that he would do, in the future, whatever needed to be done. I wanted something to come of whatever I did; Sam did things for their own sake and could not have cared less about the result. He was even, I think, beginning to enjoy himself at that stage.

The two cups of coffee took over an hour to make. We thawed out the sardines, whose oil had become thick and opaque, and I bared my feet, wrapped a towel round them, picked icicles from my socks, then dried the latter near the fire.

It was dark when we started off again.

We had seen no traffic at all. Once or twice we walked past a farm. These had been invisible by daylight, for they were well off the road, but now we could see their lights flickering through the trees. We should look, I said, for paths leading towards this river on our left and find a barn to flop in for the night. Let's push on a bit, Sam answered, and see what turns up. This was the last we said to one another for several miles.

Just after dark it began to snow. It was light, small-flaked stuff that seemed, in the darkness, to spurt gently against the skin like drops of ether. It fell into my hair, melted, and began to drip down my face in long, uncontrollable and infuriating streaks which disappeared into the neck of my shirt. But two hours after dark the snow stopped, the sky cleared and suddenly it grew intensely cold. We could see the moon through huge, expanding gaps in the clouds. The strands of my hair began to freeze together and I shoved on a balaclava helmet, preferring the constant dripping of water down my face to a frostbitten ear. Except for the echoing crunching of our boots on the fresh snow there was a deep silence into which each sound seemed swallowed, like water in quicklime. We could see the pines as black, feathery silhouettes against the blue-black sky punctured with stars. I became almost hypnotized by the silvery patches of light thrown by the soles of my boots against the snow as I trudged along and it was too cold, now, for my boots to skid easily.

It must have been just before nine o'clock when we heard the car coming.

It began as a tiny, vaguely sensed disturbance in the matrix of silence around us, growing slowly until we heard and recognized it, quite suddenly, as a car's engine. I turned, and a mile or so back on the chord across the valley where the road curved, I saw a horizontal cone of white light dipping and swinging round towards us.

'Quick,' I said, 'stand in the road.'

'Stand in the road be buggered,' Sam replied, 'he'll run us down.'

The driver swerved slightly to avoid us and swept past, the air eddies in front of the car whipping up thin gauzes of snow and drawing them across the road like the hems of bridal veils. The headlights silvered the telephone wires around the curve ahead.

'Bastard,' Sam said.

'Wait a minute ... '

The sound of the engine, almost faded into the distance, stopped.

'He's stopped for us,' I shouted. 'Let's run.'

We hobbled forward as fast as we could. My rucksack began to sway heavily until one of the straps broke and it lurched into the snow. Sam shuffled ahead while I hoisted the rucksack on one shoulder and clenched the broken strap against the other. But Sam had stopped on the brow of the hill. The road, after the curve, climbed, then dropped into a valley. There was a house on the left, then another, then two more. Round another bend and we were in a small village, walking along a main street lined with Christmas trees gay with coloured lights. One or two well-fed, fur-hatted Swedes passed us on the sidewalk and looked us up and down. The car had not pulled up for us, of course, but at some house in the village. We never even discovered the name of the place. We walked straight through it – no place for the penniless – as though we knew where we were going, struck off along a side path a mile beyond, and found a barn.

TWO

AFTER OUR NIGHT in the barn we woke cold, cramped, and ravenously hungry. I spliced my rucksack strap with a piece of rope while Sam crept out, sneaked towards the road, and stole a can of cream that stood amid milk churns on a platform by the entrance to the farm. We stirred the mixture of ice and thick cream until it was drinkable and counted our supplies – two cans of sardines, one of beans, half a loaf of bread, and a tin of Nescafé. We had no money at all. We gobbled the sardines this time without bothering to warm up the congealed oil. There was no time – we had to be on the road to catch the early morning traffic.

There wasn't any. Two cars went by, then a milk truck whose driver merely shook his head at us. To keep warm we began to walk.

As the sky grew lighter I had the curious sensation that we were back twenty miles or so, starting afresh from Östersund. There was the same wide valley cut between low hills, the same mist and dark sky, the same interminable, featureless, gently curving highway. It was colder and easier on the feet, for the fresh powdery snow provided a little friction, but within an hour I had become hungry again and with hunger there grew in me, for the first time, a willingness to discuss alternatives. We can go on like this, I thought, until we drop from starvation, exhaustion, exposure. We were in a part of the country apparently inhabited by suspicious xenophobes who would like as not turn us in to the police as vagrants if we appealed to them for help. And the police would hand us over to our respective consuls who'd confiscate our passports, label us, and send us home D.B.S. – Distressed British Subjects. So much, then, for my dreams of self-sufficiency. It would be the end of the Norway scheme and probably of my relationship with Joan, its other begetter. What love could survive such humiliation? So Sam and I would have to stay on the road and, if we persevered, we'd undoubtedly stumble into Trondheim, miles ahead, a big town with jobs, money, and shelter to offer.

But something else occurred to me. If we hit the frontier without money, bearded, hungry, and ragged, we stood a very good chance of being thrown back. And it was no use trying to enter Norway illegally if I wished to work there and make it my home. The alternative would be to find some place between here and the frontier, work for a few days, then enter by train and in comparative style. Jumping freight trains was out – there was a railroad along the valley, but again, we had to stay this side of the law.

I thought again about the Swedes – they had been hospitable enough so far – perhaps I was being a little paranoid about them. Surely no one would turn us in to the cops purely for begging at his doorstep. On the other hand, Northern Sweden in those days was unused to beggars and suspicious of foreigners, particularly those without visible means of support. But it looked as though we'd have to risk it.

We discussed all this at our midday halt. 'The safest thing,' I said, 'might be to walk back to that village, phone Robert in the Lutheran Mission at Östersund and get him to wire us some of his girl-friend's money.' Sam shook his head. 'Never go back,' he said. 'Something'll turn up.'

'Take a look at that sky,' he said later. 'We're gunna have snow up the arse by nightfall.'

The grey misty sky had grown black and sullen towards the

south and east and heavy nimbus clouds spread slowly towards us like a dark stain. The valley towards Östersund had disappeared completely ... swallowed in the cloud.

We packed hastily and buried the can. Its contents had by no means satisfied our hunger ... merely whetted it. My eyes felt gummy from the night's uneasy sleep and I could not stop myself from yawning. I knew that my body was covered in bruises from the day before. My knee-joints creaked as I got up to go, hoisting my leaden rucksack with difficulty over my shoulders. Sam was in slightly better shape, but as an Australian was more used than I was to large meals. He began to bitch as we walked slowly down the road about his empty stomach and his increasing physical weakness ... 'My gut's shrunk right up,' he complained. 'When did we eat last? ... Properly, I mean ... I don't count that bloody porridge at the mission ... two days ago ... that's when it was ... we can't go on much longer, boy, we're gunna drop in our tracks ... to think I could be back in Stockholm alonga those French bastards ... they'll be sitting in the warm, laughin at us ... stealin our women ... keep yer eyes skinned for a house.'

But no sooner had we ratified this decision to risk the cops by begging, than the opportunity to do so, such as it had been, vanished. We had begun, very slowly, to leave the wide valley with its scattered farms and frozen river behind us. The road twisted slightly and rose higher above the valley floor to work its way into a denser forest. Ahead of us, in the dusk, the road seemed to be driving towards the flank of a long, high ridge. It looked as though we were going to cross a watershed into the system of glens and lakes that wound their way to the Norwegian border. There was unlikely to be a farm for many miles. Behind us the sky was black and within ten minutes it had swallowed the grey twilight and we felt the first hesitant lash of wind-borne snow. As we got into the trees the wind dropped but the snow began to pelt down – huge, dry flakes of it, which built up on our shoulders and packs and found every gap and join in our clothing. The snow rapidly became ankle deep and then high enough to spill into our boots. The visibility sank to zero. At one point I left the road altogether in the darkness and plunged up to my waist in the ditch. Sam pulled me out and I lay panting and exhausted on the road with the snow building up mercilessly around me. With great difficulty I got to my feet, took two or three steps, then sank into the ditch again. The makeshift strap on my rucksack broke and with a savage oath I released the other strap and threw the whole bloody thing aside. I rested my arms on the edge of the drift and gasped for breath. I could see only the snow now falling rapidly in front of my face and of the road itself and the trees could see no sign. I could hear Sam shouting in the darkness. I yelled back and he lit his cigarette lighter while I called directions to him. I could see the flame drop suddenly as he stumbled into a soft drift and the light vanished to reappear a minute or so later. I heaved myself out of the hole I'd dug and lay on the snow. I no longer knew which was road and which was ditch. Sam found me and shook the snow from his clothes and hair and helped me to my feet. The snow began to settle on us as we stood gingerly in one spot, rolling and lighting a couple of sodden cigarettes.

'We're off the road,' he said. 'We must've missed the son-of-a-bitch in the dark and gone up one of those bloody farm tracks by mistake ... and now we've lost even that.'

As far as we could tell we'd ended up in a tiny clearing surrounded by an almost impenetrable forest of low pines. The tracks we'd made were now completely obscured and even the holes we'd created in the snow drifts were beginning to fill. With Sam's help I found my rucksack and ripped a dozen pages out of a copy of Gibbon I'd been carrying for sustenance, and which, of course, I'd not opened until now. We pulled a dead branch off a neighbouring pine, shook the snow off it, and broke its twigs. We snapped the branch into three pieces, laid them together on the snow, and stood over the twigs until, with the aid of Gibbon's noble prose, they began to burn. Snow hissed into the fire as we left it to round up more fuel. The fire flickered badly and its light danced back from the wall of timber that surrounded us. Our hunger had died down and left an increasing feebleness that made each step we took an almost impossible effort.

At one point I found myself gaping and dozing numbly in a

foxhole my body had inadvertently prepared for me in a snow bank by the trees. I watched myself gazing vacantly at the hissing flames, and at Sam's dancing, gigantic shadow. I heard the damp, smoking crackle of the logs. Then, with a snapping sound, and a couple of red sparks, the light went out as though it had been flicked off with a switch. Sam had dozily allowed the branches to burn through and dunk the flame they bore into the snow. I dragged myself upright and forced my way through the waist-high snow to where he stood tearing up my Gibbon and thumbing his lighter.

'It's useless,' I said. 'It'll take all we've got to keep the damn thing going. Let's find that path again and make for the farm.'

Both of us knew just how mere a gesture this would be. In such deserted country the farm could be miles off along what would now be an almost impenetrable path. But the highway, if we ever found it, would be just as useless ... there was nothing back the way we'd come and very little chance of there being a village ahead of us. The fire had shown us that the clearing was shaped like a pear and we knew roughly where the narrow end of it was. We pushed our way towards it and almost immediately became entrapped by trees. But the snow did not fall so rapidly here and the going proved a little easier. I felt my feet graze rock and once or twice I tripped on a buried deadfall and slid over the other side of it up to my waist. It seemed as though we were fighting our way around the trunks of trees, penetrating deeper and deeper into the forest. Half an hour of it and we gave up. We were far too exhausted to either go further or to return the way we came.

I shucked my rucksack onto the snow. 'Let's hole up,' I said. Sam nodded and said nothing. We burrowed under the spreading branches of a tree and, with our last remaining energy, dug out a snow cave.

'If it quits snowing,' Sam said, 'we stand a chance ... but if it goes on for a couple of days, we'll have had it.'

It was my turn to nod.

I no longer felt cold or hungry. I had begun to doze and my body seemed to be floating upwards on soft eiderdown. I could hear my own blood pulsing slowly around my body as a faint background whisper, through which I heard every now and again the creaking of a branch under its load of snow, the snapping of a twig as Sam shifted his position. This, I remember thinking, is not a bad way to die. There's none of the choking terror of drowning, or the agony of death by fire. Here one's life begins to ebb out of the body slowly and painlessly, flowing gently into the cold, dead forest. We'd disappear, that was the only trouble with it ... it might be years before we were found in this thick untravelled bushland. We would vanish like dry ice in warm air ... there would be inquiries from England ... a perfunctory search ... but no one would find us here. The cold and exhaustion had drained me of any regrets ... at nineteen I was perhaps too young to die like this, but at least I'd be spared the horrors of cancer, or the sudden whiplash of angina ... life's no joke, I thought, when all's said and done. A finite series of hot dinners, as a friend of mine once put it ... it was nothing, and neither was death.

I began to doze.

Sam Hartstein was shaking my shoulder. A light! he was saying, there's a light ahead. I staggered to my feet. Outside our miniature cave it had stopped snowing. Had we continued for a few more minutes, fighting through the bush, we'd've come out of the trees onto a huge field. I could see it now plainly – a lovely expanse of bare snow sparkling in the moonlight. At the far side of it was a house with lighted windows. With a final effort we ploughed our way towards it and bashed at the door.

THREE

THE MAN WHO answered our frenzied knocking did not gaze about him with a wild surmise. He was clearly a man of action. He rushed us upstairs into hot showers and warm bathrobes, then suggested that when we were ready for it we should join the company in the dining room. We'd struck it rich. In the kitchen were the remains of a lavish smorgasbord – we made short work of it and inroads upon a battle of aquavit. Only then, with the numbness beginning to leave our feet, did we feel relaxed enough to join the group of people gathered together in a comfortable, bourgeois room that, in itself, was a satisfactory contrast to the life we had been living for many weeks.

'They are from England,' our host said, introducing us and ignoring Sam's pained expression. 'And I think perhaps they have walked the whole way.'

We sank into deep, luxurious armchairs while an old lady in a multi-coloured gown explained what had happened to us. Had we not left the road, she said, we would have found that it bent northwards and passed through a village, the first of a chain of them, for we were now in that part of Sweden called Jämptland, a winter sports area on the Norwegian border, which, compared to what we'd come through, could be described as 'populated.' We'd stumbled on a cart track in the dark – a path that cut straight across the bend, over a low hill, and into a village. 'Now it's stopped snowing,' she told us in good, though accented English, 'you'll see the village lights from our windows. Lucky you'd kept to the left,' she said, 'or you'd've landed in dense forest and would have had a hard time finding your way out of it.'

We forced a chuckle.

'As it is,' she said, 'you can certainly stay with us tonight and in the morning apply for work at one of the hotels ... '

We nodded. We'd had enough of the road.

Then we told her about our journey on foot from Östersund and about the hut in the forest where we had tried to become loggers.

'These two are luckier than their friends,' the host said. 'Because tonight they're going to see something genuinely Swedish. Have you ever heard of the Night of Lucia?'

We shook our heads and Sam raised an eyebrow in inquiry but, just at that moment, a bowl of tiny, icing-star-decorated cakes was placed on the table by one of the women, while another carried around a trayful of what looked like small teapots but which contained hot, spiced wine.

'It's called glög,' our host said. 'Every year at this time we celebrate the anniversary of Saint Lucia – the Queen of the Light. We eat these little cakes you see here ...'

'And drink the glög?' Sam asked.

'You will see.'

My escape from an anonymous death in the woods was still rather too fresh in my mind for me to enter fully into this festivity, whatever it was. The warmth of the room, the good food and civilized company had done much to soothe me, but I had begun, irrationally, to worry about the future. How would I get to Norway? Clearly I would have to take whatever job I could find locally, but how much of a delay would be involved? I thought anxiously about Joan locked into her ghastly family and a nursing job she could not stand. To change one's life in England, in those days, needed more than an act of the will – it needed a remarkable stroke of luck; the operation, if you like, of grace.

It occurred to me that the Norway scheme would amount to very little. Already this journey had taken far too long; there was little work to be had and what there was did not last. It was not probable that things would be any better in Trondheim. I grappled with the idea of failure – failure followed by ignominious return and that unfinished business with the British Army.

I got up and walked over to the window. The farmhouse was set on a little hill so that I could see across the whole village. Each house glowed with lighted windows and small Christmas trees starred with coloured lights that reflected back from the snow in soft patterns. The December sky was black – cold and hard as polished leather. I stood for a while restless and uneasy, but thinking of nothing. There was a small commotion in the room. I turned from the blackness of the window. A door opened and a girl came in. She was young and lithe but solemn in manner: ' ... did seem too solemne sad.' There were tiny lighted candles arranged in a crown upon her head and she wore a white dress that looked like a bridal gown. There was complete silence.

Softly, with incredible sweetness, she began to sing.

Memoirs of a Gandy-Dancer

THERE ARE DAYS I feel a thousand years old. Right now, for instance, as I listen to the winter sky seep round the house, hear the scream of gulls flapping against the mist like torn rags, and watch the winter afternoon thicken into night, it seems as though I've been in this country at least as long as the Haida. Nostalgia is not one of my interests, but today I cannot rid my head of a particular, vivid image: a stranger, myself aged twenty-three, dressed in the standard British Immigrant costume of the period – tweed jacket with leather elbow patches, baggy flannel trousers, Aertex shirt, and a hairy woollen tie – wrestling an overladen rucksack and a cardboard suitcase down the gangplank of a liner onto a great plain of torrid asphalt outside the city of Quebec.

With me is my friend Jerome: deep, public school voice, sunken shifty eyes, and a chin jutting forward with a well-faked determination. Between us we possessed twenty-five dollars, eight of which went on our fares to Montreal and another three on a room near the Windsor Station. In the morning we breakfasted for fifty cents each at the Café St. Moritz, then found the Manpower office and jobs as labourers for the CPR. We were told to report to the Windsor Station later on in the day. A few stiflingly hot hours stretched before us, so the obvious thing to do was climb Mount Royal – not only because it was there but because it might offer a breeze – and for many years the controlling image I held in my mind of Canada was the view from outside the Chalet. From this height the city seemed an isolated pool of buildings in an immense wilderness – an immediate impression of thinness, of aridity, of city noise swallowed thirstily by huge distances and enormous skies. Melancholy though the landscape seemed, we enjoyed the solitude and the slight breeze and stayed on the mountain until our time was up.

At the station we were ushered with half a dozen other Europeans onto a mysterious train destined for a place called Swanson, which did not appear on the map of Canada given us by the immigration authorities but which we knew could not be far. Had not the Manpower usher told us it was in Ontario – evidently the next province over, and therefore as close as Sussex is to Surrey? But interminably the train rattled and straggled through humid and melancholy-looking half-country and we were glad, as night fell, that our faces were swept by cool air from the ventilator systems and that our nostrils were soothed by a thin, aseptic waft of chlorine. We began to doze.

Daybreak jolted us into a clear sky and a train moving sluggishly as though waiting for the line ahead to clear. Our unvaryingly slow pace came as a surprise to me, since I had always associated North America with speed, elegance, and style. We dozed again and woke much later to find ourselves surrounded by a landscape of the utmost devastation. As far as the eye could see nothing grew; stretched to the skyline lay huge, bare, slightly undulating slabs of mud-coloured granite and eroded gullies winding through small plains of baked alluvium. Here and there a yellow stream flowed sluggishly into large pools of bilious-looking water. Alongside the tracks stood in increasing numbers rickety lean-to shanties built of spars and tar-paper and sided with red or blue asphalt sheets patterned to imitate brick. A station slid into view, and the train stopped, long enough for us to get out. This new and frightening city was built crazily on a series of barren hills. It looked parched, desolate, and poverty-stricken. It was Sudbury and later that year I was to rediscover and grow to enjoy it; then, as an omen of what this country had to offer, it was irredeemably sinister.

At Sudbury the sky suddenly grew webs of cloud and the rain started to fall as we shunted out into the eroded country, which slowly turned to thick bush of white birch and spruce. Rain swept through these forests with sombre persistence. It grew darker, and suddenly it was night. At that point we felt the lurch of brakes, somebody yelled out the word *Swanson*, and a young train-man in dark uniform and quasi-military hat screamed at us to get the hell out of his train. He and a cohort threw our baggage out of the door and into the void while yet a third man shoved us down a short flight of metal steps. Somebody yelled a long and fluent oath in Polish. A door slammed shut. We stood in the jet night shivering under the rain as the train, with its cosy steam engine, bright lights and comfortable interior, chuffed off in the direction of Fort William.

We heard the distant cry of an owl, the rustling of the wind among the pines, the pattering of rain. My eyes could make out only the black silhouettes of a line of tree tops.

'*Kommen Sie hier bitte!*' a voice bawled. There was a dart of a flashlight and the voice again, once in French then in English with a strong accent. 'Come with me, you men.'

'Where the hell to?' Jerome growled.

'You speak English, huh? That makes a change around here ... well, my friend, we are going nowhere. You are in the bush.'

The stranger, no more than a black shape, flashed his light quickly around him.

'See? Bush ... and there ... bush. And look, there bush. All is bush, my friend. Now follow me.'

That night Jerome and I found ourselves in a long narrow room, part of a stranded train. Each of its cars was ill lit and crammed with a wood stove, bunks, and a trio of wash basins. Nobody cleaned these cars out – they were littered with the refuse of their polyglot inhabitants. Oddly stamped envelopes, crumpled and smudged, shared floor space with cigarette packets, candy wrappers, paper back books with lurid tattered covers, sand and lumps of soil tracked in from outside.

We entered a dim and stinking place stacked two high with recumbent bodies staring upwards at the sound of rain beating sullenly at the roof or at the mattress above them. We could have been in a Third-World army battalion or an English air raid shelter. The noise we made as we stowed our baggage caused a round blond head to move across its pillow into the dim light.

'Hey,' the head said. 'You Englishmen?'

We confessed that we were.

'How you like Kanada?' the head said, giggling, '*Scheisse*, nay? *Alles Scheisse*.'

He laughed quite loudly, which provoked the stirring of a number of bodies in curiosity.

'I haven't been in the country long enough,' I said, conscious of my voice sounding flute-like and prissy against the deeper tones of this German fellow, whose name was Paul, 'to make any sort of judgement.'

Paul laughed loudly again, as though all his Third Reich stereotypes of the effete English were here confirmed. It occurred to me that the present scene looked too much like the photographs I'd seen of the sleeping accommodations at Buchenwald for this man to laugh too smugly at us.

I smiled, climbed to the bunk next to him and, conforming to the custom of the place, lay on my back to stare first at the mattress above, then at the curved wooden roof above and to my left as though the loudly bustling rain-drops were about to come inside.

Sometime during the night the rain stopped. We woke to find that the early morning sun had drawn vapour from the earth and suspended it above the ground in a low, thin mist. I clambered out of my blankets and pushed through the throng of chattering men clustered around the wash basins and stepped outside to be greeted by a tremendous silence and tranquillity in which even this meagre human activity of maintaining a barren ribbon of steel through the bush seemed irrelevant. I lit a pre-breakfast cigarette and watched the trees grow out of the mist to define themselves against the azure sky. Somebody shouted, and we trooped along the track to another car. This one was a diner – long trestle tables decorated with huge platters of pancakes, boiled eggs, bacon, ham, toast. Big enamel jugs of juice and water. We fell upon this vast breakfast lustily, as though we'd just been released from prison camps. This was almost precisely Jerome's situation, for he had never been out of a Britain still afflicted with ration books and consequently had never seen so much food in one place. A man in blue dungarees and a striped engineer's hat came in the door, jerked a thumb, and said something in a dialect of French I had not heard before. The thumb sign at any rate was understandable. We piled out and clambered onto flat platforms fitted with wheels so as to run on the tracks. They were powered by means of long handles arranged like a see-saw and pumped up and down by a half-dozen or so on either side of the fulcrum.

'Pompah!' somebody yelled.

'Pompah, pompah!' others joined in. The handles were wet with dew and abrasive with sand but as the car picked up a clicking speed and the press-lift, press-lift motion became easier a child-like delight overwhelmed us that communicated itself even to Jerome.

'Pompah!' he shouted in his deep-voiced, Oxbridge accent, and his eyes flashed with a kind of joy.

A mile down the track we steered the pumper into a siding and picked up our shovels. A huge yellow machine chugged sullenly as though brooding over the two thin bands of steel running beneath it. Suddenly it barked, spewed smoke, roared and drew itself to its full height. From under the machine's belly we saw the track slowly lift and emerge from its bed so as to hang a couple of feet off the ground. We shored it up with a mixture of sand and gravel, stood on it, and rammed the earth under the ties with our shovels. Evidently the brand of shovel used on the first railroads were made by a company called Gandy, hence the name of this activity – Gandy-dancing. The work isn't hard, but it is monotonous, and we were all glad of the long breaks when we tidied the track up enough for trains to pass through. There were a couple of passenger trains and about three freights rigidly scheduled throughout the day. Just before they were due we knocked off and lay on the ground beside the track dozing and staring into space until they'd gone. We discovered they were usually late, so these breaks in the day might last as long as two hours.

The sun grew very hot. The peaty, swamp-like smell of the ground became parched and smoky, as though there had been a recent forest fire. A few hundred yards from where we worked that day was an expanse of lake reflecting in oil-calm water huge clouds drifting in stately processions across the sky. The long gaps in work, the chinking of shovels, the odd muttered comment in a foreign language, the sound of laughter, these became distant from me and I found myself mentally dissolving into the strange world of thick bush, almost total silence, mosquitoes, and rotting vegetation existing a few yards either side of the track.

'Work, eat, sleep,' Paul said one night. 'Is that a life? We are animals, that's all. Look at that pig there for example.'

He stabbed his finger towards a tall Greek of about nineteen who had just lit the stove. On the stove-lid the Greek was trying to fry the skinned limbs of a recently trapped hare. Acrid blue smoke rose up into an atmosphere already rank with the stench of feet and sweat.

'Hey, pig, *Schwein*!' Paul got to his feet. He was heavily built and about five years my senior: old enough to have served on U-boats during the war. He walked a few steps to the stove. 'I'm talking to you.'

Conversation stopped.

'Put that stove out,' Paul ordered. The boy looked around. His compatriots stared at the German. Impudently the boy shrugged and turned back to the stove. He prodded a hare's leg with his fork.

Paul's face went taut and white. '*Jude!*' he shouted. *Jew!* And with two long strides he reached the boy and brought a huge fist into the other's stomach. The boy fell and rolled into a ball with a high-pitched moaning sound. Then the other Greeks fell on Paul, bringing him with a crash against the hot stove and onto the floor where, heedless of the scattered embers of fire, they began to kick at him wildly.

Jerome jumped up from his bed, fought his way through the entanglement of feet and bodies, and grabbed a fire extinguisher by the door. Evil-looking flames had begun to crawl over a nearby bunk. Jerome upended the extinguisher and directed a stream of foam onto the bunk then, as an afterthought, onto the still struggling figures around Paul's prone body.

The fight died off. The men retired, soaked with extinguisher fluid, but with no visible resentment. I helped Paul to his feet. One eye was closed and blood ran from his mouth. He staggered to his bunk and lay on it with a groan, clutching a towel to his face.

The man with the flashlight who had greeted us was an amiable, multilingual Pole named Pete Sadowey. Jerome and I got in the habit of chatting with him for an hour or so after supper. The second night of this I suddenly grew aware of a strong, almost overpowering smell. I looked up. There were the remains of a man in the doorway. A man who had once been tall and brawny and whose shoulders now hunched forward as though deformed. His face was gap-toothed and disfigured by an enormous purple naevus stretching from a scarred forehead to his filth-encrusted neck. The man grinned horribly.

'You guys,' he said. 'I gotta clean up in here.'

'It's OK, Tiny,' Pete said. 'I'll sweep the floor. You take off.'

Tiny sent a malicious, small-eyed leer in my direction. He grinned again but shambled out with a parody of submission I found intensely disturbing.

'The cook's helper,' Pete explained. 'Lives only for a bottle of wine.'

'He's vile,' Jerome said, 'why don't you kick him out?'

'He's a good worker,' Pete replied. 'Even when he's drunk. Once you get outside Canadian cities,' Pete continued, 'guys like Tiny come a dime a dozen.'

Daily the work grew closer to a hamlet named Franz where the CPR track crossed the Algoma Central Railway. The place boasted a hotel and some government offices – perhaps the Department of Indian Affairs – over which, oddly enough, flew a Union Jack. For a few mad seconds I thought my countrymen were maintaining a consulate here. Pete later explained that this was the national flag of Canada. I replied that I hadn't come four thousand miles to look at Union Jacks. There was a general store called Spadoni's, straight out of a Norman Rockwell painting, complete with cracker barrels and wood-burning stove. A group of us visited the tavern for a first taste of Canadian beer.

'*Zu frisch*,' Paul said, making a face over a glass of Molson's, too fresh.

The beer seemed strangely textureless. We muttered a few

reminiscences concerning Dortmunder Aktien Bier, too much of which I had drunk in my army days. In half an hour Paul grew nostalgic about his time in the Hitler Youth – halcyon years for him. In an hour I found myself telling him that if I had been born in Dortmund (like Paul) in 1930 and not in London, I would have been in the Hitler Youth as well and turning my parents in to the Gestapo for anti-fascist remarks. I too would've been trained to use the word *Jew* as an insult. Jerome left us in some disgust, but Paul and I were sobered by this conversation, and shortly afterwards walked back to our car. I got into my bunk and read a few chapters of *Moby Dick*. The dim light came from an overhead bulb strung on leads bulgy with black electrical tape. After a while I gave up trying to read and began to day-dream. Gradually I fell asleep.

I was awakened by the Latvian in the top bunk trying to climb into his bed. He'd been kicked out of the Franz hotel and had visited one of the home-brew sessions conducted by the bull-cook. After much writhing, he got into bed and seemed to settle down. My eyes closed.

Suddenly I was awake again. The car was very dark. Something warm and foul had splashed onto my face. Looking up, I could just about see where the man's efforts to get to sleep had disturbed a portion of the mattress so that a gap showed between it and the bed rail. The drunk cried out in his sleep and turned over, roughly shaking the tier. I jumped out of bed, crept over mounds of boots and strewn clothes to the door and the fresh air outside.

The pay was ninety cents an hour. We worked ten hours a day, six days a week. The seventh day we rested, but there was nothing to do except walk aimlessly up and down the track or sit in Spadoni's. The hotel was shut. Two dollars a day was subtracted for board and lodging and a negligible amount for income tax. If you worked five weeks you could get a free ride back to Montreal or Toronto. The day our time was up Jerome and I had nearly five hundred dollars between us: not a bad stake in those days for arriving in Toronto, then a relatively cheap city. Paul and I made a ritual of my last shovelful of earth.

'This,' I swore, 'will be the last manual work I shall ever do for pay.'

I was to be disappointed in this and once, a few years later, I was so broke I went back to the Manpower office in Montreal to ask for work as a Gandy-dancer. Oddly enough I was interviewed by the same fellow who had hired Jerome and me.

'No,' he said, 'I can't recommend you for that ... it's no work for the likes of you. To tell you the truth,' he continued, 'it's no work for the likes of anyone.'

DEW-*Line*

> ... in all those cold and dreary tracts of the globe under the Arktick and Antarktick circles, – where the whole province of man's concernments lies for near nine months together within the narrow compass of his case, – where the spirits are compressed almost to nothing, – and where the passions of a man, with everything that belongs to them, are as frigid as the zone itself; – there the least quality of judgement imaginable does the business, – and of wit, – there is a total and absolute saving, – as not one spark is wanted, – so not one spark is given. Laurence Sterne, *Tristram Shandy*

I SAW THE Arctic first when the sun swung low on the horizon. The waters to the east were blue and shining and flecked with moon-white ice as though a great hand had struck flakes from a marble monument and strewn them over a hushed, enormous sea. The aircraft flew along a line of steep cliffs from which the land fell gently westwards – flat, dun-coloured, deserted. We carried supplies – giant crates of cabbage, sacks of potatoes, yellow-painted tractor parts – all of it strapped against the fuselage by heavy nets. Yet, such was the mood of childish romanticism into which this journey had plunged me, the cargo might have been silks, precious stones, and rare spices, for I had become an explorer of unknown and terrible lands – Cartier, perhaps, or Vasco da Gama – beset by calms and storms, fogs and adverse winds, travelling across a map decorated with cherub-driven sails, dolphins, and warnings about the presence of dragons.

The mood lasted almost a week before the reality principle bit my ankle. I spent much of my time on the DEW-Line watching radar scopes, sorting supplies, changing vacuum tubes, taking weather observations, and even thrusting chunks of frozen lake into a rather feeble machine supposed to crush and melt ice for a water supply. At Hall Beach on Melville Peninsula the water supply dwindled as the thickness of the ice grew on the lake, minerals dissolved in the water grew progressively more concentrated, until, by early spring, pitchers on the dining table looked as though they contained Milk of Magnesia. Even now, as I lift a glass of water, I find myself inspecting it for ice-worms. I wrote one unpublishable novel while in the Arctic and, because our fringe benefits included a darkroom, took perhaps a thousand photographs of gulls, Inuit, snow patterns, cloudscapes, and husky dogs. The short summer was filled with mosquitoes, the winters with snow, ice, and high winds. In the plane I thought that this northern experience would be invaluable to me as a writer. I could turn it into an adventure story rooted in elemental conflicts – men against nature, for instance. I found out later we were well padded and cocooned in building modules heated sometimes to suffocation and provided with elaborate back-up systems in case one of the diesel engines, sources of our light and heat, failed. Mail and whisky visited us twice a week, movies travelled back and forth along the line, we were in touch by radio and teletype with the 'South.' The conflicts were not waged between Man and the Outside, but between personalities; common sense was pitted against self-aggrandizement, life-affirmations against various forms of greed. The pay was high and, if you stayed the whole eighteen months' contract, a large and tempting bonus rewarded your loyalty. In my own case greed won out.

A handicapped friend tells me that all the questions her well-wishers ask her, no matter how caring and sincere the questioner, can be reduced to two: 'What do you do for sex?' and 'How do you go to the toilet?' That, she claims, constitutes the sum total of what people want to know about her. Checking this information against other sources, I now believe it to be true. Consider, for instance, the work of the pioneer educator, A.S. Neill, founder of a school named Summerhill. He believed that every question a child asks represents a hidden desire to know where he or she comes from. Such a dogma, surely would lead to absurd dialogues like this:

Q: 'What's the time, Daddy?'
A: 'Out of your mother's womb.'

Q: 'Daddy, why is the sky blue?'
A: 'Out of your mother's womb.'

Perhaps this is not as mad as it sounds. As I try to write about the DEW-Line I find myself answering implied questions. What *did* we do for sex? How *did* we manage the issue of bathrooms? I can tell you about the latter in three sentences: the toilets conformed to the standards you find in civilized communities. Sewage lines and septic tanks, though, were impossible to build in the Arctic because of the permafrost, so excrement of all kinds had to be directed to large tanks periodically emptied by trucks shaped like gasoline bowsers. These, in turn, were dumped out at remote sites in the open air, like garbage in the South, and allowed to freeze. When the greenhouse effect finally warms the polar regions, great floods of excrement will flow towards the equator and suffocate the famous cities of North America. This will pay them out for having taken arms against the Demon Communism.

Sex was a subtler matter, and to deal with it I must sort through the journal I kept at the time. It begins with notes on my arrival.

The plane banked into the wind and floated, gull-like, over a group of radar masts and huge, cylindrical oil-tanks glistening in the sunlight, then onto an air-strip. The pilot cut the engines, wheels hissed into gravel. The aircraft came to rest, whereupon I heard a raucous, ululating scream. I ran to the open door. Above us wheeled a massive flight of gulls – a Brownian movement on a tremendous scale, which took the gulls steadily towards the line of beach. A man shouted and pushed a wheeled step-ladder towards the plane.

Sector supervisors out first, then station chiefs, then radar technicians. After the technicians go the mechanics, followed by the cooks, scullions, and freight handlers of the Foundation Company of Canada. Inuit travellers come out last. There were no supervisors or chiefs, so I was invited to step down the ladder first. I shrugged myself into a parka, but needn't have bothered. The young man in the pick-up truck sent to greet me wore the sort of clothes – jeans and a heavy check shirt – you might wear for a hunting trip in southern woods.

'Ian Telford,' the young man said, shaking my hand. 'I'm your immediate boss.'

I muttered something in reply.

'Expecting snow?' he said, eyeing my appearance. 'Everybody does. But you won't need your outdoor clothes for another three or four weeks ... Then you probably won't use them at all ... when the winter comes, we all stay indoors.'

A dirt road carved into the tundra leads from the airstrip to the station. The ground is flat but, five miles away, it begins to tilt gradually to a sky-line of bare, rolling hills. Ian started the truck and a mob of gulls spurted into the air with a banshee wail. The station grew in size – two long rows of modules, lying parallel, connected by a short, overhead bridge and capped at one end by a spherical dome. Ian said:

'Get a glimpse of the convoy?'

'Convoy?'

'Sea-lift ships. That's how we get all the bulk supplies.'

'Didn't come that way.'

'They're seventy miles out. God knows if they'll make it here before the big freeze. In any case they'll have to wait until the harbour clears. We've got frogmen dynamiting the ice off the quays. But the damned stuff just forms again. The sea hasn't warmed up much this summer – something to do with the currents. We'll be in the shit if we can't off-load that electronics shipment.

'Anyway,' he continued, 'I'm bloody glad you got here at least. We badly need a replacement for Cam F.'

'Cam F – what's that?'

'An "I" station ... the first west of here ... fifty miles away. You'll be doing Bert Merritt's job ... I'm bringing him out on first available ... a good man, but been out there too long, I'm afraid.'

'Isolation ... '

'Right. It's a problem on those "I" sites. There'll be just the three of you. You and a couple of mechanics. Apart from the Foundation people, of course. They're in tents.'

I couldn't believe my eyes. Twenty yards off the dirt road is a small knoll decorated with what looks like an enormous bleached wishbone balanced on its legs to form an arch framing an incredibly large patch of blue sky.

'Part of a whale,' Ian said. 'Don't ask me which part. I wouldn't know. I think it's a vertebra. The Eskimos lug in what they kill and make a cache. That's the remains of a very old one.'

'Prehistoric?'

'It's all prehistory up here.'

Ian turned the truck sharply to the right so as to align it with a short ramp leading to the main entrance. He helped me with my bags through the doors to the simple cell-like bedroom. Desk, chair, bed. I might just as easily have been a member of the Benedictine order. Ian muttered something about having to get back to work and reiterated his gladness at my arrival. He wears his black hair *en brosse* – it sharpens and pinches his already lean face which looks as though too much responsibility is burdening its owner too early in life. He suggested I wander around and get the feel of the place. 'We'll meet again,' he said, 'at supper.'

Alone in my cell I stared out of the window trying to get these new surroundings fixed in my mind. Two hundred yards off, the temporary camp used by labourers during the construction phase begins. Rows of canvas-roofed huts, some of them with oil stoves burning (thin smoke rises straight to merge with the huge sky). Lower down is the line of beach – acres of flat gravel with here and there a row of oil drums neatly stacked. Past the camp and inland the country shelves upwards to a range of low hills of rock covered with greenish brown lichens dappled now in late summer with tiny yellow flowers and combed by the silver tines of a hundred unfished creeks and streams swollen with the new warmth and rushing towards the sea. Even within these modules there is the non-stop wailing of the gulls and, in the distance, the accompanying howl of dogs.

I decided to leave exploring the modules for later. In need of exercise, I walk out and back along the track towards the remains of the whale.

Ian is wrong about the vertebra, I decide. This arch looks more like a pelvis. What in God's name would a whale want with a pelvis? It is slightly taller than I am and, as a child would, I walk under its archway. On the other side is a little spring – lank grass grows close to the edges of a hole in the ground whose sides are clean and square as though chopped with a spade. Clear water runs from it and downhill over rounded pebbles dappled like the backs of trout. A thin trace of cirrus cloud wafts over the sun and the temperature drops a degree, enough to cause the mosquitoes plaguing me continuously to leave the chilly heights of my face and neck for the warmth nearer the ground. Then the sun swims out of the cloud and the mosquitoes buzz back. I smear myself with a mixture of dead insects and repellent, but a little too late. I walk back though the arch and stare at the station, now neatly framed in bone. There are five of these big complexes: PIN, BAR, CAM, FOX, and DYE, about five hundred miles apart. Between each station and the next lies an auxiliary station, and between these are the 'I' sites. So every fifty miles across the 69th parallel future generations will discover evidence of twentieth-century culture. I don't much relish being dumped so soon at Cam F. My grasp of radar fundamentals is tenuous and if something were to go wrong with the equipment I should be very quickly unmasked as the impostor I am.

THURSDAY, 12TH SEPT., 1957: There's been fog for a week and light rain. The road, we call it a road, connecting us to the lake at one end and the Foundation Company camp at the other has been ploughed to a rich, brown mud. Because of the permafrost eighteen inches down, there is no drainage, so in summer we are surrounded by vast, shallow puddles. What with the fog and a slight wind blowing at right angles to the airstrip, we've been cut off for a week now. Outside the module is a very tall mast topped by radar antennas. These are two hundred feet off the ground and betray a tendency to make their own weather. When the fog lifts a few feet you can see the antennas rimed with ice.

I share the module with the two mechanics, Leo and Larry. Leo is nominally in charge of the station. He is a thick-set, intelligent fellow well-scarred from the war. We can count two kneecaps between us – he lost his left in some battle, I lost my right falling off a mountain in North Wales. His manner is tough and truculent, but it isn't hard to challenge him. Underneath he lacks assurance; he is sensitive about what he feels is his semi-crippled state and his lack of education. He seems to find everything objectionable – the muddles at FOX Main and at Frobisher, the men on the site, the cooking, other people's brains. Naturally, it won't be long before he starts bitching about me. Larry, on the other hand, is superficially amiable – one of those people who constantly seek you out – to go for a walk, fish in the lake, play crib. He likes to touch people, slapping backs and digging ribs. Everywhere I go I seem to run across him, mouth open, waiting for me to say something to make him laugh. There is nothing about him, despite this outward behaviour, to suggest homosexuality – merely blankness and boredom. He is the eternal goldbricker – he buys cigarettes, whisky, paper-back books from the south and sells them to us for a small profit. He is full of self-serving anecdotes revealing his acumen in this regard. He's smart enough to avoid Leo. Personally, I wouldn't trust Larry with a five-cent stamp.

The sea-lift ships started to dock today creating frenzied activity down at FOX Beach. I can hear them going mad on the ship-to-shore frequency whenever I can be bothered to tune it in. My contribution is to send weather reports every hour from dawn to dusk: temperature, barometric pressure, cloud ceiling. I'm supposed to fill a balloon with hydrogen, let it loose, then time its ascent until it disappears into the clouds. There isn't much point in this, however, since I can't even see the radar antennas – so two hundred feet is all the ceiling I can give them.

The Foundation men have been complaining about the cook. As far as I'm concerned I've dined both better and worse. In any case we have our own kitchen in the module and can, if we so choose, gorge ourselves on steak and canned lobster until we sicken. However, I relayed the complaints to FOX, and back came the message that Foundation would replace the cook. It was unpleasant conveying this news to its victim. He was upset, of course, and I felt sorry for him. Soon, though, he begins telling us how little he cares because of all the money he is making in the stock market. He says he can turn his hand to any trade, but prefers to cook. A string of anecdotes follows this claim, each proving how good he is as a chef. We are all morons, evidently, for not appreciating him. He draws particular attention to his cake which, he claims, is unique and not to be obtained outside of Zurich, his home town. I've eaten his cake, as a matter of fact; it is neither good nor bad. Then he explains he is being fired because of his immigrant status. I ask him if he thinks dark forces are arrayed against him, but he lets this go in favour of a mysterious process of association leading him to moan about the difficult working conditions he has to endure. Finally, Leo gets impatient with him and kicks him out. He leaves for the south 'on the first available flight' out of here.

During the night there is a dreadful clattering on the roof. We debate whether or not it's the cook, gone mad, throwing stones at the module. But it turns out the noise is caused by great chunks of ice falling off the antennas – the temperature up there's got low enough for the de-icers to cut in, and the wind strong enough to blow the results on to us. It's like a permanent bombardment ... One could very easily get brained, so for the rest of today I've been acquiring the habit of stepping warily outside with one eye cast upwards into the fog.

Today the fog lifted, though plenty of snow fell during the night. Snow, and in mid-September! 'Is this going to thaw?' I ask. 'Sure,' says Leo. 'About the beginning of June.'

Maybe because of an association with our over-demanding main station, my mind seems filled with images of foxes. So naturally I encounter one this afternoon – he stood nobly on a mound of rocks, watchful, head erect, turned at ninety degrees to us, like some beast out of heraldry. He leapt away as we closed on him and headed south, stopping about two hundred yards off. He stood on another rock, staring at us, silver as a new quarter. Satisfied or not with what he saw he danced away in the direction of the falls. Out of a new, disturbing feeling of lassitude, I decline to follow him. My limbs seem to be stiffening up. I can see the great DEW-Line danger – immobility leading to etiolation, flabbiness, and a bunged-up gut. It's too bleak outside and cosy within. In this large equipment room, for example, I can sit at a wide desk in front of the window and stare mindlessly at our tower and the Foundation Company tents. On the ledge is a makeshift telephone, which connects us with the camp – specifically to its storeman, Bill Derby. By the window is the barometer from which I read off altimeter settings for these bloody useless weather reports. At one end of the desk lurks the VO 38, a handset tuned to the aircraft frequency and, in a dark corner of the room, is the rack containing the Doppler radar dials, glowing indicator lights bubbling and blinking as in a science fiction movie. On the whole I find it tranquil here – reminds me of being on duty in the army at night, with the office to myself.

This morning my peace is disturbed by Bill Derby who comes in unannounced, checks guiltily around for Leo, begins to talk. He remains standing so that he can do a quick bunk if Leo shows up. He can always pretend he only stopped by for his copy of the daily messages. I wonder why he doesn't just relax and forget about Leo's arbitrary rule that nobody from the camp should hang around the modules. Maybe he figures Leo will eat him.

Bill's basic complaint (everybody nurtures one) is that he does too much work for too little thanks, no promotion, and not enough pay. He is a caterwauler, proud of his high school education, and too unaware of the halitosis that discourages us from getting close to him. His moon face mounts a flat, ungracious nose, a prissy, ever-smiling mouth, and dead eyes. His voice is slow, his words clipped and carefully enunciated. A scar somewhat improves his appearance – it runs vertically from the corner of his mouth to one side of his chin. It gives his personality a spurious force. Uninvited, he embarks on an epic account of what he has done in his life so far – mostly clerical work. The hero of his epic is, of course, himself. His goal is to become chief clerk of some steady firm, though this ambition is contradicted by a desire to end up skiving in Miami, California, or New Zealand – some place with an even climate. I imagine him as a kind of thermostatically controlled chrysalis that never burgeons forth into anything else. The chrysalis is well padded in a soft, glass-wool-lined box. This box contains the thermostat. The box is also mounted on shock-absorbers consisting of moulded rubber pads. Thus, the chrysalis is fully protected against the stresses and vibration of the outer world.

A hole in the top of the box admits a glass tube inserted through the insulation. This device fully satisfies the chrysalis's breathing needs. A filter attached to the tube's top is designed carefully to ensure no microscopic foreign body can enter the breathing apparatus and disturb the inmate's peace. At the bottom of the box the chrysalis can access prepared and predigested food and it can excrete waste products into another, wider tube leading to a pan outside the box. The base of this tube is sprayed with a chemical whose smell is both heavy and pleasant – some product of coal-tar, no doubt. No other chrysalis enters the box because naturally enough it would bother, even enrage, the permanent resident. Sex is dispensed with since it would involve clambering out of the box – too much effort. Growth of any kind, including that of personality, is minutely controlled to ensure that the needs of the chrysalis require no modifications.

(Writer pauses here to wipe the foam from his lips.)

I am enjoying this bit of technical writing but it's beginning to proliferate too eerily for the purposes of describing Bill Derby. It could describe any one of us who is exchanging exile for money. As for Bill himself, I rather like him, whiner though he is.

The Beaver 'number' JZK arrived this afternoon flown by the mad pilot with the cleft palate. He carried three passengers, one went on to CAM 5, the other two stayed here for the afternoon. One of them is an engineer (whatever that means) from the Department of Health – a solid, quiet-spoken man who gives the impression of strong, uncomplicated will. The other is Bruce, the chief clerk from FOX riding out on his day off. Bruce wears a nasty wire brush of an embryo beard sprouting like an obscene white fungus at the end of his chin. In spite of this, in fact accentuated by it, my chief impression is one of baldness. His head is almost totally bald and his eyes watery and blue. His gestures and walk, his little squeaks of delight or annoyance, his habit of saying '*Oh sugar*' when dismayed, and the one *fuck* he released, contribute to his stagey and self-conscious mode of being-in-the-world. He poses as a cultured man, but he doesn't rise to any conversational bait. Instead he gossips quite vivaciously until, material exhausted, he falls silent. He and Larry enjoyed a good back-biting time together. But they clammed up on each other after half an hour.

When they'd all left and we were at the movie in the dining tent, I heard the roar of aircraft engines. I rushed outside to see a mysterious DC 3 belting off our airstrip. How in hell had it got there? Nobody had warned us it was coming. Leo and I raced down in the truck, but of course the plane had gone. Leo is very upset and has been expecting a rocket from FOX ever since.

Much airstrip activity today until the weather closed in on us. IQD made three deliveries and cancelled its fourth at the last minute. Silence descends. Peace comes dropping slow.

I'm busy watching the blizzard howl outside the equipment room window when I catch a glimpse of what looks like a couple of heavily garmented midgets. I get into my parka and step outside, hard pellets of snow stinging my face. The midgets turn out to be a couple of Eskimo children. They beam at me and point to the Foundation cook-tent. We walk over and greet the parents. A group of huskies accompanies them – these cluster around the door to lie quiescent in the snow in picturesque northern attitudes. These Eskimos are quiet, well-mannered people who know about knives and forks. According to one of our half-Eskimo labourers, they've a camp about thirty miles south and are heading for FOX. They drink tea endlessly and make strong inroads on our supply of oranges. In the evening we show them one of our movies. They appear to enjoy Jean Simmons, as who should not? They contrast rather sharply with the Eskimos one occasionally meets down at FOX airstrip on the way to Point Barrow or Yellowknife who take pictures of the white residents in the manner of tourists everywhere. One of them showed me his sophisticated Japanese camera equipped, he boasted, with a 2.8 lens. I don't know how this family found us. They must have caught a glimpse of our tower then homed in on it before the blizzard came down. This morning they've disappeared into the snow as silently as they came.

There is an amusing coda to the cook incident. Apparently he's been among the Foundation Company workers getting them to sign a petition to keep him on the site.

This morning help to unload a DC 3 at the airstrip. The sun assumed rather than seen as a dark red band on the horizon. The sun yellows the snow, which then becomes, throughout the day, a very pale blue. Walk out this afternoon to try to rid myself of what my mother calls the cobwebs grown, seemingly, all over me by getting up too early and trying to go back to sleep. Slept until midday and woke up feeling like hell.

Experiencing tendrils of depression, don't quite know why. Sexual deprivation, perhaps: I call up images of various women friends in the south, but they do nothing for me. They were 'there' once and will be again. At present I'm not in any hurry. No, I think I'm picking up these feelings from outside. Leo's increasing surliness is inducing a lack-lustre atmosphere that even seems to affect Larry, that human cork bobbing on deep waters. Checking the weather constantly, for as soon as I can conscientiously give FOX a ceiling of 1,200 feet they can send another of their damned planes out.

I walk outside and see how the top of the tower fades into the fog. Walk back inside the module where Leo lies on his bed. He's barely spoken to any of us. Merely grunts when he's addressed. Sleeps in his clothes. His emotional net is imprisoning the lot of us, and either he's totally bushed or he's oppressed by the DC 3's unacknowledged visit the night before. I send out an exploratory remark:

'There seems to be no shit flying about that aircraft.'

The response is immediate and vehement. He sits up in bed and glowers at me.

'If there is,' he says, 'I'll tell them they can kiss my royal arse.'
Whatever that may mean.

More sea-lift stuff arrived today, the weather being perfect. Sky filled with big, white, sailing clouds. Piles of stationery arrive including hordes of useless material like eight cartons of staples and a dozen of ink eradicator. Nobody uses ink here. Leo and Larry are up playing in the garage, rushing hither and yon, inventing crises. Last night they uncrated a compressor and tried to figure out how to tie in the line voltage. They buggered about with the terminals trying to find the combination that would stop the motor whenever the pressure got high enough. I lost fifty dollars betting Larry the engine wouldn't work on his system. That will teach me to bet on things I know nothing about.

I wonder if Leo's increasing surliness and lack of speech mean he has something against me. He talks these days only to old Sid Brown, the construction foreman. Sid is an old boy with an interminable supply of dull anecdotes that go on and on. He can make even the Winnipeg General Strike, in which he was involved, seem as vacuous as a parliamentary debate. His story yesterday concerning rabbits and gamekeepers made me so tense I broke the mug I was drinking tea out of by slamming it down too hard on the table. Even Bill Derby lost the thread of the story long before Sid had brought it to a close.

Friday. Still no mail. Larry's presence beginning to drive me up the wall. His nosiness, for a start. I get the feeling he's only waiting for me to leave the room and he'll be rummaging through my personal belongings. He's an over-the-shoulder-looker, perhaps harmless. He is a short, craggy fellow with a long, sensitive mouth. My manner in dealing with him is probably wrong. Lucille would say, 'Show him that you like him.' But that would be a lie – the thing that is not.

Plucked up my courage tonight and told Leo I was concerned about his mood. He was surprisingly unaggressive in return. Says he got fed up with things when Bert Merritt left.

'All these comings and goings,' he says. 'No sooner you get to know someone they go and pull him out.'

I told him I'd heard that Merritt was going to pieces and was busily occupied at FOX Main turning into an alcoholic. Leo says he knows nothing of this, that what he liked about Merritt was his cleanliness and industry. 'Always washed his clothes by hand,' Leo says. I said such a remark would look good on a gravestone. Leo gave a little smile, the first and possibly the last. 'Bert and I,' he says, 'could sit around here all day, not talking. And it'd feel good.'

Leo is clearly grieving for Bert Merritt. I realize my negative little comments on the latter come out of a weird jealousy. What's Merritt got that makes him such a satisfying companion? Obviously there existed some sentimental, Hemingwayesque attachment between them – of the kind I was not aware I craved. But evidently at some level I do. Toyed with the notion that I might, in the absence of women, be developing homosexual or at least homoerotic tendencies. Don't feel overly disturbed by the prospect. Transformations like this would certainly not be unusual up here, though they aren't given much expression. No gossip has reached me concerning anybody acting in an 'undisciplined fashion.' I think most of us have decided to repress our sexual natures – to put them on the back burner – not always successfully. I remember, for instance, Leo scorning one of the movies sent from FOX because it was a musical. 'Who wants to watch a bunch of cavorting faggots?' he asked accusingly. This, at the time, seemed an over-testy reaction.

No. Most of the men I've met are married or about to be. They're up here to save money – to buy a house, send a child to university, start a business. It is a good way to break through the chief consequences of being a wage slave – penury, monotony, and resignation. I suppose private masturbation is the chief sexual outlet, though this, like all forms of sex qua sex, is ultimately unsatisfying. What we all crave, whether we're aware of it or not, is intimacy. And in this regard men are not much different from women, though I doubt whether many of us would care to admit it. As in the army, there is much pornographic discourse, boastings, lewd castings of women in the role of whores, bitches, and insatiable vessels of random plungings, accompanied by mixed feelings of fascination and disgust. Little of it means anything – that's how we're brought up to think real men are supposed to talk. Most of it is utter bullshit, and of course most women are shrewd enough to know it. I am always amazed at women's tolerance for the psychic deformations of men.

The only problem now is that I feel vaguely jealous of this man Merritt. I don't, of course, wish I were like him, or like Leo. Both men are reticent and moody, though I've only one encounter with Merritt at FOX to go on. Drop off to sleep feeling disadvantaged, shallow, and unlikable. And with the knowledge that if I had met Leo in the south I would've paid him very little attention.

Spent today binning masses of spare electronics parts – tubes, resistors, capacitors, transformers, and so on, each done up in a neat carton covered in waxed hessian. Bill Derby mooned in to help me and, at the end of the day, saw fit to ask me to write him a reference – 'in case of need'. The message came through that Leo is being transferred back to FOX and that his replacement, a man named Alan Collette, is to come out on 'first available'. Leo mutters 'about bloody time' when I gave him the news, though I know that he is greatly attached to Cam F, his home for the last six months.

Woke at three in the morning with the alarm system howling noisily and frantic radio calls from FOX. One of the diesel generators has broken down, causing the Doppler radar to go off the air. Larry can do nothing with his generator, I can do nothing with the radar. Each of us is busy cursing the inefficiency of the other. I thought the sudden loss of power might have damaged a rectifier tube and, with great hesitation, I changed it, fighting a tendency to flap. I felt all the time I was being contrasted unfavourably with Bob Merritt. Anyhow, I changed the tube very warily, for I was scared the capacitors might discharge 6,000 volts across me. Finally I got the beam voltage back to normal, though I'm not confident this is the only problem. Ian called up suggesting he send one of the sector specialists out to help me. I say yes, instantly, then worried that this might be read as a confession of failure.

The specialist arrived and with him Alan Collette, a tall, rangy man from Saskatchewan who hums all the time and once in a while utters *sotto voce* a little burst of song:

The higher up the berry tree
The sweeter grows the berry ...

He smokes continuously and dabs cigarette ash directly onto his thick flannel check shirt. I was struck suddenly by the sheer *oddity* of human beings with a clear perception that made me gasp. I stood staring out of the window for perhaps half an hour, my mind swooning with a sense of human craziness, my own included. This reverie, or Jamesian 'vastation', comes to an end as Leo shouts an *au revoir*. I take him down to the airstrip in the truck and shake his hand.

'The best of fucking luck,' he says, perhaps all he will allow himself in the way of emotional expression – at leaving his home, at confronting his new situation at FOX, and of his detestation of Larry. Larry, Bill Derby, even poor old Sid, have invented work to do that prevents them coming down to see him off.

Thus it may have been when Ozymandias resigned his kingship.

Leo's departure has made Bill Derby restless. He reminds me about the letter of reference, so I go back into the office and bash one out on the typewriter.

TO WHOM IT MAY CONCERN: I have known William Derby for the last four months during which period he was employed as a storeman by the Foundation Company of Canada. In this capacity he showed himself to be extremely reliable and enthusiastic. He proved many times over his ability to work under the most difficult and trying conditions with cheerfulness, resource, and efficiency. His stock-keeping methods, filing systems, etc., could not, for the purposes of the job in hand, be improved upon. One of his most noteworthy characteristics is his ability to work completely without supervision. During his stay at this site he took it upon himself to reorganize the storekeeping so that it would correspond to Federal Electric Company standards, knowing as he did so that the benefits of this action would accrue not only to himself but to future storekeepers here. He has worked long hours in this reorganization without extra pay and with no instructions from me. I cannot speak too highly of his capacities and would not hesitate to recommend him in the highest possible terms to any position for which he may apply.

I signed this dubious stuff with an illegible flourish thinking, *that should keep the idle fucker quiet for a while.*

Memoirs of a Maths Crammer

I DON'T REMEMBER the exact date I first met Harold Ross, but it must have been very early in 1960, for I'd been down from the DEW-Line about a year. Back in Montreal I'd been trying to catch up on my social life, dealing with complex family matters, and considering with a good deal of anxiety my personal future. In the summer looming ahead I was due to enter my early thirties, a bad period for most people since at thirty, quite apart from the usual spiritual problems, one is either a youthful success or a middle-aged failure – at any rate, that is what I thought. I was reading Camus, then very fashionable, and was in the habit of stating that the only philosophical question of any significance was that of suicide; but since I was also of a naturally cheerful disposition and seemed unlikely to put my conclusions into practice I was regarded as insincere or, as we used to say in those days, inauthentic. But I was genuinely concerned about the future mostly because I couldn't visualize how I could make a living. Electronics nauseated me (I'd also been reading a lot of Sartre) and so did the thought of physical work. I had acquired an interest in a laundry not far from McGill and was busy watching its rapid dissolution into constituent parts of iron, salt, and water with less detachment than I publicly assumed. What with the breakdown of machinery, the business of finding the stamps I was supposed to stick into my employee's insurance books, and of remembering to deduct provincial income tax from their wages and not to pocket the amounts but to forward them to some office or other to avoid threatening letters and then the visit, on one occasion, of two sinister-looking hit-men from the government claiming to be bailiffs, the place had become a daily nightmare. I did not want to be a laundryman; I did not want to be a businessman of any kind. All I wanted was a little place on the Dordogne and perhaps a town-house in Manhattan, but I was willing to settle for a tolerable job providing good income, ample leisure, and as little actual work as possible.

Thus Harold Ross's advertisement in the Montreal *Star* for a man or woman capable of teaching maths and physics to high school students interested me very much. I had already considered becoming a teacher – in my ignorance the work sounded easy, well-paid, and padded about with pensions and fringe benefits – a consideration, after a fairly rackety decade, of some importance to me in those days. But in Quebec a man who was not a Catholic was held to be a Protestant, and if he wanted to become a teacher he had to apply to the Protestant School Board whose first requirement was a letter from his minister testifying as to his moral character. As an atheist and returning DEW-Liner I could provide neither minister nor letter and even though my moral condition in the Arctic was exemplary (there wasn't much occasion for it to be otherwise) I failed to get anybody to say so in writing. Thus the Quebec high school system lost me forever.

Harold Ross, however, clearly ran an Outsider's school unconnected with any provincial bureaucracy – a school which had the word LOOPHOLE written all over it. Intrigued, I showed the advertisement to my friend and neighbour Irving Layton, the poet, who assured me with his customary enthusiasm, that I was on to a good thing.

'My God!' he shouted, 'Ross! Why I worked for Ross after the war! Teaching veterans! John, this is what you've always wanted! A profession! A chance to influence young minds! The future! Nubile female bodies! Go after it! You'll never regret it! It's a wonderful profession!' etc., etc.

He went on to explain that Ross had started his business after the war to coach returning military personnel through the entrance exams to Sir George Williams College, from which he had acquired some sort of accreditation, the exact nature of which Irving did not make clear and which I, in later months, never entirely got straight. But Ross somehow wielded the authority to set his own exams and thus screen out students who might have slipped out of the usual educative meshes. Irving had worked there at a critical time in *his* life before he had established himself as a full-time teacher at the

Herzliah School, a poet, and a titillator of Town of Mount Royal matrons.

Heartened as I nearly always was by my friend, I phoned Ross the next morning and presented myself to him the same day.

At first glance, Ross did not cut as prepossessing a figure as I might have hoped. He was a short, stumpy man with little brown eyes embedded in sagging pockets of porous-looking flesh, and dank fronds of brown hair wiped flat over a sweaty, glistening scalp. His cheeks were pendulous and spread like thick lard over his facial bones producing an oddly shapeless effect, though the heavy lips were so definitely frog-like as to make one gasp as if to repress an unforgivable personal comment. And over the two years I worked for him I felt I was constantly fighting back such comments, as were several of my colleagues, or so they afterwards claimed. It was as though one felt compelled to intervene in his appearance in some way. This extraordinary mouth was in constant motion as it sometimes suckled and nurtured, at other times disturbed and chivvied, the remains of a cheap but fat cigar that always seemed to be in the same state of exfoliation. The cigars, probably bought in bulk at bargain prices like the Taiwanese chalk he provided for his staff, seemed to lack the elementary property of solid matter of retaining its shape. Certainly they fixed him, like photographic chemicals, with sepia fingers and a flecked and reeking upper torso. Through the remnants of his cigars you could hear Ross's wheezing breath, a noise rising in pitch as he clambered up the many staircases of his school with an odd, slow, lurching motion as though his varicosed legs, sodden with dropsy and phlebitis, could hardly bear his considerable weight. His legs and arms, even cased in their thick layers of tweed and flannel, suggested puppet limbs badly carved from water-logged maple – a wood 'seldom inward sound,' as Spenser puts it. I hesitate to claim that behind this ugly exterior there lurked a refined and humane spirit, but I am forced to in the interests of truth. You could see it often in his sudden amiability, in his delight in jokes, even of the most feeble sort. For example, I remember a student grabbing me in the hall to ask me what a Stoic was and I, half-abstractedly, replying that it was something you did to a coal fire when suddenly I caught a glimpse of Ross, unseen until then, in the background. He lifted his hand to the ghastly remnant of his stogie, removed it, dribbling a little black juice, to chuckle – wheezing and muttering like one of my own decrepit washing machines or like a boiler with a leaky valve. But this smile, and others like it, softened and even beautified his features like the mythical jewel irradiating the forehead of a toad – the weirdness, the ugliness vanished and one saw the joyous human being trying to emerge – 'pure spirit', in Bergson's lovely phrase, 'ascending against a downfalling rain of matter'. This new, spiritual, smiling Ross lumbering through the corridors of his school put me in mind of some benign and pottering gnome, happy about his woodland, his cave, his treasure.

Ross gave me his hand – an experience so like being presented with hanks of damp and tarry oakum that one was at a loss to clasp it in greeting or caulk seams with it – and asked me to run a sample class. We had arranged this by telephone and I brushed up my Archimedes' principle, the subject of the lesson, which runs like this:

> When a body is partly or wholly immersed in a fluid it experiences an upthrust equal to the weight of fluid displaced.

I trotted out this principle easily enough since I had learned it by rote in my own high school many years before, but it was greeted with blank incomprehension. It also seemed to evoke lewd chuckles over a veiled sexual imagery not obvious to me in my own schooldays. I looked over the class. Though the age of veterans had long passed, these were not high-school children – they were all of them young adults staring at me with varying degrees of mockery and hostility. The men were blue-chinned, muscular, and tall, and looked as though they would prefer to be on a beach kicking sand in my face. The women were not only nubile, as Irving had promised, but *zoftig*, languorous, and clearly as lecherous as sparrows. Why were we wasting our time doing physics, I thought. Why were we not, Ross included, getting in touch with our raging lusts?

With an effort, blushing and stammering, the centre of too much attention, I proceeded to give examples intended to demonstrate buoyancy – for instance, the loading of a flat-bottomed barge with coal. I tried to draw a picture of such a barge on the board, but Ross's friable chalk, white but with a coating of yellow, indelible powder, crumbled in my hand eliciting contemptuous sniggers. Too little pressure and the chalk would leave no mark at all, too much and it would burst all over you. It took me months to get the hang of it. But this lesson finally ended and with it the afternoon's schooling. With a whoop the class dismissed – the boys to beat one another to a pulp or to invade the local pool-halls, the girls to whisper and giggle in secret corners, exchanging trophies. Ross took me aside and tried to show me how to manage the chalk. It was also his opinion that the students wouldn't understand about coal or flat-bottomed barges. Nobody in Montreal burned the former and the latter were never seen on the St. Lawrence River. Thus my illustrations were incomprehensible. Incidentally, Ross turned out to be wrong about this: I have since tried to teach Archimedes' principle in Vancouver where coal-laden trains chug through the city each day on the way to Robert's Bank, while a plethora of flat-bottomed barges ply the Georgia Strait. But despite these visual aids the principle remains opaque to high school students and I do not believe it can ever be *taught* – only grasped in a flash of divine illumination, like an epiphany.

I left Ross with a feeling of shame and failure. He had found nothing positive to say about my performance and I could not blame him. I would not be able to winter it out as a teacher – that much was certain. I had made a fool of myself and the future looked even bleaker than it had the day before. I confessed these negative thoughts to Irving who told me not to worry – the Master Spirit was at hand and as proof of it he would read me this poem he'd written that very day. He did so – indeed, it was never very easy to stop him – but the rendition did little to elevate my mood. So the next morning I was amazed to received a phone call from Ross telling me I had already missed my first class, that he had been forced to stand in for me, and what was the matter, was I ill? And if I were not, I'd better get over to the school right away for the second maths class. I had been hired and did not know it.

Later I discovered this was typical of Ross's stance towards the world. He was never able to hire people or to fire them. Nor was he able to issue anybody with a contract. He wanted you to trust him and in return he trusted you. He thought that forms and written contracts worked against the grain of human nature considered at its optimum, as he wished to consider it, and that the people he interviewed knew, without his authority, when they were fit to work for him and when they were not. I was happy to fall in with this illusion partly because I had lied to him – I had told him I had a degree from the University of London and this was something less than the truth: I had not even *flunked* out of there; it was from the University of Wales that I had flunked. Mostly, however, it was because Ross possessed in his spiritual armoury a quality I had never met before – he was the first optimist concerning human nature that I'd met who was neither a dolt nor an unworldly Jesus freak. He was a highly intelligent secular humanist who, knowing the world, still thought of its inhabitants as fundamentally virtuous and hospitable. Such an attitude, I think, is a Gift and I was not then able to receive it.

Ross's teachers were men and women who called forth his own hospitality. He helped me, he helped Irving Layton, whom Ross remembered with warmth but whose poetry he pretended to scorn, the novelist John Metcalf, the poet Bryan McCarthy, a painter named David Silverberg, a playwright called James Harris, and so on – people who as would-be artists had defined themselves as outsiders. I think Ross saw us as people of talent and ability to teach but too high-spirited and idiosyncratic to fit in with provincial school boards, Protestant or Catholic. He even retained this romantic attitude towards his students – they were too energetic and creative, too individualistic, to be constrained by the high school system which, as everybody knows, is a prison whose purpose is to keep young people out of the job market and to delay their adulthood as long as possible. Let them have their fling, Ross seemed to be saying, as rebels against a stupid and iniquitous system, then send them to me for their education.

In theory, of course, he was quite right. You do not need six years of high school to learn the curriculum it offers. Anybody of average intelligence can master it in six weeks. The best of Ross's students took a year, however, and it is at this point that his theory broke down: only a tiny minority of Ross's students were awaiting sympathetic and flexible teachers to awaken them – the majority were juvenile delinquents, flashers, radiator clutchers, nymphomaniacs, B & E artists, car stealers, dope pushers, schizophrenics, morons, manic-depressives, hit-men, con artists, pornographers and the like. Either they were offspring of anxious, middle-class parents able to afford Ross's high fees as a last chance for their children, or of less respectable but more interesting underworld figures, such as a serious and pleasant youth whose name I remember, probably wrongly, as Petronella, whose two uncles and a cousin had been murdered by their fellow *mafiosi* for speaking out of their turn. There was a sexy girl named Marcia whose father was in 'import-export' who claimed to have been kidnapped three times, quite possibly, it occurred to me, by Petronella's relatives.

Anybody who could keep discipline in those classes could keep it anywhere. I could do it only by the most terrible of efforts and mostly by play-acting psychotic frenzies. I tried at first to be more civilized and to penalize minor infractions by setting culprits essays to write on subjects then dear to my heart: 'The Mutability of Human Affairs', 'The Void', 'Anxiety', 'Fear and Trembling Along Life's Way', etc. Alas, the little cretins didn't even understand the titles. I had to settle for such standbys as writing out five hundred times the words 'I must not open my Big Mouth in Class'. Ross did not back me up in the matter of the essays, but he supported the writing of lines. I once asked him what I should do if a student refused such an assignment. 'Send him to me,' he said grimly. 'Well, but what would *you* do?' I riposted. 'If necessary, expel him,' he replied. 'But surely,' I argued, 'that's just what the little plug-ugly wants.' Ross smiled at my naïveté. 'In some instances,' he said, '*the fees are not returnable*.' Ross's technique was to suggest to the parents at the outset that any such financial loss should be charged against the child's pocket money. A simple but effective device for keeping discipline.

I envied Ross his own effortless ability to walk into a class and achieve instant silence. This was not just because he was the principal, but due to some odd, toad-like charisma that even I could perceive. And this was the second of Ross's Gifts; he was a living demonstration that a person's authority has nothing to do with his appearance, manner, or even what he knows – it is a spiritual state or, to use a language with which Ross himself would've felt more comfortable, a condition of being. This, as it turned out, was a Gift I was able to make use of a couple of years later when I had enrolled as a student in the University of British Columbia's Education Faculty, where I was told a good teacher wore neutral clothes, had no mannerisms, looked clean, and did not jiggle chalk in his hand. I was able to stand up and denounce this for the rubbish that it is, using as examples some of the teachers who had influenced me (most of them highly eccentric, not to say demented) and the prime one of Ross himself.

By the time the school year ended I had had enough of dragging these young hoods out of the pool halls for their physics class, of preventing fights and rapes, of giving them things to write, and of growing hoarse over them. The summer, which zephyrs into Montreal with a great, liberating burst, had just arrived and I was making my own arrangements for moving into the wider world. One afternoon a student fell in step with me as I was walking home, and the following dialogue took place:

'Hey, uh, I hear you get to set the math exam.'

'That's correct.'

'And you get to mark it, dontcha?'

'True.'

'Jeez, uh, I really need to pass that exam.'

'Then if I were you I should spend the next three days in prayer.'

'Jeez, I really need to pass.' Pause. Footsteps echoing blithely along the walls of Hutchinson Street in which I lived. Birdsong. Children yelling joyously in background.

'Uh.'

'Yes?'

'Well, I was wondering if you'd have any use for, say, a new car.' Another pause. This child is trying to bribe me, I thought. How nice of him! On the other hand there was such a thing as professional pride. Would I sell my soul for a hunk of Detroit tin can? Could I ever look at myself in the mirror again? But what if it were the driving mirror of a formula K, underslung, eccentric camshafted, ultra-radial, Lotus Mark 9, or whatever they called the things? Or would he settle for laundered sheaves of hundred-dollar bills? And why be stupid about it? Whom did it hurt? Did it hurt Ross, for example? Since I didn't believe in the teaching profession, I would lose no virtue. Of course, I would have shown myself that I could be bought, but so can anybody. Oddly, it was the thought of Ross that stopped me – this mutual trust I mentioned earlier, partly, but also I was interested to see how he would react. But it's summer, I thought. How charming to own a convertible!

'I don't have final authority,' I said. 'I suggest you go and see Ross.'

The next day I asked Ross if the student had been in to see him. 'Some of these kids,' he said very cheerfully, 'think that everything's for sale.' I took it that he had refused the bribe and felt pleased. I was also amazed that a man like Ross, having grown up in Montreal, should express surprise at the thought that everything's for sale. Thirdly, I was curious to know what would have happened if, say, Petronella, or a cousin or godfather of Petronella's, had put the proposition to us in such terms that it could not have been refused, but I was denied an answer to this riddle. Almost immediately afterwards I left the school for what I thought was forever, got married, and drove with my wife along the Blue Ridge Parkway to Tennessee then back to Portland, Maine, where I was supposed to start work on a fishing boat. This project fell through and so did many others and, slightly battered, we arrived back in Montreal just after Labour Day only to discover, from my sister, that Ross had frantically been trying to get hold of me. Another Montreal winter had begun. I went back to the crammer's school situated, but only for another term, at the corner of Park and Mount Royal Avenues, a decaying building full of listing stairs, creaking corridors, and small and draughty living areas converted to classrooms. A rickety, shambolic building destined for the wrecker's ball, but I was glad to be there. Suggestive as it was of three-legged stools, scratchy nibs, dunce's caps, and barbaric punishments out of Dickens where it did not put one in mind of shady schools like Beachcomber's Narkover Academy, it was a sort of shelter to me, a place where I could winter it out after an extremely interesting but financially disappointing summer. Above all I was glad of Ross himself, for, as he presided over his odd and rather sleazy domain like a Toad Deity out of some mythology or other, I perceived him as offering a third Gift. (I am writing this at Christmas time when it seems natural to think of Gifts grouping themselves in threes.) He was the first employer in whom I did not detect the cloven hoof; he was the first patriarchal figure whom I did not experience as malign.

The Ross High School moved in the new year to an office building on Decarie Boulevard and entered a new phase of its strange career, but this time without me. My wife and I packed all our worldly goods into a car and drove slowly west in order to homestead in British Columbia – another plan that got modified by the reality principle. I do not know quite when it was Ross died. He was certainly alive in 1966, for he wrote a recommendation for me to teach in a comprehensive school in Tooting, England, an experience I would sooner forget. So he must have had to grapple with the dawn of the Age of Aquarius among the young and I would like to have known what he thought of light shows, strobe lights, marijuana, miniskirts, Vietnam, student radicalism, Afro haircuts, and adolescent antinomianism. But my conversation with him on these and related matters will have to wait.

Memoirs of a Mud-Wrestler

A Rigmarole

IT'S NOT OFTEN I read critical commentary on my own writing, partly because there isn't much of it around, but mostly because once I've written something and let it loose upon the world my interest turns to what comes next. Recently, however, a friend pointed me to an article in *Books in Canada*, a sort of brochure published in Toronto, in which a reviewer had written that 'John Mills is to the field of literary criticism what a mud-wrestler is to athletics.' I am quoting from memory and may not have got the exact wording, but that was the gist of it and, judging by the context, it was not intended as a compliment. Nevertheless I was delighted with the remark – I know intuitively what it means and I am inclined to agree with it. Mud-wrestlers are coarse-fibred souls who embark on the crushing of a novel or a poem with a kind of fat and clumsy brute force. Their idea of finesse is the hundredweight sack of cornmeal poised on the half-open door and their chosen weapons are the bludgeon, the sap, the quarterstaff. I can offer from my own experience the example of a mud-wrestler named Robert Nye who, in the pages of the British newspaper the *Manchester Guardian*, called my first novel *The Land of Is* a 'ghastly mish-mash of modernism' then quoted my publisher's ill-judged comment on the dust-jacket that I had once earned my living as a Gandy-dancer in order to say 'there's a great future for Mills as a Gandy-dancer, whatever that means.' Nye was wrong about *The Land of Is* (as was another Englishman, Maurice Wiggin, who in the pages of *The Observer*, that same week, described it as an 'august and noble work of art'), but his comment illustrates a chief mud-wrestling feature – extravagance, hyperbole, and carelessness in the service of either praise or denunciation. In contrast to Nye, myself, or even Wiggin, there is the more judicious, cooler, rope-dancing sort of critic – undeterred by abstract ideas, playful among philosophers and historians, filled with wisdom, culture, and creativity who can approach a literary work with the delicacy and daring of a surgeon cutting into a living body, and in whom, even at moments of solemn pronouncement, there gleams a kind of mad gaiety, a wild *sprezzatura*, and whose tools are the scalpel and the poniard. Examples? Well, C.S. Lewis, for one – never mind his children's books, or his Christian apologetics (though these are useful if you haven't the time to read Hans Küng) – look up *Allegory of Love*, or the work on sixteenth-century literature. Lionel Trilling – what about him? Eliot, Susan Sontag, Matthew Arnold, Edmund Wilson, Sir Philip Sidney. I admire these people but could no more aspire to their level of achievement than could my anonymous *Books in Canada* reviewer. My aspirations, my sympathies, are with another group altogether, the put-down men and women of our literary history: Mencken, James Agate, Nathan Cohen, Thomas Nashe, Robert Graves, Ezra Pound. My old professor Yvor Winters. Perhaps even poor mad Lawrence who wrestled Franklin and Whitman so deeply into the mud that their reputations have never fully crept out of it. These, if I had any culture heroes, would be mine – and I hasten to add that I don't regard myself, *qua* mud-wrestler, as fit to change their ribbons or sharpen their quills.

These two lists cannot, of course, be mutually exclusive: there is more than a touch of the mud-wrestler in Wilson, a very strong streak of the rope-dancer in Yvor Winters. But in general they represent the two categories of critic before the rise of the new technologies and the Sahelization of literary criticism into semiotics, hermeneutics, language theory, Frankfurt School obscurantics, phenomenology, post-structuralism, and so on, creating vast deserts over which many a poor graduate student, many a twitching assistant professor (as well as many a charlatan, many a band-wagonist), wander black of tongue and parched of throat in search of a T.A.ship, a merit increment, or a tenure-track appointment.

So, O most affable reader, what are you, rope-dancer or mud-wrestler? There will be an element of each in you, of course, but genes, temperament, training, and the accidents of your life will incline you towards one pole or the other. I knew, very early in my career, that I was a mud-wrestler and it was to those depths I bent my will. My own mother was a mud-wrestler to be reckoned with, and my propensities were encouraged by early years in Europe, and the friendship, in early-middle manhood, of some of the finest exponents of the art in our time: Bryan McCarthy, the poet and critic, John Richmond, the teacher, journalist, and con-man, and Irving Layton, poet and professional extrovert. What follows is a stretch of autobiography involving these people, an account of my apprenticeship under their mud-wrestling direction, and I shall call it a *rigmarole* for reasons which will become clear as we proceed.

TWO

IN JANUARY 1959 I re-entered Montreal permanently after spending eighteen months in and around the Arctic as a technician on the DEW-Line, a system of radar stations obsolete even when it was being built. There was a certain futility about such work, but I left the North with some regrets and considerable anxiety. There was enough to worry about: first and most pressing on me was the problem of how to make a living. I had saved about ten thousand dollars, but this would vanish without trace or savouring under pressure of need, like *premier cru* wine at a hippy banquet, leaving me as broke as I was before. No investment could give me a decent wage, nor could I see any business enterprise in which I might willingly involve myself. Northern wisdom nagged at me: old hands used to say *never spend your own capital ... spend other people's.* Work if you have to, they'd say; get a job. There was a respectful, even melancholy silence after these words, for men used to their freedom and the slow, easy rhythms of the outback do not speak glibly of getting jobs. Well, unless something turned up I would, to prevent my bank account bleeding itself white, have to look for one.

Furthermore, I was returning to a situation of some complexity. A couple of years before, my sister Jill had become, long before it was fashionable, a single parent. She had escaped from England and moved into my apartment on Ridgewood Avenue, a line of red brick apartment houses that snakes up the hill from Côte des Neiges to

St. Joseph's Oratory. A good friend of ours, named Jerome, who had chosen to become a student at McGill, joined us and, when it became clear that I was to spend most of my time in the North, I sent for my mother who, Jill told me, had become a reformed character. There were a number of advantages to this scheme, or so it seemed to me: the apartment was certainly big enough to contain the three of them – celibate adults, and a baby; my mother had, though one might not think so to look at her offspring, some skill with small children and in any case, in her early sixties, she needed a serious interest in life. Jerome would enjoy cheap board and lodging and supply a much needed male presence. It wasn't long, though, before my mail was containing the most desperate cries for help. As far as my mother was concerned, Jerome had become an unmitigated force for evil, part of the Devil's brood ... no redeeming social content ... never mind that she'd been taken in by him at first meeting ... that just showed the bestial cunning behind the smooth façade ... a viper, that's what he was, and what's more important he was keeping potential suitors from Jill's door ... and the first step we have to take, the most important thing in all our lives at the moment ... was to get her *married off* ... understand? *Married Off!* And what's more this creature's pretending to be a student ... at his age! When most self-respecting men had embarked on their careers! Getting married to suitable girls! Not being a trial to their families! Friends! Respectable people around them! It was abnormal, that's what it was, and the sooner I got down from the Arctic and sorted things out, the better.

I would read these pages in dim light (as befitted them) at a table illuminated only by the yellow vectors sweeping out circles on the radar screens. The Russians could've flown by in droves, squadrons, flotillas, for all I cared – let them pulverize all those little beasts pledging every morning allegiance to the American flag, all those apple pies cooling on the window sills. This crepuscular peace, this low and soothing hum of electric fans cooling the triodes, pentodes, magnetrons and klystrons around me, was too valuable to waste on surveillance. Like my colleagues, I would use the time to write letters, novels, essays, and to read fiction, text books, manuals, and dreadful letters of the kind my poor sister was sending me. How the hell was she coping? Not very well, evidently, judging by her comments that she was slowly but surely being driven insane 'by this mad woman, our mother,' and that I had 'better get down here quick and deal with this raging harpy, this demon, this poisonous and demented witch.' These struck me as expressions of considerable pain and discontent, of genuine *angst*. But I was not going to leave this Arctic womb before I was ready to, before my contract was up. And I didn't look forward to adjudicating between the needs of these people all with legitimate and conflicting claims on my loyalty. Why, I even got a plaintive letter from Jerome, that soul of tolerance, advising me that life on Ridgewood had become problematic – an almost constant screaming match – and he wasn't sure he could stand it. He looked forward very much to my return.

When it came time to leave and I found myself in Edmonton, the first port of civilization and outpost of the American military empire, I very nearly stayed there. Let them get on with it, I thought. My God, they're all adults. Why should I become their arbiter? I paid the rent, made easy living possible for them; let them learn to live in harmony. As for me, I shall go to the South of France ... sunshine ... culture ... love. I would wait here, in Edmonton, for my final cheque to come through, and not go home at all. But in two days the horrors of that town, its emptiness and banality, drove me to Montreal.

I lumbered up the stairs hefting my kit-bag and a suitcase and rang the bell. My mother opened the door cautiously then swung it wide and almost leaped on me.

'Oh my God, you're back ... I almost gave up ... it's been utterly intolerable here ... that man ... you've no idea what I've been through trying to keep that man at bay ... and your poor nephew ... poor little David ... that man's been turning him into a nervous wreck ... and your sister ... I've never seen her look so pale, so overwrought ... not her fault if she's turning into a shouting, screaming minx ... that man's done it ... it would be all right here if only he were to get out ... so thank God you've come ... he wouldn't budge for me ... idle, scrounging, good-for-nothing ... asleep all day ... on the sofa, if you please ... large as life ... if you can call it life ... broad daylight and the blinds drawn ... no food in the refrigerator ... you can't keep anything in it with that man around ... and me coming in from shopping with an armful of bags and parcels ... coming up those stairs ... and him asleep on his back with the blinds drawn ... two o'clock in the afternoon ... shook him? ... kicked him, more like it: I wouldn't touch that slimy creature with my bare hands ... up! I said. Up you get, you guzzling, swilling, idle heap of muck. Up! before I throw cold water over you ... and you know what that filthy, impudent snake in the grass had the gall to say to me? You sick, noisy old bag! That's right! Calling me names! Your own mother! Names! I rushed into the kitchen for a saucepan of water but by the time I got back with it he'd given me the slip ... just as well ... I wouldn't have thought twice about it ... soaked him, that's what I was prepared to do, soak him from head to foot ... and then I told your sister about it and you know what she said to me? *I wish I was dead*, she said to me. *Wished she was dead.* There's gratitude for you ... after all I've done for her ... after I'd got rid of him on her behalf ... because let me tell you this, my dear, she's better off without him ... in more ways than one ... '

'Just a minute,' I said, 'just a damned minute. I've only just got in the door. I've had a hard trip ... let me get this straight ... where's Jerome now?'

'As if I care where he's gone ... all I know is that he'll be back ... his filthy stuff is still here ... that's where you come in ... getting rid of him for good ... he's not wanted here ... a bad influence ... he bounces that little child on his knees and God only knows what thoughts are going on in his filthy, disgusting mind ... it's frightening to think about ... the papers in England are full of that kind of thing ... pervert, that's what he is ... he ought to be locked up ... jail ... the police station ... '

'Are you telling me,' I started to shout, 'that you think Jerome's a goddamned pederast? Are you insinuating ... '

'Insinuating! Don't you use words like insinuating with me, my dear ... and mind your tone ... I'm your mother ... you young people have no respect ... you, your sister ... that Jewish vixen downstairs ... *don't be so rude.* There he is and there's your sister, and he hasn't looked at her that way once since I've been here ... any normal man would've made a grab for her body, that's all, just for her body, and he hasn't made a move, not one, in her direction, not when I've been in the building, and I've got a sharp nose for that kind of thing, thank God ... God knows what they get up to when I'm out ... but it's little David I'm worried about ... you've no idea what being fondled like that by men of his kind can do in later life ... my God, it's criminal ... we have to put a stop to it ... you have to get rid of him ... throw his things down the stairs ... lock, stock, and barrel ... pervert did you say? Yes, and a sewer rat as well. *A homosexual sewer rat.*'

'Speak to me like that about my friend,' I screamed, 'about my sister? Your brain's diseased! You're sick!'

Sheer malice made me add, 'and I can't kick him out ... they're engaged! Engaged to be married!'

My mother gasped as though I'd just hauled off and kicked her in the stomach.

'Married? Married? What's this? Did you say they were engaged to be married? This ... this is news to me ... this is the first time I ... well, if that's true that puts a whole new light on the subject ... it's ... John! Where is he? Where's he gone? You must know where to find him! We've got to get him back!'

'That's right,' I shouted, maddened by not being greeted, furious at being dumped on the moment I stepped in the door by a woman I'd last clapped eyes on eight years before and these were her first words. 'You want me to get him back,' I said. 'You don't care who he is so long as Jill marries him ... he could be a gangster, a dope addict, a homosexual sewer rat ... it's all the same to you. Well, I'm contracting out ... '

'Wait a minute ... wait a minute ... John, where are you going? Sit down ... take your things off ... let's discuss this calmly ... an offer, you said ... she's had an offer. John ... don't go ... don't go ... come back here at once!'

But I had dumped my bags on the floor and turned on my heel. I fled down the stairs and, *en passant*, rang the downstairs apartment bell. I knew I would meet a warm welcome there. But the vixen herself was not at home. I strode instead up the hill, towards the Oratory, to an apartment inhabited by another single parent and her brother, a man named Graham Seal, where I could be pretty certain of meeting my old and valued friend Bryan McCarthy.

THREE

BETWEEN MCCARTHY, Graham, and me there was much in common. Struggling to become writers, we were each of us aware of our late starts. We were approaching our thirties, nothing done yet, nothing published, the world too much with us, no contacts in the literary world to speak of except with other would-be writers – Milton Acorn for instance ... Al Purdy ... Leonard Cohen ... none of whom had at that time achieved any recognition ... and Irving Layton. He was the only one amongst us who had at least broken into the small magazines, had had books published by arty presses with eccentric names. Irving was then at the height of his drive to power; he would recite his poems anywhere – in a classroom, in a salon, on a bus to perfect strangers. His efforts were beginning to pay off. He lived in a small house on Côte St. Luc and it was there, whenever I was in town, that I would read my feeble writings to him. I was attempting to create short stories, even though (since each seemed to contain within itself the seeds of its own growth like a grain of years) I was uneasy with the form. My first was about a young, intense student in North Wales out rock-climbing with a fellow mountaineer towards whom he feels great envy. There is a girl with them whom the hero covets, though she herself seems to covet the rival. This rival is struck by a falling rock during the ascent of some dank gully, an accident which, though badly hurt, he survives. During the rescue operation and while the rival is carried off on a stretcher, the hero declares himself to the girl. She admits to being pregnant by the rival. It was a melancholy, self-pitying tale based on my own experience. The tense, jealous, working-class boy was me, the rival a rich public school man named Roy Evans who later in 'real life' was killed in the Alps. Sad though it was, I was pleased with it and the night I finished it I took it round and read it to Irving.

'All right, I suppose,' he said. 'But it's not a short story ... '

'What do you mean, it's not a short story? You think it's a play? A villanelle, for Christ's sake?'

'It's not a short story,' the Master replied patiently, 'because it contains none of the ingredients of a short story ... no surprise ... no epiphany ... no sense of the intractable core of the bizarre in human affairs ... You don't read, my friend, that's your problem. When did you read Faulkner ... *last*? Hemingway ... *last*. Conrad ... Mansfield ... James ... Lawrence ... when did you read any of them ... *last*? It's got no tension, no shape ... it's too obvious ... too *sculpted* whilst being at the same time formless.'

'You may be a poet, Irving,' I said, 'though there are some, including myself, who might have trouble describing you as such, but you're a tyro when it comes to prose.'

The Master sat back and smiled in a maddeningly superior way. 'There, my friend, you would be wrong. I know a lot about prose. And don't be so touchy. I didn't say you have no talent. You've a good eye for landscape ... your descriptions have a certain lush, perfervid power. But as a short story your piece is a crock of shit. Go away and work on it.'

I took off fuming with anger. That this cheapjack, poetasting, gallowsglass should have the nerve to criticize a work of mine! It wasn't until I got home and reread it that I saw he was quite possibly right. Epiphany ... intractable core of the bizarre ... carefully, slowly, I began to tinker with it.

At any rate, the day I got home, I was half-expected at the Seal's. I received a warm greeting and a tumbler of Queberac, the remains of a gallon of which stood on the floor central to the three large sofas facing inward. Graham lay on one, McCarthy on the second, and I on the third. It was as though I had taken up my life again exactly where I had left off – before my Arctic travels – the three of us drinking white wine and discussing, much to the despair of our womenfolk, ways of avoiding work. McCarthy smiled crookedly.

'Glad you're back,' he said. 'We seem to be running out of booze.'

'I've got a bit of money,' I said.

'We know that,' Graham said. 'We thought you probably had just under ten grand.'

'It should last us a year,' McCarthy speculated, 'provided we don't overspend on food.'

'People around here,' I commented, 'will have to get through life without the use of my bank account. As for me, I have to get a job.'

There was a stunned silence.

'A job?' McCarthy said eventually. 'You're dreaming, old boy. There aren't any jobs. Not of the kind you could take ... nobody would have you, in any case. You've been out of the work force too long ... they don't like that. You've been a free man ... they don't like that either.'

'They'll want to punish you,' Graham said. 'I should lie very low if I were you.'

We drank for a while in silence. I told them about my mother and the violent passions unleashed in the apartment block down the road. They were inclined to discount them. Jill, my mother, everybody in Montreal who happened to be enslaved by money or the need to work each day was in the winter doldrums. Post Christmas blues ... a new year dawning and nothing accomplished ... the mixture as before ... no ecstatic vision, no promises of transcendence ... nothing but eat, sleep, drink. Work. Look after babies and struggle to pay the rent, the mortgage. Christ! Where's the joy in that? And is that what human life is all about? No wonder they're a bit touchy down there ... everybody is.

I rejected this detached, sub-Kierkegaardian point of view and suggested demonic possession. They scoffed at this hypothesis and Graham went so far as to tell me he thought my mother was rather a nice old lady.

'But where am I to stay?' I said.

'With a girl friend,' they said.

Naturally I had given this some thought. I had left town on good terms with a number of young women, but what they had done in my absence was problematical. Aviva had become more and more tied to Irving Layton, Edith and I had fought bitterly by mail, Lucille was amiable but private and rather weird. There were two others, but both had got married in my absence. I was not going back to that apartment, certainly not that night, and in any case I wanted to find Jerome.

'You should meet John,' McCarthy said. 'John Richmond. He'll find Jerome for you ... and a place to live. He knows everything.'

'*Doctor* Richmond?'

'The Herr Doktor. I've just found out he lives down the street, here on Ridgewood. I told him you were due back. He's keen to meet you.'

'Why?'

'Matters of mutual interest, old boy.'

The locution of this statement, coupled with the 'old boys' my friend had started to throw around, seemed uncharacteristic, and I later discovered that McCarthy had consciously or unconsciously adopted a Richmond mannerism. McCarthy had met him at a Jewish private school called Herzliah where they were both part-time teachers. And so, oddly enough, was Irving, whom they had both started calling 'the Gaffer.' McCarthy had written to tell me about this new star in our rather limited firmament in terms of delight and approval – it made me jealous and intensely suspicious. I doubted that Richmond was a genuine Ph.D. What would a man with such qualifications be doing, in those days, outside a university? Much later Jerome, who hated him, went to great lengths to discover if Richmond had indeed earned a doctorate from St. John's College, Cambridge, as he claimed, and drew a blank. Nevertheless, the rabbis who ran Herzliah were impressed with him as were the parents of the school's frenetic teenagers (whose vast energies were focused on minor gangsterism, cheating, establishing and defending territory, rape, destruction, and the consumption of massive quantities of junk food). McCarthy used to say it was very nearly impossible to keep order in such a place, a maelstrom, at the best of times, of screaming and violence, and a common sight there was a gentle rabbi, his head pressed to the wall, shuddering as though afflicted with the bleakest of agues. But Richmond evidently could keep order and, when I met him later that night, I could understand why. He was half a generation older than us, in his early forties, short, frowning, and stubbily built. His forehead was high and made higher by a receding hair-line. Thick spectacles made his prominent, mad eyes swim out at you like a brace of barracuda in a bullet-proof tank. The secret of his success as a disciplinarian, McCarthy said, was his ability to fly in an instant into psychotic rages, feigned or otherwise, which would amuse the children as well as cowing them and which featured hysterical screaming accompanied with wild swings of a stout walking stick or knobkerrie, an implement he was never without. He answered his door and spoke, his voice deep and patrician.

'Come in, old boy,' he said to me. 'By Jove, I *am* glad to meet you ... by Jove ... come on in for *God's* sake ... in from the icy fang and churlish chiding of the winter's wind.'

Piss on this, I thought. The Montreal winter was indeed at its bitter peak, but we were standing in the hallway of an apartment block kept, as is the Eastern custom, at eighty degrees or more. Inside his apartment, however, there was greater comfort, for Richmond had opened a window half an inch. Deep armchairs and large bookcases produced an effect of wealth and seclusion, though Richmond could not, at that time, have been particularly well off. An attractive blond woman in early middle age, rather subdued and verging on the timid, was introduced to us as his wife, Nina. This household also contained, though not the first night I was there, a child named Christie, a plump, demanding adolescent destined to blossom later into a very beautiful young woman indeed.

'Scotch?' Richmond boomed. McCarthy and I nodded eagerly. Richmond clapped his hands briskly. Nina disappeared into the kitchen and came back with a tray on which stood a decanter and three glasses. Richmond nodded, and Nina vanished into another room.

'Burra peg, old boy?' Richmond asked. 'Or chota peg?'

I selected the former. He poured the whisky neat. 'In this house,' he said, 'Scotch is not served with water.'

'Isn't Nina drinking with us?' I asked.

'She's Greek, you know,' Richmond said, his voice dropping into confidentiality. 'They know their place, old boy.'

I nodded wisely. Here was a man, I thought, clearly engaged in the practice of curmudgeonship. This is as effective a way of confronting the world as any other, though it isn't for everybody. You need a strong and commanding personality at the back of which is a violent streak, visibly repressed. You need to intimidate, rather than befriend, and you must seek victims rather than equals. You need a brass neck and little in the way of a conscience. And you have to be solemn about it: any hint that you were not to be taken too seriously, and you were done for. There are several excellent models: Samuel Johnson; Evelyn Waugh, of course; Alexander Woollcott. That ghastly Sitwell parent, Lord Whatshisname. For women there is a splendid archetype in Oscar Wilde's invention, Lady Bracknell. The trick is to surround yourself with natural vassals. Here, I think, I did Nina an injustice. Her own very quiet sense of humour allowed her to acquiesce publicly in Richmond's game, but she wasn't exactly the doormat she appeared. I discovered in her a strong compassion and general sweetness of disposition. I think she pitied her husband and nursed his insecurities as a parent does a child. I was very fond of her and, many years later when I heard she had died, I grieved for her a long time.

Richmond handed us the Scotch. We sipped it and it was good. I said something polite about his books. He began to explain some of the intricacies of his library. He'd begun his collection of Loeb classics while he was in the fifth form of some minor public school and extended it while he was an undergraduate, though his interests had slipped to English literature. The man's a fake, I immediately assumed. I was wrong. Even Jerome, who fought with him violently over some technicality in the use of the aorist tense, acknowledged, though grudgingly, Richmond's command of classical Greek, while Richmond could do something Jerome could not – speak fluent, demotic Greek to his wife, her family, and an admiring crowd of Athenians, Spartans, Corinthians, Cretans, and Macedonians at the Elnikon Taverna on Pine Avenue where we were all of us wont to hang out. Richmond pointed to a shelf of Penguin books beautifully bound in board and cloth.

'Look at these, old boy. Little man in Alexandria did them for me. A bob apiece! Imagine it! A bob!'

I uttered a phrase in my British Army Arabic, meaning roughly, *wow*!

Richmond, delighted, addressed me in a sudden spate of liquids, gutturals, alveolar fricatives, and glottals until I had to beg him to stop.

'I only learned a few words,' I confessed.

'Then I'll teach you the rest of them,' he offered. 'And Greek too, if you like.'

Suddenly he burst into a muezzinesque wail:

'Yah tah beebee, tirallal, yuhummnick, shirallah yahummnick, yah ah ahta bin ... ' and repeated it until the three of us were singing it loudly and with the strength of three or four single malt whiskies behind us. Some twenty-five or so years after the events recorded in this rigmarole I happened to sing Richmond's song to a Lebanese graduate student of mine. She joined in and sang the whole thing from start to finish. Richmond had only taught us the chorus. But it was genuine, that was the point, and I had supposed he was inventing mock Arabic to entertain us and himself.

Who was Richmond? What was he? To this day I can't be sure. I never heard him utter a word that wasn't carefully constructed to impress, disguise, bamboozle. Nothing of him that was genuine ever came through to me, though evidently it did to McCarthy, who soon became a close friend, and to a lesser extent, to Graham. His languages were genuine enough and, in an Anglo-Saxon culture where facility even with beginner's French is regarded as a sinister affront to respectability on the order of flashing, say, or child abuse, enabled him not only to be one up on his environment but satisfactorily at odds with it. Apart from his Greek, his Arabic, I'd heard him converse with sailors off the *Alexander Pushkin*, aboard which vessel he was greeted with roars of joy and approval, with editors of *La Presse* and *Le Devoir* in fluent and witty French with now and again a trace of *joual* to show he was one of the boys, in German with waiters in the Schnitzelhaus, and Hungarian in the coffee bars along Stanley Street. It was all a part of his effort to assert himself against the *pax Americana*. So one might observe him, strutting across Mount Royal, into the busy intersections of the city, head erect, stick swinging, a heavy, disapproving frown on his face, uttering loud abuse at the swishing, maniacal Montreal traffic, and he would step off the sidewalk with his cane held firmly and horizontally like a matador's killing sword as though challenging the city's demented, homicidal drivers to mow him down. Brandishing his stick he would get to the other side of the street unscathed, something that could not happen to ordinary mortals. I often wondered how it was he had escaped being broken up, flattened, and pulped by the malevolent traffic he teased and thwarted and concluded that the drivers, in their primitive consciousnesses, must have taken him for a Divine Idiot, a holy man on whom God had laid his hand, and that he was taboo. Or perhaps he touched some residual compassion in them – a man the Almighty had so drastically afflicted must surely deserve a modicum of grace.

That night I spoke again of the tearing passions of Upper Ridgewood and my own dilemmas about money. It amused Richmond to listen to me carefully whilst wearing on his face an expression suitable to a whisky priest hearing confession from the sleaziest, most deadbeat of sinners. Every now and again he would wipe a handkerchief across his brow and examine it as though for stains. At lugubrious points in my narrative he registered mournfulness and nodded compassionately. Suddenly he burst into a series of noisy, face-splitting, multiple yawns.

'I'm boring you, old boy,' I said. 'I'm sorry.'

'No, no, old bean ... no, no ... '

He allowed his eyes to glaze over and his head to move from side to side as though seeking ways of escape.

'You think I should go ahead and bugger off to the south of France?'

'No, no, old boy, definitely not.' Suddenly a look of enormous *gravitas* composed itself on his face. '*Hell is portable*,' he said. This was an expression I was to hear him use on many occasions.

Suddenly he pretended to cheer up in the manner of one perceiving the solution to a difficult problem in ontology.

'When in doubt, old boy, teach.'

'Teach? I'm not a teacher.'

'Nonsense. Anybody can teach.'

'Teach what, my dear fellow?'

'Teach what? Why, teach anything.'

'Arabic, old cheese?'

'Why not? Get a book. Stay one page ahead of the student. Teach, old fruit, that's the ticket.'

'At Herzliah?'

'Oh no, no, no, no, no, no ... definitely not. Not Herzliah. Stay clear of the rabbin.' (He chuckled at some private joke.)

'And clear of the Gaffer,' McCarthy said. His eyes had furred over noticeably, his voice was not what it was an hour before, and his nose seemed to have reddened and become bulbous.

'Particularly the Gaffer,' Richmond affirmed.

'The Gaffer hath the falling sickness,' I said in revenge for the quotation with which we'd been greeted at the door.

'Ah,' Richmond said, as though he'd caught me out. 'The Gaffer hath it not, but you and I, and honest Bryan here, we have the falling sickness.'

By now it was too late. I'd had enough for one day. McCarthy was flopping down on one of the Seal sofas. I decided to sleep on the other. Together we staggered up Ridgewood, the night cold, but clear and hopeful, and showered with a million stars.

FOUR

I'D ALWAYS thought of Jerome as sad and self-imprisoned, yet there were unexpected riches to his personality. His voice was one of the slowest, deepest, and most beautifully articulated I have ever heard. He acquired it partly from his school, partly from his habit of phoning people he admired to ask them how they'd achieved their personas. He would phone dukes, actors, financiers – you couldn't be in London five minutes without Jerome getting on the blower to ask for the address of your tailor, your elocutionist, your shirt-maker. He modelled himself on one of his victims, George Sanders, particularly as that actor had played Lord Henry Wotton, Dorian Grey's mentor, and carefully studied the gracious-living magazines together with the *Tailor and Cutter.* This immaculate being would emerge on weekends from his working-class dwelling in Pimlico (he'd been a scholarship boy) to confront the world as a suave, intimidating, English gentleman. He fleshed out the physical side of his personality with body-building and jiu-jitsu – the martial art in fashion before the advent of karate. This one might observe in the contradictions between the sophisticated lounge-lizard manner and the tough, heavily delted, triked, and latted physique. Later, in Canada, he developed karate, shaved his skull, and force-fed himself almost to obesity on scrounged protein – festoons of steak, cod, spareribs, haddock. Thus Jerome trundling down the street towards you was a figure to be reckoned with – huge gut and shoulders, shaven skull, bespoke suit, gentle expression and, by Canadian perceptions, poofter's voice, moving with the nautical roll he'd cultivated at an earlier stage in his life.

When Jerome lived with you there were only three disadvantages: he was more often than not low in funds and would feel forced to raid your refrigerator, emptying it, such was the vastness of his appetite, his sheer need for protein, at a swoop. Sometimes he would work for a living, though with understandable reluctance, as night porter, watchman, night clerk ... jobs that suited his nocturnal habits. Thus the second disadvantage was that during the day your house would be cast in shadow, for the curtains would be drawn, and Jerome, who detested beds, flat out on your sofa, mouth puffing in a series of faint snores. No remonstrance would do any good. He would apologize, sleep in a spare bedroom for a day or two, then revert to your sofa. It was like trying to train a bat, or a three-toed sloth. The third was this, that he was a lover of classical music, a mine of information on the subject, and a man of eclectic tastes. When awake he might enter your home, frisk your record collection, switch on your stereo and start to play his selection. He'd crank up the volume and settle down ... Bach, Villa-Lobos,

Janacek, Dukas ... it was all the same to him. One day he invaded the downstairs apartment I have previously mentioned. It was occupied by Aviva Cantor and its rent paid by the ubiquitous Irving Layton. Jerome found a version of *Lohengrin*, stuck it on the machine, and turned it up full blast. Within seconds this howling, demonic music smashed through the air. Irving and Aviva were in the bedroom, enjoying a quiet siesta, when this violent noise shook the entire building. 'What?' Irving shouted. 'What's this?' He leaped out of bed. '*What in the name of Christ's going on?*'

'It's all right,' Jerome assured him. 'Don't you worry about me ... you get back to bed ... I'll just make myself a cup of tea ... don't happen to have a couple of eggs, do you? Such a thing as a piece of haddock? Never mind ... toast and a cup of tea will keep me going ... ' That was his attitude. What with unpredictability and contrasts, his apparent somnambulism, the darkened, sepulchral room he liked to inhabit, he was perhaps more than most people could easily take, let alone an English working-class mother of petit-bourgeois aspirations, anxious for her daughter's matrimonial advancement, and a concern for the good opinion of the neighbours.

Where was he, that was the point. Jill, half out of her mind with desperation, couldn't even guess. I had phoned her at work – she was at that time a clerk in the accounts department of a big store and had that very day mislaid, on paper, some hundred and seventy thousand dollars and was facing the prospect of dismissal (and subsequent unemployment insurance) with less equanimity than most of us would have felt. It seemed to me that the South of France was even further in the future. I put the phone down with an oath. What in hell was the matter with all these people? I slipped down Ridgewood towards my own apartment block, dashed in through the door, and rang Aviva's bell, keeping a weather eye out for the Mother on the Stair. By the grace of God, though, Aviva was in. I crept inside the door, closed it, she shouted a delighted greeting, and we stood for the next few minutes locked in an embrace.

'Where's the Gaffer?' I asked eventually.

'What Gaffer?'

'The Poet.'

She howled with laughter and delight. Irving was a constant source of joy to her, half of it directed against him. Jerome had been in love with her, and she felt close to Jerome. I reminded her of his invasion that day of the Wagnerfest and asked her if she knew where he was. She shook her head and we played a variation of a scene that was to become commonplace in the future, particularly after I had bought a car.

'Johnno,' she said, her voice bantering, high pitched and with an edge of wheedle. 'O Johnno!'

She had retained the Australianism of adding this open vowel to first names. I wasn't sure whether I liked it or not.

'Cup of coffee, Johnno?'

'Yes, yes.'

'And then we go to Steinberg's. Eh, loved one? In a nice taxi, eh, heart's ease?'

'Nope.'

'Oh, Johnno!!'

'Not unless you pay.'

'Are you doing that tough, working-class London male again? You're such a fraud.'

'My mother says you're a vixen.'

'Oh Johnno, she *didn't* ... she *didn't* ... a vixen ... how did she say it? I have to know how she said it ... *vixen* ... does she know it's a German word for wank? I bet her eyes flashed and her teeth glittered ... like gravestones in the moonlight ... Steinberg's, my dove?'

'Nope.'

'Coffee first, my darling, then we'll go shopping. Get a nice, nice cab and go to the lovely supermarket.'

'I'm starving, Aviva. What's in the fridge?'

'Just a little cheese, my lovely. A little slice of Oka ... until we go shopping ... it's Irving's favourite ... you can't have it ... Johnno! No! I said you couldn't have it! You're so transparent! You can't have Irving's woman, so you steal his cheese ... '

'*Vixen*,' I said, my mouth full of Oka. And for her benefit and of course my own I role-played my mother saying *vixen* ... a performance that seemed to satisfy her only in the twentieth repetition. A percolator came to orgasm over the stove. Slices of toast popped forth warmly, then grew soft and limp under the ministration of butter. Cheese vanished. I sighed with pleasure. This little apartment had always seemed a haven, a warm, playful refuge where I could always recapture, presuming I'd mislaid it, my *alegría* – the human birthright, the basic, unutterable joy a child takes in its own being, its own vitality. And as for Aviva, she was fresh, joyous, and completely uninhibited. I had loved her when I first knew her, before Irving had gaffed her, then lost touch with her after I started working in the North. Irving had set her up in this apartment while he was in the long and painful process of separating from his wife. She used to crow about being a kept woman, the kind of entity her mother, back in Australia, frequently anathematized, and a factor strongly in the consciousness of my own mother whose opinions in such matters were rigid to the point of judgementalism.

Irving himself seemed to approve of the word 'kept' in relation to Aviva. He would answer the door, call her to him, then, his arms about her, would say: *How about this, then, hey? How do you like my pussy cat, eh, my friend? What do you think of this pussy cat of mine?*

'Very nice.'

'Oh, *Irving* ... ' Aviva would squirm in embarrassment, trying to escape his iron grip.

'A struggling, sensuous pussy cat ... how do you like her, hey? Soft. Furry body ... ha! and little claws too ... look at them!'

'Very nice indeed ... '

I used to see her as a glorified playmate, then as a serious contender for some sort of quasi-monogamous relationship. But I began to recognize that I existed only on the periphery of her sexual life, usually, as happened frequently enough, when she fought with Irving, grew disgusted with his slowness in leaving his wife, or nauseated with his possessiveness or solipsistic self-approval. So as a sort of defence I had chosen to discount her even though she made most of the other women in my life seem leaden, shallow, and vacuous.

I explained that I didn't think *vixen* was a German word, though it sounded very much like their expression for masturbate. But as I spoke I sounded pedantic and heavy – she had the capacity sometimes to make me feel as though I had a grand piano tied to my arse. I found myself staring at her with mouth agape in the throes of what Irving, following James Joyce, would have called an epiphany – a showing forth of the true nature of things. And the epiphany was this: *there is no reason why you should play second fiddle to Irving Layton.* His woman ought to be mine, insofar as one person can be said to belong to another. To hell with Jerome ... my mother ... sister ... I deserved Aviva. I would take her with me to the South of France. Get her to slough the Poet. And then ... Nice ... Cannes ... St. Trop' ... Porquerolles. It was purely a question of tactics. I had good reason to believe I was not unattractive to her. But soft! I knew too much to broach this serious matter in the present atmosphere – dropping the Gaffer would mean a major shift in her life's priorities. Even I, euphoric with renewed love, could see that. But I wanted her and was going to have her. Gaffer or no Gaffer.

My mood grew lighter, more frolicsome. We washed cups ... wrestled ... rolled about on the floor ... took the telephone off the hook ... deadbolted the front entrance ... visited Steinberg's ... and in all these actions my soul was as light as gossamer: the resolution underlying it as hard as steel.

FIVE

AH, BUT HOW to proceed, that was the point. One of the things I thought I knew about women was that the more you pursue them, the more they will evade you. I must remain stand-offish ... detached ... then, when the opportunity was ripe – the moment of sexual *kairos* – I would strike. But what of Irving? I had been reading Machiavelli's *The Prince* for practical advice, and what I found there was disconcerting:

> ... (The Prince) should pick the fox and the lion, because the lion does not defend itself from snares, and the fox does not defend itself from wolves. So one needs to be a fox to recognize snares and a lion to frighten wolves.

This seemed very sound to me, though difficult to translate from metaphor to action. Much trickier was the advice on fortune:

> ... it is better to be impetuous than cautious, because fortune is a woman ... and one sees that she lets herself be won more by the impetuous than by those who proceed coldly. And so, like a woman, she is the friend of the young, because they are less cautious, more ferocious, and command her with more audacity.

Irving was more than a snare and a wolf: he was an opponent with all the advantages except youth; and Machiavelli was wrong about Fortune – I was as impetuous and as foolhardy as anybody I'd ever met, and fortune had eluded me. I vowed this time to 'proceed coldly'. Meanwhile other matters called on my attention.

I found a bed-sitting room not far from McGill where I could write and be at peace. I acquired a used Morris Minor, and my friends took this as a sign that their days of riding buses and hiring cabs were over, and they made my new telephone loud with requests for rides. My complaints did me no good: if it wasn't you, McCarthy told me in a variation of the argument used by munition makers against pacifists, it would have to be someone else. I needed that car badly, however, to race around the city – job interviews, assignations, the search for Jerome. A good friend who worked for the National Film Board set me up for a meeting with a producer who outstared me and demanded to know what these short stories were like that he'd heard so much about. I said I'd send him some, and went home to make clean copies of *Dinas Cromlech* (named after the Welsh cliff where the action was located), one about reporting sick in the British Army and dying of meningitis (a true story except for its ending), another about a Salvation Army hostel in Hull. All were based on personal experience and each was about as joyous and life-celebrating as the corpse of a red snapper lying fly-blown on a polluted beach. The producer sent them back with a note to say they were of little interest. I gritted my teeth and tinkered with these stories again. I wrote one about the mad pursuit of a beautiful girl by an impoverished student newly flunked out of college (myself). She encourages him to join her at a resort hotel in Cornwall. He camps outside, on the beach, and observes her making love to a toff in the back seat of a Bentley. I was quite pleased with it and read it to the Gaffer.

'The beach scenes are O.K.,' he said. 'And I don't even mind that crap about how phosphorescent the sea is at night. But it's not a short story.'

'Fuck it, Irving,' I shouted. 'I've just about had all of you I can take. You're perverse, sanctimonious, envious, and dishonest. You haven't the faintest clue as to what you are talking about ... you're an oaf, an ignoramus. An illiterate, crass, and insensitive lout.'

'You prick!' Aviva screamed, for she too, squirming on a pouf, had listened to my recital with mounting irritation. 'You're just not a writer! You're a nothing! A man without art! Give it up! Get a job! Go back to that stupid Arctic of yours and make some money ... '

'You wheedling, treacherous bitch ... ' I began.

'Hah!' the Gaffer shouted. 'You snivelling little half-arse punk, you think I haven't better things to do than listen to your pathetic, castrated drivel? You English fart, weeping snot through keyholes, haven't you heard the good news? Where's your joy? Your energy? Your *élan vital*? You whimpering half-man, you give me the creeps ... take that idiot piece of prose out of here and go and put some guts into it ... Get your nasty, self-abusing hero murdering the man in the Bentley. Have him do in the girl for good measure ... she deserves it ... then end it with the murderer crowing in triumph, striding into his new destiny. Now get out of here.'

Furiously I snatched the story from his grasp and strode home. I reread it. It was more than possible he was right. The logic of the story demanded such an ending. It enraged and humiliated me to discover he was right again. I tried to rewrite it, but couldn't. *Things in real life just hadn't happened that way.* I hadn't even fought with the girl. Freda, her name was. Freda Webb. I'd just megrimed off, bemoaning the class system and my inability to compete with rich young men with good accents and access to power.

Hoping for a more encouraging response, I showed my *Dinas Cromlech* to Graham and McCarthy next day. But, as fellow

Europeans, they too had been brought up where writers publish or read their works aloud at owner's risk. Graham's response was normally to mock, to imitate, to reduce to absurdity any foolishness latent in a work, while McCarthy would fall into a daze broken sometimes with a sharp and adverse comment.

'Is this your personal experience?' he said.

'Yes.'

'Then why is your narrator a Welsh quarryman? You ever work in a slate quarry?'

'You know I didn't.'

'No, and that's obvious from the story. The consciousness, the tone of voice, is Clapham Junction, or the East India Dock Road.'

'Why not make him a Lascar,' Graham said. 'Straight out of a ship's hold. Then of course, he'd get the girl, and where would you go for your self-pity?'

'He'd find plenty more where that came from,' McCarthy said. 'But seriously, if you're going to write about you, make him *you*.'

At home again, I thought about it. I wanted when I began the story to make the class distinction sharper by injecting a racial, cultural difference. But I could see where this sounded fake. What if I took it out of the first-person mode altogether? I'd lose immediacy, the reader's attention. But it looked as though I hadn't got it anyway. What had I to lose? Cautiously, hesitantly, I took the first step in the story-teller's art: I imagined the action as though it took place before me on a stage. I tried to describe the events as though I were an invisible observer. What this forced me to do, of course, was to cut out my sullen hero's inner processes, his unverbalized feelings, and replace them with signs – the whitened knuckle, the sudden grating in the voice, the sharp, unnecessary movement. I began to see him from the perspective of the girl, the viewpoint of the rival. As I warmed to this exercise, against the grain though it seemed at first, I found it exciting and delightful. My hero even began to seem faintly comic.

Meanwhile my advertisement had gone into the Montreal *Star*: tutor available, Maths and Physics. B.Sc. (Wales). M.Sc. (London). My invention was stronger on creating degrees for myself than it was developing an omniscient narrator for *Dinas Cromlech.* I stopped short of following Richmond's example and calling myself *Doctor.* Even so, I was surprised to find that very quickly I had accumulated a small but loyal clientele and was making enough to pay for my room, meals, and car expenses such as gasoline, constant repair bills, and the cascade of parking tickets that deluged me whenever I ventured outside.

SIX

IT WASN'T very long before John Richmond became a frequent visitor to Upper Ridgewood. From the Seals' window he could be observed striding up the hill – bouncing military gait – through the snow, walking stick at the high port. *Here comes Uncle Mad*, we'd say, or, more concisely, *Here's Mad.* He had indeed presented himself to us in an avuncular role, not only because of the two small children connected to us, but because he was conscious of our youth – he considered himself wiser and more experienced. His natural portliness in both waist and manner gave conviction to this pose and we ourselves were comfortable enough with it.

Let us go, Mad would say. Let us go to and fro on the earth and walk up and down on it.

And we'd dress up in our Arctic clothes – overshoes, parkas, mukluks – relics of our different adventures in wilder parts, and stride with him – duffle coat, cap, pipe, stick – up through the Côte des Neiges cemetery, over the Mountain, into the Chalet for a warm-up, down the steps to Peel Street, then to the pubs and bars along rue Ste-Catherine speaking of a thousand things – money, investments, the sacraments, the South of France, what we were to do next, each of us, in our lives. We followed Richmond across intersections, plunging into the shrieking, rabid traffic, which would squeal and blast to sudden halts as Mad, chin up, stick out, scowling ferociously, strode across without fear. We stayed close to him, delighted observers, as he went about his business.

Our first day out with him was typical. I remember Mad stalking into the CBC offices on Dorchester Street and demanding, in the most peremptory of tones, to 'speak to somebody responsible'. The cowed receptionist brought down a fluttering producer who listened to a long, pompous, and irate lecture on how the word *hamartía* had been mistranslated, on some radio talk on tragedy, as 'tragic flaw', when every schoolboy knew, provided he'd attended a half-decent school, that it meant 'error'. 'Tragedy is about a good man making a mistake, old boy, never forget it.' After this we moved on to a peculiar Gothic building on Guy Street into which Mad, excusing himself, suddenly popped, emerging five minutes later with fruity apologies and a secret smile. It was only later that we understood the significance of this building in Richmond's strange career: for the moment he invented a convenient story about visiting an old student of his. We nodded and followed him into the bar of the Ritz. The barman looked at our outer clothing with dismay, but was mollified, or at least intimidated, by Mad's ultra-respectability and drill-master's frown.

It was on this occasion that we began to fence with one another concerning our futures as pedagogues. I was doing fairly well with my tutoring, but the next step for me was problematic. The job interviews, the dreary encounters with personnel managers and engineers in charge had depressed me, and I knew that my days of working for a living were over. From their point of view I was unreliable, and indeed was unreliable from my own. From now on until the day I die, I thought, it'll be a question of nip and tuck.

'I'm grateful to you,' I said. 'Without your encouragement I'd've been working for a living by now.'

'No, no, no, old boy. You are too kind. I think you would have succeeded in not working for a living well enough without me.'

'When in doubt, says you, teach. How right you are.'

'*Ex cathedra*, old boy, but not cast in stone. Let us not monumentalize our utterances, for *God's* sake.'

'But I would like to take it a step further,' I said. 'When in doubt ... *start a school*.'

He stared at me with a sort of disgust as though my face had suddenly blossomed forth in a lethal midline granuloma.

'I've been thinking that myself,' he said.

There was an uneasy pause.

'You are perfectly right,' he said. 'The next logical step for us all would be to start a school.'

'Consider it,' I said. 'I'm doing a pupil a time for four dollars. Why not two in an hour for eight? Three for twelve? And so on.'

'Exactly, old boy. Thirty students an hour at four dollars an hour each for three hours a day, five days a week, gives us eighteen hundred, times four, less rental of a building, chairs and desks, would give us about six thousand a month profit and no income tax to pay. Split four ways and we each have a living wage for one hour's work a day. The bread and butter, old boy, the jam we'll have ample leisure to pursue.'

'I can do maths,' I said. 'Physics and maths. So can McCarthy here. You could do English and languages. Graham could do philosophy.'

'Count me out,' Graham said.

'Let's get started on it, old boy. I could do with the challenge. In any case, the rabbin and I are coming to a parting of the ways.'

'So it is,' McCarthy said, 'with Irving.'

'That is what is being said,' Richmond agreed. 'So it is with the Gaffer.'

The rumour that Irving was to leave Herzliah turned very soon into hard news. Aviva and I pondered its implications.

'It may shake him out of his stupid rut,' she said. 'A cataclysm in one area of his life may provoke it in another.'

'He may get the guts to leave his wife?'

'Oh, Johnno, what else could I mean? But it isn't that he hasn't any guts: it's mostly that he's holding back, waiting for other things to develop.'

'What others?'

'McClelland and Stewart may be publishing his collected poems.'

'That's quite a coup.'

'But Johnno ... listen ... you mustn't tell anyone else but ... *he's been nominated for the Nobel Prize ...* '

I could do nothing here but nod wisely. 'Apart from the prize,' I said, 'for which he's an obvious shoo-in, what's happening at the school?'

She told me that Irving's cultivation of the mass media, his growing reputation – quite undeserved and based so far as I could see on the reiteration of certain words then taboo, at least in print, but secretly hankered after by the suburban housewives he excited and tantalized – as a pornographer and corrupter of children, his frequent assertion, reprehensible to the more orthodox of the rabbis, that he was the Messiah, and his general uninhibited behaviour, particularly in the sexual jungle, had prompted the board of governors to ask for his resignation.

'But you know Irving,' she said, 'he's not the kind of person to eat shit, rabbinical or otherwise. Come and look.'

She took me over to a desk he kept there and broached a file. There, in orderly fashion, were copies of the Gaffer's correspondence, all of it denunciatory in content and scabrous in tone. One was a bold statement of his messianic claims: tradition, he said, predicted that the Messiah would be born without a foreskin: he had been born without a foreskin. Therefore he was the Messiah. Even I, with my tendency towards making wild and unsupportable statements could see that the Gaffer's conclusion did not follow from the premise. But the letter went on to suggest penalties adumbrated by various Old Testament prophets for failure to recognize the King, descendant of David, and these, most of them blood-drenched and bowel-bespattered, would be visited on the rabbis. There were several addressed to a publisher who had turned down a manuscript. *You could have achieved honour and fame in your lifetime and immortality beyond it as the first to recognize the greatest poet of the age. You have missed your chance, my friend.* Another, in similar vein, was sent to a producer who had rejected a radio play of his.

'Sad stuff,' I commented.

'Megalomania,' she agreed. 'Sometimes I think he's a great genius, at others that he's off his head.'

This led her to speak of the Gaffer's selfishness, insensitivity, what we now call male chauvinism, and acts of what seemed deliberate cruelty. She followed up with descriptions of the kind of things she had to endure and grew emotional, vengeful. I hugged her while she sobbed out grievances and disillusions. Things are going very well, I thought: this was the first time I'd heard her denounce her lover. I considered pressing home my proposal: that she should dump this zany and elope with me to the Mediterranean littoral. But I decided to let these insights into Irving's character mature, and the impulse to elope come from her. One should approach a seduction, as Lao Tze must have put it, as one prepares a little fish for the table.

Jerome, whom we'd given up, reappeared quite suddenly. He phoned Aviva, explaining that he'd been lying low due as much to pressure of work as to my mother's animosity, but knew I must by now be in town and would like to see me. As for him, he was quite comfortable in his new lodgings: a friend of a friend had found him a bed in a basement curtained off from the furnace on one side and by boxes of old newspapers, telephone directories, and *National Geographics* on the other. There were no windows and not much air, which suited him, but no means of consoling himself with music. He arranged to meet me in the Kiltie Lounge of the Laurentian Hotel.

This was a bleak and darkened bar, almost always empty, hung with fake tartans and plastic claymores. It was as close to being a catafalque as one could get without closing the lid. It suited Jerome, of course, for with his etiolated appearance and sunken eyes he never seemed much further than a hand's clutch from the charnel house.

'I wanted to lie low,' he explained. 'You must understand that my life in the Ridgewood apartment was growing steadily insupportable.'

'I can see that, Jerome. You took a lot of abuse.'

'Yes, I did, and I would've walked out before had I not felt guilty about leaving Jill to face that termagant alone. I say, I'm most awfully sorry.'

'About what?'

'Calling your mother a termagant.'

'It's the least of her problems.'

'A sick old woman, in my opinion. But of course, one ought not to judge.'

'She had plenty of names for you.'

'I know.'

'Vicious, lazy sponger.'

'I know.'

'Fat slug.'

'Yes.'

'A homosexual sewer rat.'

'I hadn't heard that one. What a warped mind she has!'

'She thinks your presence in that house has probably screwed up David's future sexuality.'

'It's a wonder to me, given what must have been your upbringing, that you're not a homosexual sewer rat yourself.'

I explained that his absence had not improved matters with regard to the relationship between the two women in the house; they spent their time together in mutual recriminations, going over old wounds, insults, failures of loyalty, etc., and Jill was almost totally worn down by it. Then I took a rash step, one that was to have the direst consequences.

'Jerome,' I said, 'would you consider going back to Ridgewood?'

'My dear fellow, your mother has made that quite impossible, surely you must see that.'

'I shall ask her to leave.'

'You can't do that.'

'Kick her out.'

'She's your mother.'

'And Jill's my sister. And they're driving one another mad. One of them has to go.'

'How will you kick her out?'

'Find her a place nearby. She can have my room in fact. Down by McGill. It's begun to give me the creeps.'

'I don't know, my dear fellow, I don't know.'

'My nephew needs you there: particularly since I won't be around myself. I'm heading off to the South of France very soon.'

'Lucky you.'

'I have a couple of irons in the fire,' I said, deliberately not mentioning Aviva. 'But it'll be the situation as before ... back to the days before my mother arrived.'

We ordered more drinks from the mute and pallid waiter, and I left Jerome there. As for me, I was anxious to deal with events transpiring at Richmond Academy.

We had placed a carefully worded advertisement in the *Star*, and it wasn't more than an hour after that paper came out that calls started to flood in and the first appointments were made. I sat with Richmond and McCarthy, all of us dressed to the nines in Richmond's book-lined study. The bell rang, we smiled grimly at one another. Richmond ushered in a couple (Westmount, middle-class, I would've said) and a tall, bespectacled male teenager of unprepossessing complexion, lank hair, and dangling hands.

'Not doing very well at school,' Mad said after the preliminaries. 'What do your parents mean, you're not doing very well at school?'

The boy shrugged.

Mad's voice suddenly took on a kind of thunderous growl.

'Are you failing your examinations?' he asked.

Shrug.

'Are you failing, yes or no?' Richmond suddenly screamed. His face had swollen in a trice, turned red, apoplectic veins knotted on his forehead, tendons bulged and quivered in his throat, his stick, in his hand, began to vibrate. 'Yes or no!' Richmond shrieked, 'and if you shrug again, sir, I shall crack your skull! Yes sir, crack your skull! With this stick! *I shall crack your skull.*'

Christ, I thought, this evil bugger's headed for the bin.

'Yes,' the boy muttered. 'I can't seem to concentrate.'

'Concentrate!' Richmond bellowed. 'Well, you'll concentrate in *my* school if we decide to admit you. Yes, we'll teach you how to concentrate, don't have any illusions on that score. He's not as stupid as he makes out,' Mad said, turning to his parents, 'just idle, pampered, and over-indulged. We can knock that out of him. Give me your phone number and I'll call you when we've made our decision.'

With a good imitation of badly concealed contempt for the three of them, he showed them out. 'Damn it,' I said as the door closed behind them. 'Is there a sense we might possibly have overdone it?'

'No, no, old boy. They'll be on the blower again. Within twenty minutes. You'll see.'

And indeed he was right. McCarthy took the call in the next room as Richmond, shrieking with demonic frenzy, threatened the next candidate, a plump and sullen girl, with twisted arms and shattered teeth.

SEVEN

IT SEEMED to us that Richmond's exit from Herzliah, timed so precisely with Irving's, was too fortuitous to be ignored. We ought, McCarthy pointed out, to include the Gaffer in Richmond's academy. Accordingly he got on the phone and was greeted by the most enthusiastic reception he had experienced from the Poet in a very long time. They set up a meeting of the four principals for the following evening.

We gathered, then, *chez* Seal, on what might be termed neutral ground. Mad entered first – short, stern, batrachoid as to mouth – then Layton – white sports shirt open at neck, black chest hair, hairy forearms – slightly out of his element here; at home, in Côte St. Luc, he could stand close to a bust of Beethoven, an artist with whom he felt a great affinity, and defy the elements and human animosity to do their worst. Here, on Upper Ridgewood, he was among people who were as lunatic, and therefore as unpredictable, as himself. Perhaps that is why he had brought Aviva – light, frolicsome, dressed in a low-cut blouse and dark blue pants that hugged her half-way up her calves. Graham had declined to join us. Bryan McCarthy was there already – red of beard, blear of eye, but at this stage of the proceedings, clear-headed and acute. Then there was myself, slightly above middle height, long of hair, shifty of expression, and twitching with needless jokes and smiles.

McCarthy took the chair.

'We are here,' he said, 'to discuss ways in which we may pool our expertise. Each of us is an experienced teacher; each of us is dissatisfied with the present school system. We are therefore to discuss possibilities of creating some form of educative alternative. For my part I have to tell you that I am in it for the money.'

After this unwontedly long but characteristically honest speech, McCarthy helped himself to a tumbler of Queberac, a gallon of which stood on the coffee table, and as the session wore on retreated into silence.

'And I am not in it for the money,' Irving declared boldly. 'I am in it for my principles. I have taught in the school system and found it destructive of body, soul, and spirit. It crushes creativity and celebrates mediocrity. It erases courage, individualism, and ambition, and affirms servility, incuriosity, and the mentality of the herd. The public school system is an abomination and a disease; the private schools, at least Herzliah, are chaotic, undirected, and controlled by eunuchs and poltroons. I want to set fire to the imagination of the people of this country, to inspire them with a love of life, a delight in art and poetry; I want to prepare them to recognize the Master Spirit ... '

'By whom you mean yourself?' Richmond could not resist saying.

'By whom he most certainly means himself,' Aviva said loudly, 'have you any objections?'

'I do *not* mean myself, wench,' Irving said. 'I am a prophet, a *vates*. I prepare the way, the path, the wide road along which Dionysus shall one day stride.'

'But I've heard you claim to be the Messiah,' Mad said. 'And now you also want to be John the Baptist. Come, come, old boy, you cannot strive to be both.'

McCarthy grunted, either to conceal a belch or to express approval at this rather cheap quip.

'Well, let's hear from you, John Richmond ... *Doctor* Richmond ... let's hear the word from the groves of Academe. Let's have the moderate, detached, judicious, and unexcited point of view. You think what I've said utopian?'

'Oh, utterly, old boy, utterly.'

'Then tell us, you pompous bullfrog,' Aviva screamed. 'Tell us before I piss my pants in anticipation.'

'I am finding it very difficult to make my point. And will you, Layton, not endeavour to control that vile trollop of yours.'

'Just talk, old boy,' McCarthy said. 'Never mind the noises off.'

'Under normal conditions,' said Uncle Mad, 'I would support the idea of a school where a core curriculum has been re-established. And by this I mean a suitably supervised study of the classics – particularly Greek. Never mind the cant about the will of the child – that is so much liberal wish-wash. Greek is all a man needs to get him through life. Is he unhappy? Let him learn Greek. Unfulfilled? Let him learn Greek. Does he question Providence? The problem of evil? Greek. Divine justice? Greek. His own purpose in life? Greek, and again, Greek. Make him learn Greek, sir, do you follow me? Greek ... Greek ... Greek.'

'Are you saying,' Aviva said through clenched teeth, leaning well forward, as though intent on grasping the subtleties of this message, 'are you saying you want the little buggers to learn Greek?'

'He's being idiotic,' said the Gaffer. 'Take no notice.'

'But conditions are not normal,' Richmond continued. 'What we have in this country is a lack of cultural base. We have the melancholy spectacle of parents afraid of their own children, writhing in a constant state of guilt as to whether they are bringing them up correctly according to current liberal notions. With the result that discipline has gone out of the window and they are unable to get their children to learn the simplest things like the alphabet, or the eight times table. Unable to stop them haunting the streets, fighting in gangs, mugging pedestrians, falling into the hands of the policeman, the magistrate, the probation officer. They want their children taken in hand, force fed, caned if necessary, so long as they don't have to do it themselves. They want to relinquish to stern and capable hands their own parental responsibilities, which they no longer have the courage to administer. That's it, old boy, in a nutshell. They want a return to the days of spare the rod and spoil the child. And for this they are willing to pay good money. I propose to set up a school where we can give them what they want, educate their brats, their cretins, their morons to pass these really very simple government exams, and relieve them of their disposable income.'

'Caned, you say,' Irving muttered.

'Yes, indeed, old boy. Caning if necessary, but not necessarily with the cane.'

'I see it all now,' the Gaffer said. 'I've often wondered about you. You're a simple sadist, that's what you are, a man who disguises his sexual inadequacies under a guise of moral rectitude and love of discipline, order, and reason. What's the matter, Richmond, can't you get it up? Is that what your walking stick means? Is it a substitute penis? Is that why you thrust it at the traffic? What's a car to you, a ravenous, insatiable female equipped with *vagina dentata*? You're a coward, Richmond, afraid of a mere automobile – a cheap thing of plastic and tin.'

'Try putting your cock in splints,' Aviva yelled. 'Tie it between a brace of chop-sticks.'

'Sir,' Richmond roared, 'you are a mountebank with the mentality of a street urchin.'

'And you, sir, with your deformation of the sexual impulse have the sort of mentality that leads to war, genocide, the rape of the environment!'

'Shut up the pair of you!' I screamed, unable to contain myself any longer. 'You couple of glib and paltry maniacs. I came here to discuss turning an honest dollar, not for facile cultural analysis.'

There was a silence that rather shocked me. I was unused to being listened to. Perhaps I was learning what the others knew by instinct – that a forceful and brazen manner will, regardless of content, secure attention.

'What you are observing, old boy,' said Mad, turning to me, 'is the locking of horns of two impotent bulls of Bashan ... '

This was a shrewd stroke. Irving's method of attacking people who disagreed with him was to accuse them of being undersexed. Richmond, though a mud-wrestler, was – unlike the rest of us gathered there – no guttersnipe. He could manage the well-turned phrase, but his notion of abuse was of the sir-your-wife-under-the-pretence-of-keeping-a-bawdy-house-is-a-receiver-of-stolen-goods variety. Thus he was too literary for this rough-and-tumble city: epithets like *cockatrice* or *bolting-hutch* hurled at taxi drivers, etc., seldom produced a reaction. Yet oddly enough the simple device of turning the charge of sexual inadequacy against its originator was enough to trigger a quite violent response.

Fuming and bubbling with rage, foaming at the mouth and punching the air before him like a brain-damaged pug, Irving shouted, 'Impotent! Speak for yourself, you over-bred, ineffectual bully-boy from the rabbit-chinned, asinine, and twittering class of petit-bourgeois, counter-jumpers, vestrymen, and lounge lizards. Where was your power when my people were rounded up and gassed? Where were you when the Warsaw ghetto was pulverized by the Nazis and betrayed by Stalinist thugs? Where were you when Hitler strutted into the Rhineland and began the massacre of the Jews? Busy sucking the likes of Neville Chamberlain when you weren't masturbating or stealing the straw from your mother's kennel.'

The conversation had taken what to me was a quite unexpected turn. It was a sign of Irving's discomposure that he had resorted to the oldest stand-by in the book – the charge of anti-Semitism.

'Irving!' Aviva pitched in noisily. 'He called you a mountebank. You know why? Because you mount banks! You take sides! You don't sit with your arse safely tucked across a fence, facing both ways ... '

'I was deprived of all those delights you mention,' Mad replied acerbically. 'I was neither at the hot gates nor at the Iron Gate; I was neither in Warsaw nor the Rhineland. I did not have the pleasure of putting your family to death.'

'*Putz!*' Aviva bellowed, turning on the Poet. 'How much longer are you going to tolerate these worthless and preposterous squares? When are you ... '

Irving, too far gone to hear, began another tirade with the words, 'You Nazi, Jew-burning, culture-hating psychopath ... ' when an extraordinary thing happened. Richmond started, quite literally, to bark. The noise was sharp, loud, and a cross between the yelpings of a seal and a dog.

'Ha'karf,' he barked, standing up. 'H'ruff! ... k'chah! ... h'roof! ... kah! ... k'chah!' He reached for his stick, ' ... h'roof ... woof*kaff*! ... ' and he was out of the door.

He left the rest of us in a stunned silence. For a moment I wondered if, in the give and take of argument and persuasion, one of us had gone too far. Then I thought of the frogs in Aristophanes ... kr, kr, kr, kr ... koax, koax ... and said so. McCarthy smiled amiably. The Gaffer and Aviva, good humour restored, were chuckling and feeling one another up. McCarthy said he didn't think Richmond's feelings were discomposed, but that he had better traipse down to lower Ridgewood and find out. He poured us all a *deoch an doris* from the fast failing Queberac jar and we all parted with many expressions of mutual regard.

Two days after this encounter, Irving astonished us by leaving on a jet plane for Paris. He had left Herzliah, his wife, their house on Côte St. Luc, and a letter for Aviva, slipped under her door on Ridgewood.

> Well, Pussy Cat [he wrote]. By the time you read this I shall be in Europe. Paris! Then on to Rome! Athens! Florence! Venice! What names these are for my imagination to conjure with! I have taken out my small savings, sold a bond or two, screwed the school of severance pay, and got an advance from McClelland and Stewart. And that's the most exciting thing of all! My first book with a commercial publisher! An epoch-making event, the beginning of a new age in literature. At any rate, do not worry that I will not have any money. I have more than enough for my modest needs. I shall send you postcards with exotic stamps.

Aviva phoned me in a state of great turmoil. That this utter bastard should take off to Europe, finally leaving his wife, and she – Aviva – not worth much more than a postcard. The thought of these legendary places, though she had in her time seen them all, drove her mad, for one of her favourite fantasies was of steering her lover around Europe ... hand in hand along the quais ... gondola to

Torcello, snuggled on cushions ... roistering with Cretans to bouzouki music ... making slow and tender love under the cypresses of Capri. Treachery! She embarked on a description of the Gaffer's character that even divided by four seemed utterly damning. I put my arms about her and kissed her gently. 'I've finished with him,' she said. She kissed me back. 'Forever and forever,' she said. She sobbed bitterly. 'Johnno,' she whispered. 'Are you still going to France? And do you want me to come with you?'

I paused for reflection – the game had gone entirely my way without any effort on my part. The enemy, as Machiavelli pointed out, may in his confidence overreach himself, bringing about his own downfall. I did not fully believe that this could be Aviva's last word – no attachment as strong as hers and Irving's could be dissolved by a mere oath. And if we went away together all kinds of exciting, but also terrifying possibilities opened up. My pause lasted a full second and a half.

'Not France,' I said. 'We're too likely to run into the Gaffer.'

'It's a big place.'

'Mexico!' I said. 'Let's go to Mexico! We'll leave Europe to the Gaffer! Vera Cruz! Oaxaca! Yucatan!'

With delighted cries we got out maps and atlases and made plans with energy that took us far into the night.

We couldn't, of course, go immediately. There was much to be done ... much unfinished business. I began winding up my Montreal affairs. A morning's work and *Dinas Cromlech* lay on my desk – finished at last. I read it over to McCarthy and Graham a couple of hours later. I was greatly moved by it – the young man's longing, his bitterness, came over as strongly as it did before, but the omniscient narration made clear the *inevitability* of the situation: much as the woman in the story might have liked or admired the hero, she was pregnant by his rival. I uttered the last word with a sign. Then I looked up at my friends. Graham giggled slightly, then fell silent. McCarthy stared at me with a kind of stony severity, as though my upper lip bore traces of a carelessly wiped nose.

'Why is he telling all this?' McCarthy asked.

'What?'

'Why's he going to the trouble of telling us this story? What's its point? What question does it address? Why should I be interested?'

'And I for one,' Graham said, 'am not. What's the subject?'

'Are you kidding? Do I have to read it all over again? It's about a young man in love with a woman who turns to somebody weaker, more effete than himself. It's about class antagonisms ... it's about ... '

'God help us all,' McCarthy said.

'Amen,' said Graham.

'Your plot and your characters are trivial,' McCarthy said. 'Everybody knows that there are class antagonisms. Everybody in Montreal knows that if two men compete for the same woman she will gravitate to the materially better advantaged of the two. Everybody on this street knows that the loser will be upset. What's the matter with you?'

Graham said, 'Your real subject, the thing you really seem to want to write about, is North Wales – its steely grey cliffs, dark skies, and deep, mysterious mountain tarns. Take the people out, and you may have something. Or even better – put in another person, the narrator. Put it back into the first person, but a person acting as a minor character in the action.'

I swore at them both and stalked out. On the way down to Côte des Neiges I dropped in on my mother and told her, as gently as I could, that I was coming back into the apartment, and so was Jerome. There wouldn't be any room, I said, for all three of us. It seemed also that she and Jill were not hitting it off. There is no need to describe this interview in any detail: suffice it to say it was long, painful, and acrimonious, but in some ways unnecessary. My mother had already decided to leave, and had found a room for herself on Bishop Street. I left her; I felt exhausted and at a loss. Further down Ridgewood I called on Uncle Mad to inform him that, since I was about to leave for Mexico, I would no longer be associated with Richmond Academy. He accepted my resignation with false sorrow – he knew I would be a source of dissension. We parted with expressions of mutual good-will.

I got back to my room and began packing my few belongings into my Morris Minor. Some I would take to Ridgewood and store there, the rest I would need for Mexico.

The phone rang.

'Johnno!' Aviva said, her voice breathless and delighted. 'You'll never guess what happened! He *phoned!* ... Irving phoned! He's sent for me! He wired me the fare! Oh Johnno, I'm so happy ... so delighted ... he's left her! Given up the house! ... Johnno, come over here and help me celebrate.'

I raced over. She was already packing ... stuffing books into cardboard boxes from the basement ... dismantling shelves ... wrapping pieces of china in newspapers ... hanging clothes in garment bags for storage ... a whirlwind, a flurry.

'Christ!' I screamed. '*What about Mexico?*'

'Johnno ... Johnno ... don't you understand? I got a call from Irving! He's sent for me!'

With growing desperation I pointed out that the previous night she had cursed him roundly, up and down, sideways and across, to the effect that she never wanted to see him again, that her most fervent wish was that he would come down with typhoid fever, or botulism, or salmonella, or die of the bloody flux in Venice, unnoticed and unmourned. And I reminded her how we had spent the previous night, working out the best route to Oaxaca, a place sacred to her through its Lawrentian connections. She looked at me as though I were a moron.

'Johnno,' she repeated, '*he sent for me.*'

'It's not good enough,' I wailed. 'What about me? Self? *Ich?*'

Suddenly it was as though a wave of comprehension washed over her; as though, yes, she had remembered some vague commitment to elope with me. 'Let's sit down,' she said.

We stared at one another; the expression in her eyes resembled that of a doctor who tells you in one breath that you are terminally ill, in the next that he is conducting a rollicking affair with his receptionist.

'Johnno,' she said, 'you're a man. It's a very good thing to be a man. But Irving is a God. Do you see now? When he calls me, it is as though I were being invited to dance – by Dionysus. You must see that. You're a man ... but Irving's a God.'

I thought about this. How wrong they were, McCarthy and Graham. The woman did not gravitate to the better off of two suitors. She went straight for the Godhead. There was nothing to be done here, I could see, but declare myself *hors de combat* with what grace I could muster. I stood – an unaccommodated mortal: we said good bye. I wished her, in all sincerity, the joy of Irving and her journey to Europe in his company, but I regret to say I left the champagne she had bought for us deliberately untasted in the glass. Thus we parted – with many expressions of mutual regard.

EIGHT

THAT NIGHT I left for Mexico on my own. When I returned, some months later, it was fall. My mother had left for England; I saw her there, a few years later, when she was dying of cancer.

I began teaching at a crammer's school run by a man named Ross and, with a friend from the DEW-Line, invested in a laundry on Burnside Street that cost about six thousand dollars and was eventually sold for one – whereof quit.

Before he retreated into silence, Bryan McCarthy published a fine book of poetry *Smoking the City*, and opened a café on Stanley Street called The Place. It was a run-down building awaiting the wrecker's ball, which the landlord allowed him to use for the remainder of its limited time. For a while, and despite the impoverishing bribes paid to fire marshals, cops, tax-men, bailiffs, etc., it thrived ... one of the first 'alternative life-style' places in the city – late Beat and early Hipster. There of an evening one might observe the literati; Leonard Cohen, then going through an Oscar Wilde phase – trilby hat, tweed suit, nosegay carried and ostentatiously sniffed; Milton Acorn presenting a picture, on the whole deceptive, of a solid working-class poet who had got himself together; Al Purdy, a lurching, unpredictable presence who never seemed to me wholly sober, never wholly drunk. One day Richmond and I stopped off at The Place on some errand or other. We checked my laundry, strode along the busy street in the direction of Park Avenue. Without thinking about it, Mad raised his cane to the horizontal and, still speaking to me with great animation, stepped off the sidewalk.

There was the customary squealing of brakes. Then another. A car swerved to avoid him, squealing, almost sideswiping a panel truck trying to overtake on the inside. We were almost across, but I could sense trouble. A car had moved forward quickly to cut us off from the far curb. I saw the driver's face – it was frozen into a diabolical expression of hatred and ferocity. He moved his vehicle forward very slowly, then swung it at Richmond's legs. Scowling savagely, Richmond brought his heavy stick down on the car's hood as though firmly rapping its knuckles. The driver jammed on his brakes, flung open the door. He began to scream, rounding the hood with clenched fists. There was no mistaking his intention – it was to beat Mad to a pulp with his bare hands, dig his steely fingers into his stomach, rip him open from crotch to sternum, then stuff liver and lights down his tormentor's gullet. Richmond fled. He dropped the stick and scuttled for the nearest doorway; it was a pharmacy. The insane driver, business suit, tie, but big and clearly rendered psychotic by a day spent in an office, went after him like a stoat after a shrew. Richmond yelped, ran the length of the store, and literally dived behind the pharmacist's counter. A man in a white coat held off the gibbering pursuer, police were called, traffic tied up for several miles, the demented driver hauled away, Richmond questioned and pushed around a little by the police. I took him off, clearly shaken to his deep heart's core, to irrigate him with whisky at a convenient bar.

A few years later Nina, presumably unprotected by the magic stick, and after a married lifetime of being metaphorically crushed by her husband, stepped off the sidewalk of Côte des Neiges and was flattened by one of those speeding cars Mad had so teased and angered.

Perhaps half a decade on, Richmond himself died. He had left the teaching profession and, in that little office along Guy Street, had set himself up as a marriage counsellor. He became a hot-line broadcaster, then wound up as the literary editor of the Montreal *Star* where he exercised, though personally grown more mellow, his own dark power. He choked on a morsel of food in a restaurant and died of a heart attack.

Fallings from us, vanishings.

After many stormy and bitter years, Irving and Aviva separated. I have, I regret to say, totally lost touch with her. I encounter the Gaffer once in a while. A year or two ago a rather unreliable biography of him was published in which my own role in his life was mentioned, quite inaccurately, and where it is stated that I 'hated' the Poet. My attitude towards him was not simple, as I hope I have shown in this memoir, but hatred was certainly never a part of it. I did not show him my final version of *Dinas Cromlech* because I failed to complete it – the narrator became, following Graham's suggestion, a minor character in the action. He so interested me that I could see no alternative to writing a novel about him – a novel I have never yet attempted. Irving would in any case have reiterated his unanswerable comment that 'it wasn't a short story'. I knew now that his concept of the form was a classical one derived from Henry James and from Poe's theory of 'the single emotional effect.' Accordingly I wrote a piece called *Joust in Eight Rounds* in a new and totally artificial form I called rigmarole. It consists of a number of narrative threads, all of them autobiographical, drawn together and interwoven then divided, quite arbitrarily, into eight parts. *Joust* dealt with the Ross School, the endgame with my old flame Edith, and that truly dreadful laundry on Burnside Street.

'It's good,' Irving admitted, 'in parts. But it isn't a short story.'

'You maladroit bumbler,' I shouted triumphantly. 'Of course it's not a short story. It's a rigmarole.'

It took the wind out of his sails, I could tell that. But I think he saw the point of it. Rigmarole is designed to reflect a vision of life as constant *peripeteia*, change of fortune, as the source of what he called 'the intractable core of the bizarre in human affairs', together with my growing conviction that we are caught up in a universe essentially playful – *deo ludens.* I wrote two rigmaroles and they were published in a little magazine called *Evidence*. At about this time I had the pleasure of reviewing for another journal Leonard Cohen's *Beautiful Losers*. Thus I embarked on my career as a mud-wrestler.

Canadian literature entered the modern world with Layton's *The Swinging Flesh* and Leonard Cohen's novel. Prior to these events fiction in this country was disguised journalism of Victorian overtones, poetry milk-and-water imitations of Wordsworth, Edward Thomas, or Coventry Patmore. Literature and criticism of literature were hamstrung and thwarted by a cult of politeness, of coy and smiling self-ingratiation. Cohen is not a mud-wrestler, but he wrote a mud-wrestler's novel. Layton was and, praise the Lord, still *is* a mud-wrestler – for this Canadian literature owes him a debt, as Gulley Jimson says, that can only be paid in cash, and it is to him this Rigmarole is dedicated.

Memoirs of a Bishop's Man

A RISK PECULIAR to being a teacher of English is the effect that confessing to the trade at social gatherings produces on innocent bystanders. 'What do you do for a living?' someone might ask. 'I teach English,' I say. There is a stunned and rather shocked silence. Someone might cough noisily and change the subject, as though I'd just boasted of an act of cannibalism or of violating a corpse. Others may hang their heads in embarrassment and mutter, 'English was always my worst subject at school.' Breezier and more self-confident people might respond, 'Oh, then maybe *you* can tell me ... When is it correct to use "which" and when "that"?' To these I explain that I'm not to be held responsible for grammar – except, perhaps, to the great Examiner in the Sky where I might easily fail – and that I teach English literature. 'Well, *that's* all grammar, isn't it?' may come the hot retort. So over the years I've found it better to admit to being a bait-digger, hodsman, or money-launderer, for these are regarded as certainly more honest callings and somehow more *real*.

An even greater embarrassment has confronted me since 1976 when, after decades of militant atheism, I became a Christian. At first, the problem of self-identification wasn't quite so pressing – though strangers will ask you what you do for a living, few at a first encounter will ask you what you believe and those who do are either New Agers, Jehovah's Witnesses, guru seekers, guru flackpersons, etc., easy to detect and deflect. But the Christian, unlike the English professor, is called upon to spread the good news and, where possible, convert the sceptic. And the main problem here is that this activity seems to require an attitude on the sceptic's part that is at least neutral and without preconceptions. So it was discouraging to find that most people have made up their minds about what I believe even more firmly than they have stereotyped my profession. I announce myself a Christian and there is the familiar stupefied silence; someone coughs and begins a discussion of the weather as though I had confessed to child abuse or ritual murder. Others stare at me in a combination of fear and horror as though, before their very eyes, a chancrous bubo had sprouted from my nose. The more assertive might say, 'Oh yes, Jimmy Swaggart; that the kind of thing you mean?'

It's a peculiar business; in the sixties I could always, if I felt mischievous, make a lecture audience twitch by uttering the word 'fuck'. Now I can achieve the same result by uttering the word 'God'. People shift uncomfortably from buttock to buttock. They remain polite, but you can tell they wish I hadn't said it. You can smell the fear, the terror of men and women who suspect some dreadful, moralistic trip is about to be laid on them. It's more intense than a possible concern that I'm about to correct their grammar; what they fear is that they've encountered someone who is absolutely certain how to live, who is monolithic, totalitarian in his certitude in which there are no cracks, no misgivings.

Most responsible for this stock response to Christianity are, of course, Christians themselves. We have by our sermons and actions given the Faith a bad name through the centuries; generations of men and women have had their minds warped by fables about hell, about how easy it is to get there, how the walls are ten thousand miles thick, and the flames hotter than the sun, the screams everlasting and unheard through those walls, and how if you get flattened by a truck as you cross the road on your way to confession (but not immediately from it) you will find yourself in that hell faster than you can say Amen. Furthermore, we are supposed never to be satisfied with distorting the minds of our young believers, we do it to innocent strangers: we force native women at gunpoint to put on Marks and Spencer's underwear; we torture virtuous pagans and burn them when they don't convert; not only do we persecute Jews, but we are responsible for the Holocaust. And for the genocide of native peoples, for the white male supremacist system, for the rape of natural resources, and the devastation of the environment. Clearly there are grains of truth behind these accusations and perhaps there is some justice in resting the burden of proof on modern Christians that they won't burn, torture, or maim someone. At the same time, Christianity is no more invalidated by the inadequacy, indeed, malevolence, of some of its adherents than Islam is by figures like Khomeini. It is difficult to persuade non-Christians that the Faith is by no means monolithic, that not all of us are fundamentalists, or friends of Jimmy Swaggart; that not all Christians are implacably opposed to abortion, or the ordination of homosexuals, or to movements of national liberation which, in modern times, we helped reinvent.

But once in a while I come across a lapsed Christian or an articulate secular humanist with whom discussion moves quickly onto a more personal level. Given the facts of human history over the last two thousand years, they say, how is it that you can swallow the dogmas of such an outmoded and discredited faith? One that casts no light on our modern predicament? Did you (as Martin Luther recommends) 'tear the eyes out of your intellect?' Is it age? Fear of death? Weakening of the critical faculties? Or what?

I try to explain that 'reason' has at first very little to do with it. I have met few people who come in later life to religion by way of rational conviction, nor do I know many Christians bound to their beliefs through the letting go of their intellects; faith comes upon us and is maintained by a different, and to me much weirder, faculty than that. In my own case, it did not come entirely without prior notice, for I became aware, whenever I taught Chaucer or Spenser, of my attraction to the medieval picture of an ordered, harmonious, sacramental cosmos – one that seemed to have nothing whatever to do with the modern world – a 'discarded image', as C.S. Lewis called it, but charming in its way and a concept I could admire at a distance as I can admire a picture. Then in the late sixties and middle seventies a number of small and isolated experiences began to move me in my present direction: a folk mass in Cuernavaca, Mexico – the huge and ancient church echoing to mariachi trumpets, drums, and the delighted singing of perhaps a thousand people; a half day in the new and magnificent cathedral at Coventry in England in which the remains of its blitzed predecessor form part of the design. (I remember vividly the bombing raid that destroyed Coventry, and there among the ruins was a plaque celebrating the post-war activity of German volunteers who had come to help rebuild it.) I choose these three (out of many) because they illustrate a particular pattern: in the first two my response was an aesthetic one, and aesthetics, as Kierkegaard pointed out, is often the first 'stage' in a journey towards religious faith. In the case of Coventry Cathedral I found myself moved by the more complex issue of Reconciliation about which, as I was to discover, Christianity says a great deal. When I returned from England I underwent a series of conversion experiences of a more or less conventional sort. Though there is an abundance of literature on the subject – for instance, William James's *Varieties of Religious Experience* – these experiences are not really communicable. In my atheist days, for instance, I was ready to put down even my own childhood encounters of the numinous (I describe one of these in my non-fiction 'Unicorn Evils') as a sudden 'defamiliarization' of the kind that transforms us when we read poetry or gaze at a painting. A hard core of greater wisdom, though, managed to retain a sneaking existence in my mind until I was ready to consider these childhood memories again, when, in fact, and to use James's useful word, 'vastations' began to happen to me.

Over a period of several weeks each day would start with a feeling of great and delighted expectation – something entirely wonderful – miraculous – was going to happen. Throughout my waking hours each tree, flower, grain of earth, human face seemed to burst out towards me renewed, vibrant, and intense as though I were on an acid trip. But acid deforms reality, in interesting and entrancing patterns maybe, but deforms it nevertheless. Within these drugless experiences of mine everything I saw and touched was not only real to me in a way I never experienced so fully before – I also knew that I was in communion with things as they actually are. This knowledge was accompanied by what I can only call a *feeling of blessedness* – as though I truly was, in Hildegard of Bingen's lovely phrase, 'a feather on the breath of God'.

These perceptions faded, though they recur from time to time, but the knowledge they brought did not. I could see what lay behind the common imagery of God's presence you find in the Bible – He

(She, It) appears in tongues of flame, clouds, whirlwinds, flaming bushes – there is a violence about these manifestations that results in one great injunction – *you must change your life*.

At about this time I found myself rereading George Orwell's essay 'Inside the Whale', a work of literary history and criticism whose title for some reason or another stayed in my mind on this occasion more than the contents. What would it be like, I thought to myself, to be swallowed by a whale, to find oneself inside the huge cosmos of a whale's belly, walking across the fields and streets contained within it, encountering cities, strangers, and foreign shores?

I imagined, inside this whale's belly, arriving at a bar. I sit down to drink with a group of people in the midst of an argument about whether or not there is such a thing as a whale.

'A whale must exist,' one of the speakers says, 'because there has to be a cause which is not in itself an effect, and therefore there needs to be entity which is a whale that has not been created by other whales or by anything else, for that matter.'

'What you're saying,' somebody replies, 'is that there cannot be a series without a first term. But there are such series – the series of negative numbers, for instance, or the series of positive fractions. Therefore your argument is invalid.'

'But,' said another, 'if Whale exists it is by definition omnipotent, omniscient, and all-loving. Yet we are confronted on all sides by Evil.'

'There is no such thing as Evil,' a voice claims, 'Evil is an illusion propagated by the Anti-Whale.'

'Then we are in Error,' counters a heavy drinker, 'and therefore Error exists and why does an all-loving whale allow it to?'

And so the arguments rage, far into the night, debating the existence and nature of the Whale that carries us – atheist and theologue, Jew and Christian, Buddhist and Hindu, Moslem and Taoist, male and female, planets and stars, time present, past, and future – nurtured and protected, on its vast and mysterious journey across the universe.

Following this set of experiences and fantasies I became a Christian. The Faith was, so to speak, at hand. It 'resonated' with my childhood, and returning to it was like returning home. I have said that one aspect of conversion experiences is that they are not easy to discuss with those outside a belief system. This is also true of Christianity itself and here, I must say, is that edge of certainty that no real Christian can be without. When my atheist friends, for instance, tell me that I was suffering a nervous breakdown – all I can offer in reply is my knowledge that they are mistaken. I can also assure them that after these episodes are finished with, and one embarks on the actual work of trying to become a Christian, one is involved in a relationship like marriage – though troubles of a certain kind may be over, troubles of another kind begin.

Consider, for instance, the issue of the Church. One of the major features of Christianity is the emphasis it places on the idea of *ekklesia* – an assembly, my dictionary says, 'called out of the world'. Thus the Church is intended to be a community of men and women in which there are no distinctions of race, class, or sex, united by a *telos* – a sense of purpose or end-state. It is exceedingly difficult for a man or woman of ordinary sensibility who is also equipped with strong opinions to stay within such a community; yet it is not possible to be a Christian outside it. Here is an illustration: Christianity calls me to radical pacificism, yet I know enough about myself to recognize strong impulses towards violence. Therefore I need the support of fellow Christians as I struggle with this duality – and that is the kind of community the Church is supposed to provide.

I discovered that though the Church is united by a shared *telos*, it is divided as to finer details. It was not obvious to me in 1976 that the Church is strained between the inertia of traditionalism on the one hand and the forces of renewal and reform on the other. That Christians fight with some bitterness among themselves came as news to me. I knew, of course, about the wars of religion and the burning of heretics, but I had supposed that in these days, when Christians are very conscious of being outnumbered by secular humanists, where they are no longer part of a top-dog belief system, and where they perceive themselves as a remnant, that differences between us were minimal and subject to rational debate. I believed this until, a few years ago, a small but significant episode demonstrated that I was mistaken.

One morning the mail brought me a letter from the Archbishop of the Diocese of New Westminster inviting me to become a member of a group called the 'Bishop's Men'. At first it took me a while to associate this with anything Christian, for when I was growing up in London it was the name of a gang of race-track hoods operating out of a pub called the Elephant and Castle. I asked around in my home parish and discovered that these Bishop's Men constituted a group of about a hundred and fifty members of the diocese, who paid a couple of hundred dollars a year each to the Bishop's discretionary fund and met once a year at a banquet held at the Vancouver University Club. I didn't like the sound of this at all and wrote to the Bishop quoting Groucho Marx's dictum that I wouldn't want to belong to any organization that would admit the likes of me, and that no one of my politics ought to find himself in anything as establishment as the University Club. The Bishop wrote a charming note back asking me to put aside my fears, for the Bishop's Men Organization was only a device to secure extra money for worthy causes not covered by the diocesan outreach funds, etc. I was lulled by this and sent the Men's secretary my two hundred dollars.

In the fullness of time I received an invitation to the annual banquet. I had, however, some reservations about the title of this organization – not only did it sound like the name of a London gang but it was sexist; it excluded women. Why not, for instance, follow contemporary fashion and call it the 'Bishop's Persons'? To make such a change, however, we might need to rethink our policy with regard to women, for at present the group was all male and so was the University Club. So for a start what about opening the whole thing up to women? I suggested this to the Bishop who seemed vaguely supportive. After he'd made his report to the diners after the banquet, he said, I could bring the matter up under 'any other business'. He told me that in the U.S. there were many groups like the Bishop's Men open to women and called names like the Bishop's Associates. I said I would make a little speech in support of this suggestion.

The banquet opened with a general milling around, then prayer, then an indifferent meal. As you would expect from a body of Anglicans, enough wine flowed to create a mellow feeling. The Bishop made his report, and I made my speech. 'Let's get out of here,' I said, after a brief introduction, 'to somewhere more human, let there be women around us, and let it be known that we are the Bishop's Associates.' I sat down. Two people applauded but fell silent almost instantly. This boded ill, for in Vancouver you can get up on the stage anywhere and play the comb-and-paper and receive a standing ovation. Somebody coughed, the Bishop shifted position, and I fielded a number of rather hostile stares; it was as though I had suggested we spend the rest of the evening getting laid.

There were two responses; somebody argued that women ran the Church already and that men needed somewhere of their own to go. Another stated that he had been in this organization for many years, so had his father before him, that there had been no changes within it except for Bishops who had come and gone, and he was quite happy with the way things were. Sporadic clapping broke out at this, the question was called, and my suggestion defeated by a vote of 118 to 3. Then the meeting dissolved and the milling about began again. An elderly gentleman buttonholed me and asked what the hell I thought I was doing. 'Women run things,' he said, echoing one of the speakers. 'They run the Church through the Altar Guild and by petticoat government. Their influence on doctrine and ritual has been unrelenting, pernicious, and utterly debilitating.'

'That's right,' argued a third party, 'it was through their lobbying that the Church had to get rid of the prayer book.'

'And got us that Green Thing instead,' a fourth chimed in, referring to the colour of the *Book of Alternative Services* which was intended to supplement (but not replace) the red-covered *Book of Common Prayer*.

I began feeling aggressive, for a number of other men were closing in on me for the kill. 'So women got you the Green Thing,' I said. 'What other horror do you think they might force on you?'

'I'm not scared of *them*,' someone claimed. 'I'm not scared of any woman alive.'

'Then let women into your rotten club.'

'Listen,' a fifth man reasoned, 'that's not the point. They have their own organizations, as this other gentleman tried to point out to you, and they make policy. This is our own place here, the place we can relax.'

I tried to say that it sounded as though these men wanted either a whore-cum-coffee house of the eighteenth-century sort, or to belong to some male-bonding group of the kind Robert Bly runs where men try to contact their inner warriors then go out into the woods to beat drums.

'And what's wrong with that?'

'There's nothing wrong with that – but this is a Church-based outfit and ought to be inclusive.'

'Maybe what *you* want is to be cosseted and dominated by a bunch of women.'

At this point I made a tactical error and instead of quoting St. Paul, for instance, to the effect that in Jesus Christ there is neither male nor female, freeman nor slave, Greek nor Jew, I tried to link their exclusiveness to fear of women and to trot out all the old clichés about sexual fears and castration phobias. It didn't go over too well.

'I'm a grandfather,' someone said indignantly.

'It's you who ought to worry about castration,' a menacing friend of his said. By now I was at the centre of a small but hostile knot of Bishop's Men and suddenly felt vulnerable. Seek not to know for whom the knives are out, I thought, and how do I escape from here? By a great stroke of luck, however, or by the operation of the Holy Spirit, we heard someone loudly calling for order so as to propose a toast. My would-be tormentors stood to attention as somebody gave them 'The Queen' while I seized my opportunity and sidled away.

I tell you this story not to denigrate Christians, with whom I feel great fellowship, nor to mock the Anglican Church, which I have grown over the years to love, nor even to sneer at the poor-man's upper-class twittery of places like the University Club, towards which I feel much less hostility than I did as a youth, but to illustrate a not always acknowledged truth: that contention between

Christian and non-Christian is mild in comparison with debate among believers, shared *telos* or no shared *telos*. To the non-believer, after his or her initial shock, the Christian is perceived as a harmless freak on the order of a channeller, let's say, or a thirty-year IBM man. The Christian, however, is surrounded on all sides by people who feel with strength the urgency of such questions as: Is belief in the virgin birth necessary for salvation? Is homosexuality sinful? Is the acquisition of property immoral? Do the scriptures *actually* suggest women are to be held inferior to men? What about abortion? etc. The answers to these and many other issues of hermeneutical or ethical importance are not simple, though most of us behave as though they were. In the specific acrimony that surrounded me that night with the Bishop's Men I felt the peculiar irritation and even rage that people within an ekklesia can manifest – an irritation and rage all too often overlooked in the more pious descriptions of how Christians behave together. At the same time, however, I felt just as strongly an awareness that *sub specie aeternitatis* these rages, these disagreements between one brand of Christian and another, and between those who are Christians and those who are not, are tied together in one vast ironic knot, then mellowed and dissolved by the operation of grace.

Compassion Practicum

ONE OF MY favourite passages in the Gospels describes a man kneeling before Jesus to ask him what he must do to inherit eternal life. The scene isn't hard to visualize – the road through Judaea to Jerusalem with the little spurts of wind off the semi-desert lifting dust up to eye level, the parched fields, the sun already hot enough to sear the skin, the little knot of travellers, then the rich man (in Matthew's version he is a youth) riding up on his camel personally to get the word from this already legendary, itinerant teacher. He rides up (his camel 'sore-footed and refractory', as Eliot says somewhere about another occasion), leaving his wife, his concubines, his mansion in the suburbs, and the Palestinian equivalent of sushi bars, designer clothing, boutiques, hair-styling salons, Thai restaurants, far behind with all those life-style magazines – *Look, Gloat, Envy, Bask, Sneer, Get, Desire* – scattered about on his coffee tables, in order to follow the promptings of his spiritual dimension and find out what he must do to be saved. I can imagine him mulling this problem over in his mind: *What's it all amount to? Say a few prayers, perhaps. Straighten out my ritual. Write a cheque to Oxfam. Send a letter a month to a foster child in Guatemala, or some other distant place. Compose a letter to the papers denouncing a book, or a movie, or somebody's moral failings. Take a firm stand against abortion, maybe. Or another against the ordination of gays. Or perhaps* FOR *the ordination of gays. Where in hell should I stand on these matters?*

So he rides off, asks questions, tracks Jesus down just as the latter is enjoying a break after completing a speech taking a tough line on divorce.

'Teacher,' the young man says, 'what good deed must I do, to inherit eternal life?'

Jesus, knowing full well how wrong the question is, summarizes the Decalogue for him.

'I have been doing these things all my life,' the man says.

'Right,' says Jesus, 'you lack one thing, go sell what you have and give to the poor, and you will have treasure in heaven; come, follow me.'

Then the text (Mark 10:17-21) concludes with this lovely remark:

> At that saying his countenance fell and he went away sorrowful for he had great possessions.

Yes, indeed. Well might his countenance fall. Jesus' answer is utterly devastating and uncompromising – never mind the side issues of divorce, abortion, writing cheques out of your great abundance to charity: sell up, give *all* your money to the poor, trade in your camel for a good pair of sandals, and join us here, on the road. He follows this doleful message with the story about the rich man, the camel, and the eye of the needle as though to say, Sorry, but there it is. You want to be 'saved'? *That's* how you do it.

The one great advantage of Christianity (if you consider it merely as a system of ethics) is its simplicity – divest yourself of your wealth and identify yourself with the poor, the oppressed, and the marginalized. Its one great drawback is that hardly anybody's ever done it: it takes either a rare, inborn disposition, or a conversion experience on a massive scale, or, as in Tolstoy's case, a sudden attack of senile dottiness. It seems to run counter to what a study of history shows to be the human predilection for sin, for dog to eat dog, to cut throats, to kick the opponent when he is down, to aggrandize, rape, and pillage, and in short, pursue the allurements of the Id. Nevertheless, this divestment of wealth remains an ideal, and one that has begun to attract me more and more.

Not that I consider myself rich, though I *am* rich, I suppose, even by North American standards, for my salary is within the 10 per cent range of highest wages in the country. But I don't *feel* rich and I don't suppose I ever would, even if my income were doubled. Nevertheless, I know in my head I am wealthy and therefore one of the oppressors. I am a middle-aged, comfortably off writer and teacher of luxurious tastes used, over the last twenty-five years, to being cosseted and enriched by a society whose basic values I despise. Even my colleagues, amiable and thoughtful people for the most part, express themselves, at least to me, only on such matters as tax shelters, travel money, computer time, teaching load, and registered retirement savings plans. Perhaps they sense I am secretly fascinated by such things. Yet as I sit writing this in my comfortable if squalidly untidy study, I am morbidly aware that a large percentage of the world's population is starving to death, an even larger permanently hungry, that well over half of it lives in substandard housing without adequate medical facilities, little schooling, and chronic malnutrition. What's more, I know that men and women who have become conscious of their own oppression enough to try to do something about it are either in the hills or disappeared into jails being beaten, raped, castrated, scourged, and cattle-prodded as I sit here, calmly changing a typewriter ribbon.

So what must one do to inherit eternal life? A Hindu might spend the latter part of his life, after completing the family part of it, in the forest; then he takes his begging bowl, sandals, and saffron-coloured garment on the dusty road to renunciation and enlightenment. And there is something very tempting about that – sell off the house, pay out the mortgage, donate the money to the poor, and retire to a life of holy contemplation – perhaps in a monastic community sworn to poverty, obedience, and chastity. No more cappucino bars. No more summers in *la belle France*, Aprils in Portugal. That's one alternative. Another, as I contemplate 'retirement' a few years away, is the more customary one in our culture of the gilt watch, the cursory handshake, the garden in the suburbs, the two years of watching telly, followed by the dropping dead. I know that retirement will never be like this for me – at the very least I would try to finish Proust – but those are the choices: the mendicant on the road, or the aging writer under the loggia. Either/Or.

I found it useful, while I was living in California last year, to mull this over with my friend Terry. He is a tall, vocal, speedy, bespectacled, and macrobiotically thin young man of thirty-seven. His talk is fast, witty, and sardonic, and his prominent Adam's apple, sharp as any pen, bounces delightedly in his throat as he engages in almost constant speech. The problem was that we did not immediately share the same language. This was not because we were of different generations, but because my own tradition pretends to lucidity and precision in the use of words. Terry, on the other hand, is a New Ager and thus an adept at *theobabble* even while sceptical concerning its abuse. While I, for example, might seek to define words like *kingdom*, or *kerygma*, he'd be content to use, in my view loosely, words like *cosmic* and *creativity*. Terry never tells you anything – he shares it with you. He uses *and* when he means *but* as in sentences like, 'I agree with everything you say and I dispute to the death your right to say it.' Often such a statement would end on a note of interrogation as though to render it less aggressive. He can speak volubly of feeling 'empowered' by a lecture or a book, and is happy attending *needs assessment seminars*. He and I would take care to 'affirm' one another, though sometimes Terry would use the word 'celebrate', particularly whenever one or other of us had 'owned' his feelings. Terry rarely thinks things through: he 'revisions for a new paradigm'. He can sometimes, particularly when sitting down 'intentionally', 'get in touch with his dark side'. I too grew skilled in the modern theo-babbling practice of communicating feelings by blameless and non-judgemental phraseology like 'when you tread on my foot I feel some irritation'.

On one level, language like this, which exists and is spoken at the interface of theology, popular psychology, and Age of Aquarius *Kindersprach*, is formulaic, reductive of feeling and response, dishonest (for it hides the speaker behind jargon, hindering self-revelation and establishing a power imbalance between speaker and audience), and cheap. It reduces the language to a collection of mindless counters. Terry recognizes this, of course: I once told him how on the streets of Santa Cruz one evening I happened to hear one young man say to another, 'Hey, man, I can really co-passion with how you must feel about that.' Terry's first impulse was to round up a squadron of Hell's Angels from the Oakland chapter and visit Santa Cruz. At the same time, both of us can acknowledge that speakers of theo-babble are trying in their dim way to express a reality: if, for instance, you believe that words have power, that they change things, that human relations are affected by them, and you wish also to participate in the positive, transformative aspects of creation, then you will take care to affirm, to seek out and express the positive, to celebrate life and not put it down or do dirt on it by heaping on it negative words. By the same token, if you perceive the human in front of you as a sacred being, or, in Christian terminology, a 'Royal Person', you will again want to affirm that person and celebrate his or her existence. As in the Rule of Saint Benedict, a more traditional way of putting it, you will want to 'receive the stranger as though he were Jesus'.

Terry started his life in and around Pittsburgh, as an engineer. Then he dropped out to become a door-to-door salesman, then a manager of a health food store. He knows more about tofu, miso, tempeh, organic carrots, hidden carcinogens, pesticides, and irradiated foodstuffs than is probably good for any one averagely paranoid human being to know. He was attracted to the program in Creation Spirituality in Oakland (which my wife was also attending) because it seemed to explore the connections between the alternative society he was used to and the tougher, more disciplined theological adventuring he was not. Thus, along with my wife and perhaps ninety other men and women from a variety of backgrounds, some in religious orders, some missionaries, many therapists, counsellors, professional conflict resolvers, artists, aficionados of theology, Huxleyite Perennial Philosophers, and so on – he found himself in this master's degree program run by a Dominican monk named Matthew Fox, the author of *Original Blessing* and *Breakthrough* (translations of and commentaries on Meister Eckhart).

Part of the course involves choosing some area of social service, working therein part of the week, and reflecting on the experience. This was called the 'Compassion Practicum'. Thus a student may decide to spend a few hours in a hospice, a children's hospital, or at a soup kitchen (of which, in this age of Reagan/Thatcher New Reality there are more than enough to go around, even in a relatively small place like Berkeley, where we were living) or, as in my wife's case, helping a group called the Catholic Worker to build a safe house for Salvadorean refugees.

Terry and I gave much thought to his choice of Compassion

Practicum. Salvadoreans didn't appeal to him, nor did working with the sick. He was tempted by the Berkeley Styrofoam Cup Project, then busy trying to convince junk-food outlets and cafeterias that there exist alternatives to devastating the ozone layer in the upper atmosphere, but thought the work involved might be too reminiscent of his proselytizing days as a nutrition freak. The ongoing protest at Concord against the rail transfer of nuclear weapons interested him, but the difficulties of actually getting there by public transport proved insurmountable. He chose instead to work at a drop-in centre for the 'homeless', hordes of which had appeared on Bay Area streets following budget-cutting legislation by the Reagan government.

It is impossible to avoid these 'homeless'. They sleep in doorways, culverts, public parks, abandoned automobiles, BART station entranceways, and so on, and one need only take a few paces along any given street in the Bay Area to be panhandled by them. Berkeley is beginning to look like the Third World – Calcutta, Mexico City, São Paulo – where the homeless starve in their cardboard jungles, or like the conurbations of Europe or the Eastern seaboard. Or London, swinging London, where unemployed youths shiver in the wind that blows under the viaducts by Charing Cross. Or New York and Boston. Who are these homeless? Some of them are obvious dope victims, others bag-people, some quite respectable men and women down on their Reaganesque luck. Others work, but do not earn anything above a minimum wage, so cannot afford the Bay Area's inflated housing prices for even a room in a tenement. Better and cheaper to live in a doorway – at least one can eat. Many are drifters, just out of jail, others are inmates of the newly shuttered mental institutions. So you might see a man standing perfectly still on the sidewalk staring into space suddenly twitch, shrug, froth, and scream – perhaps for fifteen seconds before reverting to his daze. A bag lady might totter into you with loud advice to fuck off, while another might collapse against a wall in a deep fit of terrifying and uncontrollable giggles, pounding her fist on the concrete.

Thus the victims of the 1980s dog-eat-dog, war-of-all-against-all, *sauve-qui-peutisme* are out there, on the street, their presence an eyesore to the business community, an aesthetic blemish on the tourist trade, an embarrassment to the politicians who put them there, and a test of one's own *caritas*. Now they are visible who once were safely tucked away out of sight, tranquillized to the eyebrows, dazed and stunned with behaviour-modifying drugs, lobotomized, shocked, and flown far out over and beyond the cuckoo's nest.

GO SELL WHAT YOU HAVE, Jesus' words keep ringing in my ear, AND GIVE TO THE POOR.

OK, OK, but let's get this straight – I sell my house, renounce my pension plan, unload my stocks at bargain-basement prices, and what happens? I wind up on a bench in People's Park, or in a culvert under the McArthur Freeway. And for what? Divide my wealth equally and every person officially designated as 'homeless' in the Bay Area gets a raise of about a nickel.

'That's not the point,' comes the answer, 'the point is to act paradigmatically.'

'What's *that* mean?'

'Go help Terry with his Compassion Practicum and find out.'

Accordingly, I offered Terry my assistance. He was glad enough of it, and together we made our number with a young social worker named Dave who showed us around the shelter, the large hall of an Episcopalian Church.

Here was God's plenty. Here were our putative clients in various stages of animation from comatose to the hebephrenic. An insanely violent game of table tennis waged between two hyper-athletic black men threatened the too-close spectator with decapitation in one corner of the hall, while in another three young and dirty youths stretched out in sleeping bags against a cold radiator. A large cluster of men and women sat by the television, while others formed a ragged group of smokers on the fire escape.

'They'll tell you their story,' Dave said. 'You don't have to believe them. Just be who you are and let them be in the space they're in – like, *it's* OK. Don't give them money, or even tobacco. *Just be present to them.*'

Dave, then, was also a theo-babbler. I nodded at Terry as though to say 'one of us'. Babbler or not, though, he knew his job. Slowly and discreetly he showed us around the place indicating the various less subtle signs whereby something could be learned concerning the histories of these people.

A tough-looking black man leaned coolly against a wall, displaying an upper arm decorated with a tattoo of a sun with three rays emerging from it; inmates of prisons, Dave told us, will tattoo one another in this manner – one ray standing for one year of a sentence. Three rays out of a yellow sun, then, meant a trey at San Quentin, or somewhere perhaps a little less vicious. His heavy muscular development was another sign: body-building is evidently a common prison sport, and so is the habit of playing cards, particularly the game called 'spades', with that peculiar intensity – the attention with which men in the slammer play for cigarettes – 'snout' as they are called in Her Majesty's forces and in British prisons.

'Consider this poor twitcher by the door – ragged, very thin, swelling abdomen, prematurely wrinkled, few teeth, tattooed forearms. These,' Dave explained, 'are the characteristics of speed users; speed thins you down, bloats your liver, and consequently your abdomen (while alcohol inflates the stomach). You can lose your teeth on speed, though a full set of teeth is not a counter indicator; for jails and psychiatric wards offer free dental care. Or used to. The tattoo marks on the forearms show an attempt to hide the track marks of intravenous drugs.'

We nodded and moved to the next exhibit. This was a woman of indeterminate age shuffling towards the washroom, her jaws in constant motion. As we watched, her tongue suddenly lolled out, flopped, then withdrew into its dark home as unexpectedly as it had left it. 'Get close,' Dave said, 'and you'll probably smell urine.' Urine and onions. Loss of bladder control can indicate either alcoholism or schizophrenia, though many alcoholics who don't want their addiction noticed eat onions to disguise a breath redolent of booze.

'The tongue,' we said, 'what about the tongue?'

Tranquillizers, evidently, like phenathiazine, cause you to open and close your mouth spasmodically and create an over-relaxed, irresponsible, separate being of your tongue. Dave nodded at us and went off to answer the phone.

Just be present to them ...

I took this to mean play cards, table tennis, chess or just talk – twenty years ago we would have said *rap*. It was with the greatest difficulty that I kept my eyes off people's forearms, their abdomens, their tongues. I tried to strike up a conversation with an elderly and toothless (speed? caries?) black man sitting lonely on a bench against the wall, but he shook his head at me as though he thought I was cadging snout. Terry wasn't doing any better. He sat at a table looking rather discouraged – his Adam's apple lay passive in his throat and lines deepened at the corners of his mouth. I could feel a kind of hopelessness myself. It was *his* Compassion Practicum – I was just along for the moral support. At least down at the Catholic Worker safe house I could practise my bad Spanish. I experienced an unworthy urge to get out of there and let my mind drift over a cappucino at The Coffee Connection.

Terry was suddenly standing in front of me. '*I've done it*,' he crowed. '*I've made contact.*' He jabbed a thumb over his shoulder at a shapeless, shambling young white man whose sallow face was decorated with a streak of dried blood. 'This here's Mike,' Terry said. 'Inviting us for a game of spades.'

I felt a sudden wave of relief. Contact at last.

'What are you doing?' Terry asked.

'I've made no plans,' I answered. 'Just sitting here trying to get in touch with my inward hunter-gatherer.'

'Well, cut it out. Let's get a fourth player for the game.'

I stood, nodded, and grabbed the arm of a nondescript black youth. 'Game of spades?' I asked.

'Sure, man,' he replied.

It was easy. The four of us sat down while Mike and the black man, whose name was Stanley, taught us the rules of the game – quite simple, a variation of whist. Stanley played carefully and intently as though some screw armed with a shotgun stood over his shoulder. Mike was extroverted, slapping down each card violently and crowing with triumph if it made a trick. Terry and I lost steadily, but it didn't matter. I felt bathed in the warm and fragrant oil of self-congratulation – this is what we came for, this was our little contribution to the alleviation of the world's misery. And it was both simple and pleasant – no penance required, no self-abasement to inherit eternal life, *just be present to them*, the losers, the homeless, the *anawim*. A volunteer came around with a try of doughnuts – gift of some charity organization. We munched them hungrily. All around us the noise, the activity, began to mellow into a low buzz of happy conversation as our clients grew more comfortable with their surroundings. At nine-thirty the place closed, and the clients were redirected to another church hall to sleep. This place didn't have the right kind of licence evidently.

At half-past nine, then, there was a sudden burst of activity. Men and women took off, very quickly, for the hall of the sleepers. Terry and I stood up – as volunteers we were expected to clean, sweep, and stack chairs. As we began to fold up the tables, both Mike and Stanley, to my utter amazement, raced for the cupboard to grab brooms and dusters. *They were volunteers like us* ... and like us they must have been congratulating themselves on making contact with the poor and disenfranchised. *That thin, lined guy suffering from chronic malnutrition, possibly a speed-user*, they must have thought. *Let's play spades with him. And that poor old fart with white hair come in off the street* ... LET'S BE PRESENT TO HIM. Probably run out of food stamps ... no wonder he guzzled that doughnut as though he hadn't eaten in a week ... poor old bugger. I ought to have offered him mine as well ...

Terry and I parted from our card partners with many expressions of warm regard. We walked back to my lodgings amused but slightly befuddled by our experience. Terry was inclined to think it meant nothing; I, on the other hand, used to teaching English and therefore in the habit of deciphering, or trying to decipher, poems and narratives, start from the position that *things mean things*. Almost automatically I began trying to formulate a Midrash on the text, a commentary on the episode. One could, for instance, entertain the notion that what had happened meant no person need be anxious about identifying with the marginalized – the act of identification was being carried out, on one's own behalf and by other people, quite gratuitously. Ah, but this was a special case. Well, what about this? *One's own well-being can never be a permanent condition.* At any moment a man in good health, proud of his bank balance, can be precipitated into poverty. I'm told, for instance, that the handicapped think of the fit and well as the 'temporarily able-bodied'. Exactly: though we may walk on two legs at noon we will be walking on three at sunset if we're lucky enough to walk at all. So it is with riches. I have long considered myself 'temporarily affluent'. Throughout my adult life I have had a fantasy of ending it as I began it – sleeping outside railway stations and bus depots with a newspaper over my face and being rapped on the soles of the feet by police night sticks, moving me on.

And that's what those other volunteers, my companions in spades, were clearly picking up. I had been assigned to the ranks of the twitchers, the shufflers, the tongue-lollers. Now it looked as though I might finally begin to 'appropriate' the other hard, unambiguous, Gospel saying: 'Do not be anxious.' Take no thought of the morrow, consider the lilies of the field, trust that all my wants will be supplied. Get mellow, then, relax – and if the worst comes to the worst there'll always be someone out there, some frustrated idealist on his or her Compassion Practicum, to take up the slack.

At the same time Jesus' plain, clear words to the rich man – 'Go sell what you have and give to the poor' – crept (and creep still) into my mind. Surely Jesus couldn't have *meant* this; there has to be a way in which I can pretend to misunderstand his harsh doctrine so as to continue in my comfortable, materially blessed mode of life. What we need is *a discourse of deliberate misunderstanding*. And this, it occurs to me, is one of the chief functions of theo-babble: it helps us to evade the truth; it cons us, for example, into believing that 'but' means 'and'. And in my own profession, the discourse already exists in the form of literary theory, which holds that meanings are obscure, nothing is what it seems, that there is always some deep 'signified' waiting to be deconstructed from the text, that all statements are machines for generating interpretations. So – let's go to work on it; 'Sell all you have' must mean 'Get a job where your talents will be amply rewarded'. 'Give to the poor' means 'Charity begins at home', and 'Come, follow me' means 'Attribute all your desires to the operation of the Holy Spirit' and therefore 'Do as you please'.

Two Epitaphs

Milton Acorn Remembered

'HEY, MAN!' Milton Acorn bawled amiably, catching me by the elbow. 'You're the only guy I've ever met who looks like me!'

I cannot say I felt greatly heartened by this news; while I had never thought of myself as handsome, Milton Acorn was, out of all my friends and acquaintances, the one that most deviated from classical standards of good looks. His body was wide and heavy, his face broad at the top, pointed at the bottom, and his mouth, rather thin lipped, drooped violently at one corner – the result of an attack of Bell's palsy. His eyes were small, the colour of McEwan's Export Ale, and almost concealed by protuberant welts of inflamed-looking flesh. His forehead was low and heavily wrinkled, and the high, prominent cheekbones made his face appear as though carved from teak by an absent-minded carpenter of inferior talents and this wooden look, coupled with the solidity of his torso and his upright, rather stiff posture, created an earthy, durable, rooted effect. A man who looks like this, I thought when I first met him, must be in touch with the Eternal Verities: not for him the glitter of our society with its false promises and debased values. Ah no:

> *Leave me, O love, which reachest but to dust ...*

and the poetry written by such a chthonic figure would have something important to say about life and art.

Nevertheless, I approached the mirror that night with more than customary misgivings. Much as I respected him, much as I admired his poetry, *did I really look like him?*

The first winter I met him was also the one my wife and I rented a cabin in the Laurentian mountains just north of Montreal. It was a quiet, small place and towards the end of our stay there we invited a number of guests most of whom had to sleep on the floor. Stepping among those recumbent bodies was the restless, insomniac Milton, his thoughts focused on God knew what underground visions, his torso stripped (for the house was, in accordance with customs of eastern Canada, extremely hot), his intestines rumbling from some bacterial infection. Thus one could observe the chunky, earthy quality of his body, disfigured, to the critical eye, by a couple of pendunculated warts, one on his back, the other just above his belt and to the side. There was a coal-heaving, navvying look about this body, at odds with an extraordinary delicacy not normally associated with those groups, which he manifested on this occasion by accompanying his frequent visits to the toilet with *running the tap* in the bathroom sink.

Milton's approval of the working class was as unfeigned and as profound as is possible only to a person not born and brought up in it. There was no hesitation in his allegiances, no doubt in his mind about the future: it would involve a dictatorship of the proletariat – a *good* thing. Government would eventually wither away – an even better thing – and the result would be a classless society, the best thing of all. Meanwhile he chose to romanticize the working class and to adopt, much as George Orwell would leave a top fly-button undone and drink tea from a saucer, what he thought were its habits. He would appear at poetry readings dressed in heavy ankle boots, thick greenish denim work-pants which, out here in the West, he would cut off just below the knee in a style he associated with loggers. Thus he turned himself into an extraordinary and powerful figure, short pants, logger's boots, wooden though forceful body – prancing about the stage bellowing forth 'I shout love!' the opening line to one of his most popular works.

'I can see what he means,' my wife said. 'Something about the eyes.'

'Thanks very much.'

During that Easter we spent at the Laurentian cabin it rained heavily, so some huddled in front of the fireplace, others went walking among the dripping trees crunching underfoot the dirty remnants of the winter's snow. Milton disappeared and I thought the earth had swallowed him, claiming its own. Then I saw him. He was standing among trees on top of a small hillock, staring at nothing, perfectly immobile as though he himself grew tall and strong from the thin, Laurentian soil. Shortly afterwards I lost touch with him and did not see him again until his arrival in the West, a year or so after my own.

By then I was an undergraduate at the University of British Columbia and was writing, among other things, a column for the student newspaper. It happened there was a conference of Black Mountain poets on at the time – Charles Olson, Robert Creeley, Robert Duncan, and some others were there in person together with a clutch of home-grown imitators who used to meet together and produce a magazine called *Tish* of which another friend, Irving Layton, once said, 'Twenty issues they've sent me: twenty issues of a poetry magazine and not a single poem in any one of them!' He roared with laughter and added he thought this was quite an achievement. I was inclined to agree with him. At any rate, I attended the conference and listened to a recital by Robert Duncan. This was a dreary experience, for I had rarely come across so much verbosity, pretension, wilful obscurity, and self-approval in the service of nothing. I had heard Milton read in a pub the day before and stated, in my column, that Milton stood out among this flaccid Black Mountain bunch like an oak cask in a supermarket, a comment that elicited a certain amount of hostility from the campus poetasters and sparked a controversy that occupied my attention for a few weeks to come. But I recognized that to say such things of Milton was to deploy critical clichés. It seemed impossible to speak of the poet's work without being affected by his appearance, so that one found oneself writing up images drawn from trees, earth, roots, the solid, the old-fashioned, the virtuous and serviceable. It wasn't until much later on that I came to realize that much of Milton's enviable centredness and air of repose was an illusion and came from the discomfort he felt in his own body.

Nevertheless, Milton Acorn, in contrast to most of the people I was meeting at U.B.C., seemed to me a genuine poet as opposed to a man or woman who goes in for poetry as a device to secure fame, riches, and beautiful lovers. After all, the work looks easy: all it appears to need is a pencil, an eraser, a Roget. It doesn't consume much time (unlike the writing of fiction) and one risks nothing, for audiences are enthusiastic, uncritical, and happy to take the poet at his or her own valuation. Milton, in contrast, wrote out of a love of language, a coherent world view, a deep and genuine urge to change the consciousness of his fellow creatures and move it in the direction of love, peace, and social justice. He desired to communicate a perfectly reasonable vision in language as simple as he could find consistent with his own joy in complexity of language and image. The very last time I saw him he did not comment on our fancied (I hope) resemblance. It was on Charles Street in Toronto, not far from one of the world's ghastliest corners at Yonge and Bloor.

'Hey, man,' he shouted. 'Your hair's gone white.'

'Hallo, Milton,' I shouted back. 'What've you been up to?'

'Oh, living the life of a poet, living the life of a poet.'

Milton lived the life of a poet. For him – and I think for me – there can be no finer epitaph.

Let the Trumpets Sound for Bill Sellers

BILL SELLERS WAS about the first person I encountered when I was hired by Simon Fraser University. He was a tall, skeletal, grey man with a crew-cut head and a leathery Humphrey Bogart face filled with projecting teeth. I was a lowly instructor and he an associate professor and the difference in rank between us was emphasized by Bill's great height. My eyes seemed to be focused at the level of his tie – a rather shoddy blue affair decorated with white lines that looked like print. I examined them more closely. They *were* print. The words TO BE OR NOT TO BE THAT IS THE QUESTION TO BE OR NOT TO BE THAT IS THE QUESTION flowed in an endless chain from the knot to where they disappeared into his jacket. The rest of his clothes were commonplace and even shabby, for they smacked of dollar-forty-nine day at Woodward's, but the voice was astonishingly deep and resonant, the voice of a Chateau-Yquem cheese-and-walnuts don who could, were it not for his American accent, have stepped from the pages of C.P. Snow. I took him for a man of fifty, but he turned out to be a genuine thirty-nine. I was surprised to find out he was a Canadian. He was born in Manitoba, emigrated to the States, and wound up at Oberlin, from which unlikely place our first department chairman had winkled him early in 1965. Later that day, while I was prowling the corridor, he invited me into his office.

'I'll be glad,' he boomed, 'when all this opening ceremony bullshit is over and done with. What I like to do is get hold of a course and hang onto it. Like at Oberlin. I was the Shakespeare man, see? Shakespeare. Those are my lecture notes.' (He pointed at a row of yellowing files on his shelves near his desk.) 'One for each play,' he boasted. 'Wouldn't be without them. They date back to my first year's teaching.'

'Do you ever add to them, Bill?'

'Are you kidding? After all the work I put in on them?'

'But they must,' I said in my naive way, 'be out of date by now.'

'Is *Hamlet* out of date? Is *Macbeth* out of date? Let's talk about sex.'

He opened a drawer and pulled out an envelope. 'Read *that*,' he commanded.

The letter was from a girl. It was a nostalgic letter. The young lady was still at Oberlin and she regretted the passing of her liaison with Bill and reminisced, with a wealth of anatomical detail, about their adventures in the library stacks.

'I'd get her up against the bookshelves,' Bill said. 'I'd spread her legs with one hand and pull down her pants. I'd unzipper my fly, get my cock out, then ram it up her until it touched her shoulder blades.'

'You did what?' I asked, quite taken aback by this sudden switching to a mode of discourse I had not engaged in since my army days. I glanced at Bill's shelves – Shakespeare: *The Complete Works*. Samuel Johnson: *Rasselas*. Dante: *The Divine Comedy*. Auden and MacNeice: *Letters from Iceland*. The *Meditations of Marcus Aurelius*. Bill peered at me solemnly over his glasses and repeated what he'd just said, word for word. 'Male chauvinist pig' talk is what we'd call it nowadays. What made this odd, though, was Bill's evident detachment, his inward elation. His eyes seemed to buzz with more than sixty-cycle flicker, while his voice was deep and unhurried as though he were carefully explaining to me the difference between a villanelle and a triolet.

'I don't want you to think,' he said, beginning to elaborate, 'that there was any pause in my movements, any jerkiness. It was all done with one, flowing, unbroken gesture with my right hand while my left hand was over her mouth to keep her moans under control. Usually there was some young bastard in a carrel ten yards off working on the poetry of Andrew Marvell, or some such twit, whom we wouldn't want to disturb. But we'd be in there, every lunch hour, a knee-trembler up against the stacks ...'

I thought to myself, right, it's the *game* aspect of sex that allures him, together with the lesser game of *talking* about sex. I was at that time considering writing a pornographic novel, just to make some money. This vocabulary, these images, were part of the skin novel convention – I could learn something from this. I began to listen with greater care.

'Here's a photograph,' Bill was saying, ' ... dig the negligee ... get a load of those boobs! ... in glorious Technicolor! ... look and see what's written on the back ... *To Bill, from your juiciest Grad* ... juicy's the word ... we used to joke about it ... see, what I'd do is I've give her a feel in the elevator on the way up, just for starters, particularly if there were other people in the elevator ... you know how people in elevators just stare up at the numbers ... I'd stick my hand up her crotch a couple of times ... she'd collapse against me ... hardly able to wait for me to ram it to her ... here's another picture ... one *I* took ... no, wait a minute ... that's another ... the girl I had before Joan ... yeah!'

Bill's eyes lit up with the sort of joy that, in Renaissance paintings, shines out from the eyes of men and women caught up in religious ecstasy. I felt a sense of awe – here was a man at the delighted interface of lust and aesthetic response.

'Just feast your eyes on *her*,' he said, his voice slowing, becoming even deeper, a jaguar purr. 'Isn't that a sight for sore eyes? I'm getting a hard-on just thinking about her ... same thing though ...

lunch hour ... in the stacks ... usually in the Middle English section ... that being the least frequented ... students all round us, heads in their goddamn poetry texts. Piquant, wouldn't you say?'

He turned back from this art appreciation lesson to the more solemn litany of the pornographic novelist: ... steaming thighs ... thrusting breasts ... engorged nipples, members ... *jobs* of different descriptions including hand and blow ... garments ripped in the enthusiasm of lust – blouses for instance, or underpants ... penises like iron bars. I had read a fair amount of porn as preparation for my novel, but had usually been oppressed by the humourlessness of it: the pornographer, I was beginning to learn, has to be in dead earnest. Any hint that the author is sending up the tradition and he or she will upset the reader and is done for. Bill at least saw the comic dimensions of the mode.

'Here're some more letters,' he was saying, 'photographs ... nude babes with Shakespeare and the poets of the thirties ... in fact that's how I'd gather them in ... reading the spicy bits out loud ... have 'em creaming their jeans right there in the seminar ... my advice to you, boy, is to get your course ... one with a bit of love poetry ... get your student, get your Middle English section in the library, and you're away. Matter of fact I'm thinking of going up to the library right now ... kinda check things out.'

Almost every day I'd pass his office and each time he'd call me in to show me letters, photographs, testimonials to his sexual skill. Each night he would go alone to one of the more scabrous *Nachtlokalen* on Hastings Street, such as the Smilin' Buddha, and sit and drink, waiting for something to happen. How much of his Oberlin love-life was fantasy, I'll probably never know. Certainly the material he produced looked genuine. Yet the men and women I've met over the years who were students at Oberlin during his time there never heard any sexual gossip connected with him: laziness, yes; lechery, no. At Simon Fraser I heard no rumour to substantiate his fantasies, but that may have been because everybody's fantasies were beginning to be realized on a scale beyond adolescent dreams: it was the mid-sixties and affairs with students, considered so turpitudinous a few years before, were almost marks of status, so that a man could barely expect tenure without a list of sexual adventures on his C.V. Only a few approached the subject with any sort of outdated machismo, and I remember an argument I had with a colleague, Stanley Cooperman, about the evils of the grading system.

'Whaddya mean, flunk students,' Stanley snapped, flapping his arms. 'Of course I flunk students! That doesn't mean I hate 'em! Sometimes I go to bed with students! That's nothing to do with it! You wanna know what I tell 'em? Darling, I tell 'em. You're great in bed but you're lousy at English literature! How's that! You like that? How d'ya like *those* apples? You can't write for beans, I'd say. So I'm gonna have to flunk you! That's what I say! That's my attitude! I fuck 'em ... *and I flunk 'em!*'

This febrile angst was not Bill's style. For one thing, his fantasies were delivered in a slow, rich voice full of rolling cadences, and for another, they seemed more an aspect of deep joyousness, an inward hilarity, than an evidence of some neurotic need to prove himself. A world, one imagines him saying, in which such adventures are possible, such physical contortions feasible, cannot altogether be a bad place. He derived almost the same enjoyment from the feuds and intrigues of the English Department as he got from observing the eccentricities of the human flotsam down at the Smilin' Buddha. This gave him a certain poise and detachment which now and again I would find irritating.

'But *Bill*,' I'd say to him, 'can't you *see* that Professor X is a complete arsehole?'

'You mean just because he dresses up in his wife's clothes?'

'No, no, because of this memo he's just mailed out, and in any case that's only a rumour about him wearing his wife's clothes.'

'He does,' Bill said, his leathery face creased delightedly, his voice beginning to bubble. 'He does, he does. You can take my word for it ... *that's how he gets his jollies* ...'

'Who wants to be a department head,' he said on one occasion when, dissatisfied at the way in which the department was falling apart, a group of us had approached him in the hope of plotting a *coup*, to topple the head and replace him with Bill. 'My role,' he said, 'has always been to befriend the chairman and try to prevent him from making a jackass of himself.'

'Publish or perish?' he used to say. 'Why should I write anything? Everything worth saying about the literary canon has already been said a hundred times and I've nothing to add.'

Nevertheless he pottered about among his five-by-three cards and finally produced an article on W.H. Auden. Sometime in the early fall of 1966 he called me into his office and showed me another letter. This time it was from the most prestigious journal in English studies, the PMLA, and it was a letter of acceptance.

'Bunch of pricks,' he said, barely able to conceal his delight. 'Fancy them accepting the damn thing.'

At that time Lawrence was for Auden the chief 'healer,' the visionary who could lead man out of the wasteland by restoring him to his long lost psychic balance ...

I was listening to these words, or words very much like them, being read almost inaudibly from a kind of pulpit by one of Bill's closest friends in the department. Bill himself lay in a plain wooden box on the floor of a utilitarian funeral parlour situated in the ratlands of Burnaby. It was the most conventional of days for a funeral – overcast sky, driving rain, fog rolling in from the Fraser River. We were somewhere along the Burnaby section of Kingsway, a long street that winds its way through cut-rate electrical supply houses, used car lots, McDonald's hamburger shops, Pay 'n Save gas stations, finance companies, Dairy Queen ice-cream stands – the detritus of a dying, entropic sub-civilization. A good time to be cremated.

... Some of the difficulties of interpreting THE ORATORS *result from Auden's own early idiosyncrasies; in the brief prefatory note to the collected poetry (1945) he describes* THE ORATORS *as 'The fair notion fatally injured' by youthful incompetence or impatience. Some of the allusions, for instance, still defy meaning and will probably continue to do so until, as G.S. Fraser remarks, some industrious 'thesis-manufacturer' asks Auden himself for enlightenment.*

Bill keeled over one night playing, of all things, ice-hockey. He died of a broken aneurysm of the aorta – just a few days after receiving that acceptance note. The superstition, I thought, that lies a skin-thickness between the rational agnostic secular humanism of academics is going to prevent us all from sending articles off. There'll be no publish *or* perish for us. What would he think of his article now – intoned bloodlessly over his corpse? His attention would not be on that, of course, but with charmed approval on my friend Professor Fox who had brought to the funeral his babysitter, an inscrutable girl of about seventeen, with whom he'd been amusing himself while his wife was on some trip back East. I made a vow that if ever I were to meet Bill in the afterlife I would tell him about it. While that clap-trap of yours was getting spouted over your bones, I'd say, there was Fox feeling up his babysitter under a coat they'd placed over their knees.

> THE ORATORS *remains the key to the Auden of the thirties. Although in* THE DANCE OF DEATH (1933) *he dabbled briefly and rather self-consciously with the Marxist solution to contemporary problems ... the informing ideas remain essentially those first explored in* POEMS (1930) ...

Every once in a while I attend the funeral of a colleague. They never fail to oppress. Bill's was the worst, but Philippa Poulson's, at a Unitarian Church with Khalil Gibran read over her corpse, ran it a close second. Stanley Cooperman's, in a synagogue, was conventional but dreary beyond belief, since nobody, not even the presiding rabbi, quite knew how to eulogize Stanley's life and thought. But then and there, in that dim, Burnaby hole, I thought, 'How Bill would have hated this aseptic, bloodless exit!' Behind that retired basket-ball player's exterior there lurked an anarchic roisterer bubbling on the verge of escape. I imagine him now during his solitary excursions to the Smilin' Buddha, alone at a table with his Scotch-on-the-rocks, solemnly eyeing the seedy drunks, the whores, the pot-belly crowd – a man of grey leather secretly roaring with laughter, covering his fellow men and women with a vast sympathy, inventing for them within his imagination a gamut of sexual postures.

What can I say about Bill in the way of an obituary? Was he 'the most unforgettable character I've ever met' and should I send these pages to *Reader's Digest*? He wasn't, and I shouldn't. But I can say this, that dead though he was he seemed more alive to me than the rest of us in that place, more alive than the solemn young man hastily recruited to speak in the order of Bill's departure, more alive than Fox's baby-sitter out of whom, Bill would've agreed, a seducer could expect little mileage, and more alive than I felt. Some years ago I inherited, after it passed through many hands, his office – he was its first occupant – in the deliberate hope that some of his basic sanity, some of his joyousness, would rub off on me. He was lecherous of mind and bawdy of soul – he was beloved of his students, not because they were sexually attracted to him (though some of them may have been, unlikely though that seemed), but because they knew he was subversive and on their side. Above all he had fulfilled the task required of him by achieving, without harm to others, an intensity of being ... *Lord, now lettest thou thy servant depart in peace: according to thy word ...*

Unicorn Evils

Faith in their hands shall snap in two,
And the unicorn evils run them through;
Split all ends up they shan't crack;
And death shall have no dominion.

Dylan Thomas

Landfall

I MIGHT NOT have returned to England as early as 1966 had it not been for Californians and my mother's illness. My memories of the country where I was born and which I left thirteen years before with an oath, hurling my ration book into the River Mersey, were almost entirely negative. But during the period I lived as a graduate student at Stanford I met many people who not only swore by the place but who went there every year almost as though they were pilgrims of some sort. I was so busy agreeing with them, since most of them were my wife's customers and she a Fuller brush saleslady, that I talked myself into a condition of nostalgia. Thirteen years is a long time, this was the kind of thing I said to people, and things have probably changed. The brush buyers agreed. They were all of them rich and anglophiliac – the first explains their freedom of movement, the second Jocelyn's success in selling them expensive rubbish. Their love of English institutions often transcended the borders of absurdity – men and women in black coal-scuttle hats, scarlet jackets, and shit-catcher trousers used to prance on horseback in the field near our house chasing foxes they'd probably imported for the purpose over the brown, dusty hills around Palo Alto. They rode with packs of beagles and were presumably led by a Kiwanian or a Shriner disguised as a master of foxhounds. But their enthusiasm for things English was genuine and contagious and I spent half my time around Atherton and Menlo Park encouraging a reluctant population to support the Boston Tea Party and to vilify George the Third.

Paranoia had kept me away from the country for thirteen years. I'd always supposed somebody would 'get' me if I ever set foot there. An income tax official, perhaps, or a recruiting sergeant who'd press-gang me into the army for a second time. These fears are not as mad as they sound, for though my father died in 1944 we received a dunning letter in 1952 warning him that he owed thirty-two pounds eight and threepence in taxes for the year 1941 and that he should govern himself accordingly. Very much against my mother's wishes I wrote a self-indulgent letter back informing them of the old man's death and suggesting that if they wanted the money they should Burke-and-Hare his corpse out of its resting place in the Battersea cemetery and see if we'd left anything in his pockets. As for the army, I was once sent a rail ticket from London to Crowborough, Sussex, with instructions to report for two weeks with the reserve. At the time I was working near Franz, Ontario, and could thus afford to send officialdom a brisk, not to say peremptory reply. *They* had undoubtedly filed those letters and the possibility of repercussions caused me a twinge of anxiety. Basically, however, I felt unwilling to face England as I remembered it – a land of mean streets, sodden skies, scowling class-obsessed populace, queues, shortages, Sunday boredom, and rain. Ah, but you should see it now, my friends said, things are *happening* there ... Carnaby Street, mini-skirts, Mary Quant, the Beatles, the Stones, explosions of pop culture ... new energies have been released. The dreariness, the quiet desperation, had vanished. The land of virtuous gloom has become unzippered and euphoric. This is Tir-nan-Og, they said, the country of the young.

Jocelyn and I had moved from California to British Columbia in the summer of 1965. A new university, Simon Fraser, had opened up and I was offered, and I took, a job there. But a few months later I heard that my mother had been admitted to hospital and operated on for cancer. I had last seen her six years before when she had spent a year in Montreal during a period when nobody I knew was in very good spiritual shape so that we had parted on bad terms.

Since I believe it important to arrive at some rapprochement with one's parents where possible and where the latter allow it, I was glad I had the time and the means to visit her. It was as well I did so, for six months later and two months after my return to Canada she died in a Brighton nursing home.

I had met Jocelyn at a secluded resort in the Laurentian mountains just north of Montreal. It was called La Chaumine and I immortalized it much later in my novel *The October Men* where it appears as 'La Cabane'. Jocelyn was British working class in origin but had achieved a certain social mobility, as had I, by passing the right examinations while at school and jumping, or more accurately staggering, over the various educative hurdles existing in the days of our youth. She became a physiotherapist and was strongly urged by her teachers to acquire a genteel accent so as to cut a more convincing figure in what was then still a very middle-class profession. So when I met her I mistook her for a woman two or perhaps two and a half risers above me on the social staircase. Subsequently, it amused us both to discover that her parents were, if anything, even lower than mine. At any rate that day we met we began to talk as though we had never been strangers: we rowed on the lake close to its rocky banks shaded from the mild October sunlight by copper-coloured foliage, speaking freely of our lives and beginning to fall in love. I was twenty-nine, at the end of more than a decade of frenetic, unconsidered activity, and I knew myself to be tired with the deep inner exhaustion that expresses itself in paradoxes: a need to withdraw from the world coupled with a need to seek out a purposive way of life, a desire for solitude and silence, but a desire also to reveal myself and be open, vulnerable, and yielding. I didn't know it then, but I was going through one of those periods when we are highly sensitive to signs, visions, and significant encounters by which the pattern we so fervently seek seems to be made evident to us, when black cats cross the paths of the superstitious, or, for the rest of us, when the branches of trees form letters and write words, or the face of an old friend, last seen fifteen years before, darts into your consciousness and there he is, when you go home, standing on your doorstep, or when a woman you fall in love with turns out to have the same initials as you do, or when she is someone you visualized, in your fantasies, years before. To most of us these coincidences, these synchronicitous events, mean nothing except as reminders of the stupidity and destructiveness of acting on them; to others they are the signs, the everyday symbols at your door, by which we can read, or think we can read, the inner truths of the world. I was not conscious of this at La Chaumine: what I *did* know was that I had entered a moment of peace during which I could try to set straight the course of my life.

Jocelyn worked for the Canadian Arthritis Society, but she had decided to give up her profession and train for something else, though she wasn't clear what this was to be. We were alike in that she had let go of a past way of life without fixing on an alternative but, at that point in time, her youth, high spirits, and confidence caused her to believe she would eventually find one. She was tall, brown-haired, slender, and straight-backed. She moved gracefully and laughed a lot. I thought her slightly excitable, a little frenetic, but I put this down to a flow of adrenalin of the sort I was experiencing myself. I may very well have seemed manic to *her*. At any rate, our states of mind seemed to correspond; we attracted one another, became lovers, and then, a year after, a married couple. Knowing what I know now, and taking all the subsequent disasters, her deepening depressions, her eventual suicide into consideration, I would still have said 'yes' to this fall day on the lake and to everything that followed it.

And now, in January 1966, we set sail from New York to visit England, land of our origins, home of our problematic parents, together for the first time.

A man travelling to England in those years, and sailing up Southampton Water, would have seen, to the east, a huge red-brick Victorian eyesore, a quarter of a mile long, topped and bookended by Gothic minarets. It lies some two or three hundred yards back from the shore and was used, in my day, as a military convalescent depot. Many years before I had been sent there in order, as the medical officer put it, 'to rest up a few weeks'. This phrase made me think of deck chairs, *A Farewell to Arms*, lawns and sun-decks where I would spend the hours between reveille and bedtime sipping chota-pegs and burra-pegs brought to me on trays by starched and sexy nursing sisters. I'll recover there, I thought, get my strength back sufficiently to grapple with the army to some purpose. This'll be a sanctuary – nobody kicks sick men around, not in England. I'll read, laze, and smoke myself back into shape. Instead I came upon Netley first in the way one always confronts new things in England – under drizzling skies and after a train journey of many changes. Six weeks in bed had not improved my stamina so that after lugging a heavy kit-bag over a mile from the station I was shaking with exhaustion and self-pity. A Welsh sergeant in the Hussars met me at the entrance and immediately put me on fatigues for being improperly dressed. I got signed in, issued blankets, and released into the bowels of the hospital, which was less a hospital than an unheated greenhouse, for one's first impression is that this is a house of glass. Tall glass partitions separate the rooms from the corridors which, stretching the entire quarter-mile length of the hospital, open out to Southampton Water through huge windows. Biting winds swept the corridors and a damp cold nuzzled its way into the rooms to lurk there despite the fires one was allowed to build under certain conditions, and the conditions were these:

1. No fire will be built before 4:30 p.m.
2. All fires will be out by 7:30 a.m., the grates cleared, dusted, and brought to a high state of polish.
3. No coal, wood, paper nor any other combustible material will be kept in the rooms at any time.

If you could resolve the contradiction between the building of a fire and condition 3 then you were in clover.

There lay fifteen not always comfortable years between the paranoid convalescent and my sleeker, thirty-five-year-old self –

running to fat, short in wind, comparatively affluent – now cruising into Southampton on the *United States* under conditions of luxury that a lean malingerer would have found hard to visualize. I watched the hospital slide past the ship and picked out the line of shingle where we used to go beachcombing – scouring it three abreast in the hope the seas would wash us up something we could flog – but all we ever found was a menu from the *Queen Mary.*

There was another man on deck staring over the rail. I borrowed his binoculars and focused them on Netley's façade. I began telling him how grossly I once hated this building and started to describe that first day at Netley, fifteen years before – the bleakness, the cold, the voices – whining, disgusted, very English. But I quickly bored him and found myself alone.

'Fer fuck's sake less get this bleedin fire going.'

'Oo's that on the bed?'

'Git olda some dry wood, Dogsbody.'

'Soddin road walks ... musta done abaht fifteen soddin mile ... '

'Ay,' a Yorkshire voice bawled in my ear. 'It's uhff puhst foh-uh.'

'So what?' I answered sleepily. I'd found my assigned room, dumped my kit-bag, lain on the one vacant bed, shivered violently for a few minutes, then dropped off into a nightmare-ridden doze.

'Well, dorntcha want no sooper?'

I could see men in overcoats, breaths steaming, trying to light a fire with slivers of driftwood and wet slag. The cold penetrated two shirts, an army sweater, a thick serge tunic, two pairs of trousers, one civilian and one issue, both made out of stout, bulky wool, an overcoat, and three available blankets. My teeth began to chatter.

'Eddie!' the Yorkshireman bawled. 'Coom on ... it's sooper time.'

A heavily built man lumbered over as I got to my feet. His back was very straight yet he walked with a lurch and seemed to have difficulty moving his neck.

'It's not me military training wot's given me a nice straight back,' he said as we walked up the stairs and joined a noisy queue fighting at the dining hall entrance. 'It's a fuckin great plaster cast stretchin from me ip to me shoulders.'

'What's that for?' I asked.

'Slipped disc,' he said. 'Or some other fuckin thing. Ow the fuck would *they* know?'

'Might get your fuckin ticket.'

'Fuckin ope so.'

We got our issue of supper. That *Queen Mary* menu was to put us all in touch with a life one might have supposed would be going on on another planet. Dover Sole, Lobster Thermidor, *Entrecôte à la Sauce Béarnaise* ... whereas in the cookhouse at Netley they used to empty cans of pilchards-in-tomato-sauce into a long wooden horse-trough and mash them to a red paste to be served with potatoes and cabbage they'd boiled in brine and under pressure for twenty-four hours. Once I saw one of the cooks lift his white smock and piss into the pilchard-brimming trough, stirring it well in.

'*Dafi booncha boogers*,' he said, cackling. 'Fancy eatin that ... '

As for me, I dined in the NAAFI that night – eggs, beans, and chips.

It's all over now. All gone. There's no longer any conscription in Britain, which is in some ways a pity since, as I shall try to show later, the British Army represented a nadir of experience from which one could only ascend. I pointed this out to Jocelyn, who claimed that her life as a student nurse in Britain functioned in the same way. I think she was wrong. You can always stop being a nurse ... you cannot, without risking a lagging or a stretch, get out of the army. Or at least it seems that you can't. At this point I can hear the reader's angry voice raised against me; *you should think yourself lucky*, I hear him say, *you were in during peace time. What if you'd had to grapple with trench feet, gas gangrene, lice, frostbite, and chaps running towards you with bayonets?* I answer that disease is a natural enemy, like aging and death itself, that the bayoneteer is a hireling who doesn't necessarily hate you, and that your true enemy is to be found among the officers and NCOs of your own side and that nothing I've read in the history and fiction of the great wars has convinced me that I'm wrong.

At any rate, for a few years after World War II, Britain retained its large army – thin red line or end of wedge – by means of the Conscription Act. Most young men of my age accepted, though many of them gloomily, the fact that they would have to spend eighteen months as guests of His Majesty. I did not accept it and, as soon as I reached the critical age, took off for Europe (as we call it in England) with my eyes darting from side to side. Things did not always go too well on the Continent and now and again I would return to my austerity-ridden, ration-booked, coal-shortaged, army-threatening homeland for recuperation. I could not, without exercising more caution than lay within my talent, work there legally, so, when an understanding developed between myself and a young woman from Liverpool, I left for Scandinavia hoping to make money either in the Swedish bush as a logger or on the Norwegian whaling fleet. I promised this girl that I would send for her as soon as I'd made our fortunes, but nothing worked out in Scandinavia either and I was back, penniless, vowing that I would for her sake allow myself to be conscripted. Readers may be inclined to forgive my stupidity when they understand that I was only twenty years of age. In any case, I found myself one morning in May 1950 being lectured by a very young officer with a cherubic face, Eton accent, and buck teeth: 'In the King's Royal Rifles,' he said, 'we think fahst, we ect fahst, and we *shoot*-damn-straight.'

There followed ten weeks of rather pleasant, cops-and-robbers, cowboys-and-Indians work around Winchester with Bren guns, grenades, and an extraordinary device called a PIAT cocked, if one were strong enough, by an enormous spring. I was thrown out of the KRR's after ten weeks and into the Royal Army Education Corps from which I got turfed, mainly for lack of High Seriousness, in late October of that year – a disaster that coincided with the seeding, budding, and final blossoming of a misunderstanding between myself and the young woman.

Thus I found myself, by November, a lowly clerk in the Service Corps, the most despised and underdog branch of the army, with prospects neither of promotion nor of access to graft, locked into National Service on behalf of a woman who would no longer speak to me, for a period of service increased to two years because of the

Korean War. A classic, but nevertheless dismal, A.E. Housman situation to which I responded by contracting meningitis and going into a coma. On my survival I was sent to this convalescent depot at Netley.

Cruising now into Southampton, I saw that the hospital was deserted. At this time of day there should've been knots of convalescent soldiers outside the building, waiting for supper, scraping their feet in the gravel. I should've been able to hear them bitching, even at this distance. It was a ghost building, that was what it was, and I could imagine the corridors, once clamorous with army boots, the bawling of NCOs, the thumping of hand-drawn polishers, now empty and silent, beginning to silt up. I saw the windows smashed and vacant to admit the full force of the wind, which would streak down the quarter-mile corridors tumbling in front of it fag-ends, part-one orders dating back fifteen years, carbon paper, shit-house roll, and documents relating to the Korean War. I could see it now as a sanctuary of the genuine sort, as a doss house for bums, pad for kids on LSD, and as a stoating ground for the young lovers of southern Hampshire.

After supper that first night we breathed life into the fire, shoved some of the wet slag we used for fuel over it and waited, crouching, until it began to generate some heat. We spoke of the no-man's land we occupied between the status of patients, who were kept in warm hospitals, fed amply, and issued a pint of beer a day, and that of soldiers who lived in barracks, ate pigswill and not much of that, and whose access to beer and skittles was as limited as our pay. We discussed the inhabitants of our limbo – appendectomies, pneumonias, underweights, busted legs, spinals, rickets, and vitamin deficiencies. We spoke with morbid relish of disease and of the miraculous door it opened – the possibility of working our tickets.

'You was lucky,' Eddie said. 'You might've ad to spend Christmas in ospital. Down ere you'll get leave wiv us in a few days time.'

'How long does one stay here?'

'A mumf,' somebody answered. 'Supposed to be. But if you box clever you can stay ere as long as yer like. Bin ere six mumfs, me.'

'But you adta box clever.'

'Ho yus ... I adta box clever.'

The fire grew brighter and we watched the flames spring up and grow so that they became reflected brilliantly in the panes of the glass partition. I asked them why they tried to stay on here. They pointed out it wasn't hard to dodge authority in limbo.

'It's fuckin cold, that's the only bleedin drawback.'

'Not in E-block it ain't,' Eddie said, referring to the new building at the back. 'They got central fuckin eatin.'

'The food's fuckin rotten,' someone warned.

'It is everywhere.'

We all nodded wisely. A very tall, hoarse-voiced corporal crept into our circle saying:

'Wot you ad wrong wiv you, cock?'

I told him. 'Jabs!' he whispered in horror.

'Dintya get no bleedin lumber punkcha?'

'I've ad *them* fuckin things,' Eddie said. 'As a matter of fact I've ad three. You lie on yer side wiv yer knees drawn up an they shove a soddin great needle up yer spine.'

'Worse than that,' the man known as Dogsbody said, 'is an enema. Know wot I mean? Enemas, see? Tube goes up yer arse, in goes the Persil, and fer three weeks arter you can shit froo the eye of a needle.'

'Ow long yer bin in the Kate?' somebody asked.

'I got eighteen months of it to get through yet,' I answered.

'I dunno wot's up wiv you National Service blokes,' said a private in the Ox and Bucks Light Infantry. 'Bitchin abaht eighteen bleedin mumfs ... I signed on, I did ... pissed as a soddin newt. Five wiv the colours and seven wiv the reserve. And ere's you whinin abaht eighteen mumfs. Are you a man or mouse?'

I thought about it. '*I'm a mouse*,' I said.

'Bloke last week got is ticket wiv meningitis,' Eddie said.

'Yus, yer wanna try fer yer ticket.'

'Tell em you get pains in the fuckin ead.'

'Black-ahts is favourite. Geezer I know got is ticket wiv black-ahts. E was always blackin aht, see?'

'You wanna try it, cock,' the corporal advised hoarsely. 'They discharge a dozen a week ere. Discharge on medical grahnds, know wot I mean? yer ticket.'

'My ticket,' I affirmed.

An hour later I walked down to the beach, fully dressed plus overcoat and two layers of newspapers I'd wrapped between skin and shirt. I shivered in the light, insistent drizzle. I pottered down to the sea's edge, my feet dragging through a mixture of mud and fine gravel. The water was a suicide's black. Across the inlet I could see the lights of Beaulieu competing with the yellowish smog that began to roll up the estuary. I was surprised to find myself weeping uncontrollably. They were tears of self-pity but, thank God, also of rage. From now on, I swore to myself, I'm their enemy. I saw myself as the Free Human Spirit engaged in the eternal conflict with the forces of Oppression and Regimentation, though to put it like that is to mock myself as I was then. You'll notice, for instance, that I have given those abstractions capital letters. This is supposed to distance the writer from what he writes – to inform the reader that the author is a sophisticate who has achieved an ironic view, and that he is inviting the reader to share in the joke at the expense of all the insufficiently motivated passions of the young.

Utterly diabolical, in my opinion, since my enemies were certainly real enough – fat, beer-drenched sergeants; shaven-headed and bull-necked corporals; rabbit-chinned and treacherous subalterns and remote, 'justice'-dispensing colonels who were waiting desperately for a war to start to give their lives meaning. But a man's enemies are not exclusively figures of authority but also those in his own group who lose their nerve and incorporate themselves into the system and thus perpetuate it. I'd watch them change from ordinary, decent civilians into insane supporters of the army's power structure – they had become, in other words, Eichmanns, lick-spittles, time-servers and garotteers. And I might have felt differently had I thought they constituted a powerful and efficient army, but this they manifestly did not. Had it not been for the

Russians and Americans Hitler would have overwhelmed us within a year of Dunkirk. Thank God we were not at war, and I didn't have to fight alongside these stupid, cowardly, and treacherous men.

I swore on that beach an oath to escape them all and I warmed to my room-mates huddled over their fire and saw them as Nyms, Pistols, Bardolphs. I began to love every inch of their cunning, malingering heads. Like them I'd concentrate on working a medical discharge, preferably with a pension, and if I failed, and the War Office wanted me that badly then, by God, let it watch out, I said – I'd be an asp in its basket, a fifth-columnist dedicated to its overthrow by means of passive resistance, rebellion, and sabotage.

Having shouted all this into the wind and greatly relieved by its expression, I returned, purged, to my room.

We were queuing, for this was England again, to get off the ship. The longshoremen were the cause of the queue – they ambled with dignity, refusing to be hurried, through the chaotic piles of trunks and packing cases. Customs men were too few in number to adequately badger the thousand or so passengers. It was raining quietly and there were groups of bedraggled and badly dressed people on the quay. I scanned the pale faces rapidly for any that resembled the photos I'd seen of Jocelyn's parents and, drawing a blank, sidled with relief to my place in the line. Outside, my feet on land, the cold, knowing it was supposed to be in England, suddenly grew intense. With laughable ease it penetrated three sweaters, a jacket, my Arctic parka, and two pairs of trousers. Jocelyn, who had caught the grippe in Montreal, suddenly began to cough uncontrollably. The sky darkened, lights were switched on, night fell. What we want, I said, is a centrally heated hotel. By means of porters and heavy tipping we transferred our baggage to a cab and drove to the Dolphin, a fine, Georgian pub towards the centre of town.

The Dolphin was carpeted and bow-windowed. A huge fire blazed in the lounge. Tweedy ex-public-school boys turned salesmen sat around drinking vodka and lime. The management directed us to a room 'with central heating'. What this meant was that a towel rack in the bathroom was at a slightly higher temperature than the surrounding air. We ate quickly and Jocelyn took to bed with her bottles of ascorbic acid, Contac-C, and cough mixture. As for me, I walked out into the street to discover whether or not the pub life had changed.

The fine drizzle that had accompanied us from the pier had frozen on the sidewalks producing a thin layer of treacherous *verglas*. Street lamps lit the deserted city with a ghastly sodium yellow. There was no one about, so that the pedestrian, journeying to his lukewarm beer, felt alien and furtive, a Jack-the-Ripper. I slunk into a public bar and, after a double Scotch with which I silently toasted myself, Jocelyn, central heating, gourmet cooking, survival from the war and from virulent disease, demobilization from the army and the Canadian citizenship that rendered me immune to governmental attack, I began to think about the immediate future.

It seemed both menacing and auspicious. My stomach churned slightly at the prospect of visiting my mother, whose moods even in good health were hard to predict, and Jocelyn's parents about whom I had heard nothing for my comfort. Probably Jocelyn had told me too much about them: she had depicted them as narrow, bigoted, suspicious of strangers, foreigners, and of English working-class men and women who had escaped. I told her I thought she must be exaggerating (we tend to see other people's dreadful parents with a sympathetic and objective eye *sub specie eternitatis* – or so we hope. What the hell have *you* got to worry about, we say. Think yourself lucky you weren't afflicted with *my* lot). 'My own mother,' I said, 'would make yours look like a saint.'

'Your mother's had a hard and tragic life,' Jocelyn riposted, 'what with being married to your father. And in any case the poor old girl's been sick: she's probably dying. You need to be gentle with her.'

With this I agreed. It wasn't going to be easy – there was a certain amount of unfinished business between my mother and me. But I was happy to be in England, despite this issue of relatives. I looked forward to enjoying the role of spectator – as though I were an anthropologist or sociologist observing a culture towards which he experiences a mixture of fascination and recoil. And the England of this trip was still recognizably the England of my youth. On my next visit, in 1974, this country of the past had vanished: the currency had changed, the freeways had been built, the elms and hedgerows decimated, and the people and cities had become as Americanized as their Canadian counterparts.

I sat in this bar huddled in my parka, my hand clutching a Scotch-and-soda that needed no ice to cool it. A Hampshire yokel crouched at the other end of the room: a heap of old clothes confronting a pint of dark and headless beer. A television set over the bar jumped and spluttered. 'The News' was being broadcast and a man commented on the intensity of the cold spell then afflicting Great Britain. I remembered my last winter in the country of the Great Pea Soup Fog and how cold it was and how, at peak hours, the available electric voltage drops so that the heaters emit only a few wan calories, kettles sit on electric rings for half an hour without boiling, and the picture on television tubes shrinks to about half its normal height. And now, oddly, the same thing was happening to this television set in front of me. What made it odder still was that a spokesman for the regional electricity board was being interviewed and was busily claiming that there was plenty of electric power and that his organization was prepared for the coldest possible January. What he didn't realize was that his face on the screen was no more than three inches high but the full width across so that he looked like a bullfrog with its head squashed in a vice.

Then I asked about Netley.

'It's all coming down,' somebody said. 'It's finished.'

'Finished?'

'Ah. They used un fer an ospital ferr a woil. Did you know it were desoined ferr India?'

I knew it, but I thought I'd let him tell it.

'They wanted two ospitals,' he went on. 'One ferr India, t'other ferr England. Well, the Croimean war were on at the toim ... '

'Arr, Zulu war, Jack ... '

'Zulu war were it? One a they wars – anyhow there were a lot of argument and the plans they got mixed up, like, and the one desoined ferr India they built over ere.'

I could imagine what they built in India. A yellow brick stables with windows carefully pre-smashed, floors designed for polishing with toothbrushes, grey-veined and shattered porcelain toilets with rusting fixtures, rooms tested for the production of low temperatures, no provision for fireplaces or stoves.

'It's the end of an era,' I said.

Arms and the Poltroon

IT WAS AT Netley that I gave some thought to the problem of escape. Desertion was the simplest, most obvious method, but this would involve leaving England forever – a step I was at that time reluctant to take. The second possibility was the 'mature' one of staying out my time and 'making the best of it'. On the face of it, however, this was absurd since the army was the proverbial sow's ear notoriously hard to craft into a silk purse. The third and most adventurous option was to 'work my ticket' on medical grounds. I had a head start, so to speak, on this course of action since I was still weak from my illness, prone to headaches, very depressed, and unmilitary enough, in a conformist society, to pass as mad. There was another factor. Across the fields from the depot was the new building called E-Block, which contained, apart from conventional hospital departments, a psycho-neurotic ward. If I were to play mad I would not have far to go. I was already 'on the doorstep'. Apart from anything else the place enjoyed central-heating – a consideration, in this bleakest of army winters, of the greatest decisiveness. Each malingerer coveted a stay in E-Block. We would sit huddled over our meagre fires plotting means of egress. A room-mate of mine, suffering from a mild case of 'flu, pretended, at my suggestion, that he had meningitis. I knew the symptoms. One of them is an inability to straighten a bent leg. Accordingly he reported sick with fever and added this matter of the leg. He was whisked instantly to E-Block from which he returned about a week later, cured and somewhat chagrined. I had forgotten to warn him that they would probably test his spinal fluid by means of a lumbar puncture. He had thawed out, over there in E-Block, but he was, on the whole, disinclined to be grateful to me.

The rest of us got on with the job of malingering quietly and without fuss. Some were fortunate enough to be permanently disabled. Eddie, for example, whose torso was encased in plaster, was given his ticket and went marionetting out into the Free World with an army pension for the rest of his life. Another man, pretending to be anaemic, stayed in E-Block for nearly three months. Dogsbody, a regular soldier who'd undergone a late conversion to the concept of liberty, convinced Them he was allergic to khaki, then disappeared into some research centre where, for all I know, he malingers still. But it was by no means so easy for everyone: a man reporting sick with headaches, depression, or just plain dottiness ran a discouraging gamut of shock-treatment, insulin, lumbar puncture, strait-jacket, pentathol, and long psychiatric examinations. You had to watch your step, all right. You had to box clever.

In the early evenings the reading room of the Southampton public library was filled with soldiery engaged in learning by rote the symptoms of his choice. I, for one, spent a week there poring through well-thumbed medical treatises acquiring a knowledge of allergies, megrims, back ailments, blood conditions, kidney malfunctions, brain tumours, paranoia, manic depression, and hebephrenia along with a taste for medical literature I have not yet lost. Few novelists can invent such deadpan, wildly funny (except, of course, for the patient) narratives as exist in medical journals. Consider, for example, the following case history:

> One afternoon in February 1956, he suddenly experienced a sensation as if he had received a blow in the stomach, and soon afterwards there was a pulling sensation in the jaws, followed by an impulse to dress in female clothes. On the way home from work, he bought some female underwear and secretly put it on when he reached home. He then felt 'completely calm' for a few minutes, then he experienced a feeling of revulsion and later that night

> burnt the clothes ... On all such similar occasions this desire was ushered in by epigastric and jaw sensations ... It was now impossible to hide the transvestite activity from his wife and though he worked efficiently at the bank all day, he would spend his evenings at home completely dressed in female clothes, using cosmetics and adopting female mannerisms ... on examination there was no physical abnormality except for a subcutaneous nodule behind the left ear. (Davies and Morgenstern, 'A Case of Cysticercosis, Temporal Lobe Epilepsy, and Transvestism,' *Neurosurg. Psychiat.*, 23 1960, pp. 247-49.)

I doubt if even Nabokov could cap that subcutaneous nodule – it is a *master-stroke.*

In the juvenescence of that year I was ready to act. I overstayed a weekend pass by one day and got a chit from a civilian doctor to the effect that I was too scared to face the journey back to Netley. He'd also written me a prescription for a sedative. The chit was accepted and the MO called me in for an interview. 'What's all this?' he said. I remained silent, withdrawn.

'It says here you were frightened to come back by train. Why?'

'Sir.'

'Whaddyer mean, "sir"?'

I shrugged. 'What is it about trains that upsets you?' he asked in a friendlier tone.

'I don't know,' I said after a long pause. 'The noise ... the way they sway from side to side ... the compartments are so small ... '

'You could've come back by bus,' he said, with what he may have thought was devastating logic.

'It ... it was the thought of coming back here, I suppose ... what with everything else ... just one damned thing on top of another ... '

'Nobody in his right mind,' he said testily, 'wants to come back here after going home on leave. What's the matter with you? You think I like coming back to this place? But I don't get the better of some poor, innocent, civilian quack and go around flourishing a chit.

'Oh, well,' he said finally. 'You've got a chit and I suppose I'll have to respect it ... get any headaches?' he asked suddenly.

I nodded. So did he. He scribbled something on his pad ... with any luck 'this man is a suspected Bedlamite'. Then he kicked me out.

'You done wrong,' one of the malingerers said, back in my room. 'When e arst you abaht them eadaches you shoulda give im the fuckin works.'

'Not *im*,' another critic said. 'E done juss wot e shoulda done ... don't overdo it, thass always my motter ... keep the fuckin bastards guessin ... '

'Yuss, I'm in fiver a that ... *course* yer gotta keep the bastards guessin ... but now, see, wot e's gotta do, see, is ter get ter see the bleeding doctor again ... '

'That's under control,' I boasted. 'Tomorrow morning.'

The morning room inspections were carried out by the fat Welsh sergeant who'd greeted me on arrival and taken such a dislike to me. That morning he strode into the billet, little pig eyes darting from side to side, sharp creases in his trousers, gaiters nicely blancoed, and his boots in a high state of polish, as they say. Two corporals marched in behind him. '*Shun!*' he squeaked. We tottered to attention. He caught sight of my unmade bed and blenched. 'Voss diss?' he shrieked. 'Voss diss, you?' I fixed him with a stony glare then bent down, picked up a boot, and threw it at the partition. It sailed across the room, smashed its way through a pane of glass, and landed in the corridor and slid on its side amid its shards along the floor's highly polished surface until it came to rest against the far wall. As soon as the Welshman was able to regain his breath he did the correct military thing and ordered the corporal behind him to fall in two men and march me to the guard house.

This lay three-quarters of a mile down the long approach drive. The progress of escort and prisoner was by no means as regimental as it should have been since one of my guardians was anaemic, the other limped from a recent cartilage operation, and the corporal himself was convalescing from pneumonia and had to abandon us after a hundred yards or so and I could see him, as I looked back, sitting by the side of the road with his head in his hands.

The charge against me was dismissed. I was forced to pay for the window, and sent to the cookhouse where, it was thought, I would be kept out of trouble. It was clear that my presence there, after a day or two, was an embarrassment to the head cook who forwarded me to the boiler room. This was warm, silent, and deserted. For over a week I stoked my furnace gently every half-hour and occupied the spare time in trying to learn Spanish from a book. After I've worked my ticket, I fantasized, I'll go to Spain ... somewhere where there's sun, warm seas, and lovely towns. Somewhere where a man could live off the land away from this drizzling sky and from the sights and sounds of industrial civilization in which a man can acquire dignity only through learning to malinger. I made a reclining chair out of a pile of coke and thumbed through my irregular verbs. The present disappeared and daydreams took its place.

E-Block was to us what the Grail was to Arthur's knights. I achieved it shortly after my relegation to the boiler-room and for two days felt lulled by its warmth, food, and lack of pressure. I lay silently on my bed trying to hide an elation inconsistent with my reputation as a depressive and observed the other inmates. They were a mixed bunch. One of them imagined he was the skipper of an ocean liner and would pace thc long, well-buffed floor with his hands behind his back peering keenly always through the same window as he guided the course of his vessel over the ice and snow of a Hampshire field. Mostly he was silent and intense though once in a while he would bark an appropriate command such as 'Midships!' or, 'Steady as she goes, number one!' Another feigned religious melancholy and, like myself, would lie most of the day on his bed uttering the occasional hollow groan. Sometimes he would anathematise the 'bloody city of Lichfield' in the manner of George Fox. I suspected that he, like the skipper and the man we all called the 'sex-maniac', was an impostor and this turned out to be correct for they were all of them kicked out of the P-N ward about a week after my arrival. Their behaviour contrasted rather sharply with those, a majority, who were genuinely ill. These men seemed superficially normal and it was only by means of small signals – the flickering away of eyes, an over-excited shout at a card game, a sob caught in the throat – that one knew there was something wrong. If I want to survive here, I thought, I must practice subtlety.

Let me put it this way. Suppose you were asked at a party to perform in a charade and that the role you were assigned was that of 'madman.' You would have immediate access to a number of largely comic stereotypes – the man who sits on a piece of toast and claims he's a poached egg, the zany with lolling tongue and uncontrolled eyeballs, the imitator of Napoleon, or Jesus, or Alexander the Great, etc. These are *conceptions* of what madmen are like and they do not correspond very much to reality. Nevertheless I think you would choose one of them because your conception is shaped by the audience. Thus, however you played the role, you would be playing it for laughs – you would render your madman as a *grotesque* and the audience, appreciating your skill, nevertheless recognizes that you are a man playing a role. Thus the skipper and his friends were Brechtian actors *demonstrating* madmen whilst themselves preserving an alienated distance from their outward behaviour.

It occurred to me that if I could sense this alienation within my malingering friends then so, on a good day, might a psychiatrist.

Accordingly, I sought for what I later discovered was called *the method.* It was not simply a question of imitating the less spectacular forms of psychic disturbances – catatonia, radiator clutching, total withdrawal – but of concentrating my mind on those recent experiences that had depressed me in the first place. These were many and included loss of freedom, the break-up with the girl in Liverpool, the weather, the army *mise en scène*, and the series of humiliations dealt me by authority, many of which, as I was now beginning to realize, were due to my own stupidity. Whilst deliberately increasing the bleakness of my inner life, I thought it important to participate fully in the social life, such as it was, of the ward and in other ways act normally in the hope that I would create the impression of a man trying hopelessly, though rather gamely, to cope with the external world against considerable odds.

This course of action met with some success, but there was a complicating factor. I found it increasingly difficult to ignore certain more positive manifestations: the first sunlight of spring gleamed on the grey waters of the Solent and daffodils began to thrust their way out of the soil around the elm trees now filling with rooks. The air grew warmer, blowing in from the sea. There was that spring flavour of things to be done, of journeys to be made. I had recovered completely from the disease that had originally brought me to Netley and, like any other moderately healthy youth, I was beginning to react against uselessness and inactivity. Besides, They were treating me as though I were genuinely sick and this, perversely enough, I began to resent. As February of 1951 turned into March, I became increasingly uneasy.

And the March of 1966 came in like a lion and went out the same way.

Jocelyn and I had been in England for four months and our boat was due to sail back to Canada on the eighteenth of April. We found that there had indeed been some changes in the tone of English life but that these changes affected only the young and comparatively affluent. The poor stayed poor and conditions for people like my mother, whose life was visibly coming to an end, remained abysmal. Our time in England had been dramatic and emotionally harrowing, but I had re-established some rapport with my mother so that, though this trip was to haunt me in many ways for years to come, I had to consider it successful. Jocelyn and I were utterly exhausted by it, however, and as early as February we had begun to count the days much as one counts them in jail or in the army.

I failed to work my ticket. The psychiatrist assigned to me maintained the stance that depression is a healthy reaction to army life. 'It makes *you* depressed,' he said, 'it causes me to wake up at night screaming in nightmare.' He went on to describe his nightmares and to provide me with interpretations, Jungian in tendency, for some of the more extravagant ones. Though his facial tics and over-reactions to any unexpected noise made me at times suspect him of malingering for the purposes of stealing his patients' thunder, I felt that here was a man whose burdens were even heavier than mine. I liked him and came clean with him so that one afternoon in early April I found myself dumping my kit-bag in my old room and walking out once more along the deserted beach. I'll get posted abroad, I thought: Trieste, Gibraltar, the Sudan ... what did the army deprive me of? Nothing. Nothing, since a man who values his freedom is everywhere on the run ... the army made very little difference. I had just over a year left to do and I had jibbed at that. I'd been a self-pitying child and victory, had there been one, would've been hollow.

I gazed across Southampton Water, this time with approval. On the other shore lay the New Forest, through which I had cycled when still at school. I had found it good – the thatch of old roofs, the inns encircled by clumps of trees, the grass-grown dockyard of Buckler's Hard where Nelson built his ships – and I should certainly visit it again. I faced the future with optimism.

My unit was in Germany and, though I spent a tolerable year there, it took a long time for me to develop a detached attitude with regard to the army. On one level it is perfectly iniquitous that two years should be carved from the life of a free man; on the other, that same man is taught valuable lessons, which stand him in good stead in the capitalist Land of Jobs. The army teaches a man to lie, cheat, steal, and look after Number One. He learns the inner meaning of the French verb *se débrouiller.* At first sight the private soldier is a victim – pushed around by cringing lance-jacks, sadistic corporals, fell and bloated sergeants, thuggish warrant officers, commissioned baboons. But since he is *lumpen* and lowly the private soldier has nothing to lose. He is blithely unconcerned with promotion since he knows it is out of his reach. He enjoys security, if you can so describe three ill-planned and poisonously prepared meals a day, and the ulcers and heightened blood pressure of responsibility do not trouble him. He is as a child – feckless and pampered. *Queen's Rules and Regulations* protect him and enfold him like a nurse's arms. He is not supposed to know this, of course – QRRs are supposed to be available only to officers – but he quickly finds it out as soon as he gains legitimate access to the company office and then he becomes a barrack-room lawyer. He grows needle-sharp protective spicula, from which potential enemies, with rank to maintain, recoil in fear.

The British Army provided one other major service to its temporary victims. It created an environment that, given normal social conditions, *must be the worse the soldier will ever encounter.* So long as he had the intelligence to keep himself out of military prisons, the private soldier knew that whatever happened to him in later life could only be an improvement on his present position. Outside of Buchenwald I defy anybody to show me anything worse than life in Salamanca Barracks, Aldershot. As I have said elsewhere, each of us needs a nadir: the underprivileged aristocrat can look back with loathing on Harrow or Charterhouse, the middle classes on their family life, but what about the sons of the sly and undeserving poor? No. I am on the whole grateful to the army for giving me if not an image of hell then at least a sense of anti-paradise. What can ever take its place? I suppose the present generation has to make do with prisons and approved schools but these are not quite the same thing. A young offender has to work quite hard to get into prison these days and, once in, he is soothed by social workers, idealistic chaplains, issue-mongering Members of Parliament, enlightened screws, book-struck education officers, and governors with humanistic values. Those of my students who have been lagged on drug charges complain of the *blandness* of Canadian jails. Once in a while they will come across a screw of the old school who will obligingly work them over with his truncheon, but on the whole the accent is on what liberals call *rehabilitation.* There are even agencies who will look after them when they've finished their time. I put it to the reader that this presents a totally different picture from that of the army. The prisoner is quite often a man guilty of breaking the law; the private soldier is plucked from his environment without a by-your-leave and is innocent. There are no agencies or half-way houses for the army man; he is kicked back into civilian life as though to the knacker's yard. The prisoner often enjoys a feeling of solidarity with other prisoners or at least with those convicted of similar offences; the soldier stands alone and every man is his enemy.

I learned to live with this situation by treating it as a game. One day I found myself given the task of pasting in amendments to *Queen's Rules and Regulations.* These amendments were endless, issued almost daily, and incomprehensible. One was supposed to cut each from its sheet and paste it into the appropriate section of the manual. I found that fertile, evocative conundrums, *non sequiturs*, *poèmes trouvés*, witticisms, and obscenities could be created by pasting a given amendment to the wrong paragraph. If caught out at this harmless sport one had the cast-iron defence that one was a private soldier and, therefore, a being of negligible intelligence.

Soon I discovered other clerks and skivvies engaged in similar activities. Some of us got together and formed a group. Together we read Kafka, sometimes aloud, and tried to master the art of perpetrating bureaucracy. One of my colleagues did extraordinary things with a kit-bag full of army clothing left in the barracks after the owner had been taken into hospital with appendicitis. My friend surrounded the incident with the appropriate paper work and then deliberately lost a memo. He wrote himself another memo that ordered the kit-bag to be forwarded to central stores, Bielefeld, under the Y-List regulations, then got it transferred to England under the forged signature of some fictitious supply officer. From England he moved it to Cairo, then back to Germany *en route* to Singapore. The paper work grew exponentially like a 'red tide' and suddenly there was a mess which no one could straighten out, though two courts of inquiry were held. An inextricable, bureaucratic knot had been created, which was still ramifying cancerously when I was demobilized a year later. It was out of small, arcane pleasures such as this that we made our lives tolerable.

Two days before we were due to sail, we took a boat out onto the Serpentine in Hyde Park. The agonies and problems of this particular journey were over with – unresolved, but temporarily at an end. Perhaps, I thought, one endured them just as one endured the army, for the sake of the condition of euphoria I was just now, rather tentatively, beginning to feel. Many times over the last few weeks I had had occasion to remind myself that at least I was no longer a member of Her Majesty's Armed Forces. The stratagem had been effective. But at the same time the joy I was experiencing was nothing compared to that wild elation I felt the first morning the army was behind me when I awoke, like the narrator of a Chaucer poem, with the mid-May sun brilliant in the panes of a lattice window. Nevertheless the sky above the Serpentine was utterly cloudless and the wind, our implacable enemy throughout the winter, blew now from the Channel and across the Downs – it had dropped and mellowed and felt faintly warm against the skin. Primroses bloomed on the banks of the artificial lake and above the budding trees you could see the old, greyish white buildings of London basking in the sun.

How the Poor Die

IT HAD BEEN seven years since I'd seen my mother and that was in Montreal under circumstances neither of us wished to recall. She lived in Brighton, on Eastern Road close to a region of Georgian and Regency houses, some picturesque and graceful, others tottering into slums. The city council had cleared some of the famous slums of Edward Street, which leads into Eastern Road, to make way for one of their bland, Americanized main streets lined with concrete lamp standards from the tops of which monochromatic sodium lights glared malevolently. But the buildings on the other side of St. James led down to the sea front and were well kept and nicely painted and turned into private hotels and boarding houses, empty now in the winter season. We arrived at my mother's in time for tea. She answered her door and fell into my arms, crying my name. I felt no joy, only an overwhelming sadness – and a feeling of irritation as I sensed, behind me, Jocelyn's uneasiness. My mother looked tiny and frail – silvery hair a wispy cloud around her head, sunken and very piercing blue eyes, nose as sharp as an arête, and the skin of her temples brownish and flaky. Her energy had begun to return to her, enough at any rate to spark a number of feuds; and her laughter, loud and breathless and entirely without humour, was as I'd remembered it. Her room, up two flights of stairs, was like a skid-row itinerant's – full of knick-knacks carried about in trunks, unpacked from one battered caravanserai to the next. She lived in what in England is called a 'bed-sitter' and in Canada a 'housekeeping room.' A woman named Mrs. Swain presided over the rest of the building; short, white-haired, bland-faced, with a soft voice and ingratiating manner – decayed gentlewoman, perhaps, or one who would like to be taken for such. Downstairs she kept a neat, highly polished, well-carpeted hallway, but once behind my mother's door you were in the world of the old, the poor, the unwanted. There was a boarded-up fireplace and in front of it an electric fire, a 'two-bar' whose meter ticked menacingly and expensively to the left. A tiny kitchen area, washstand, sink, hot-plate and electric kettle lay curtained off opposite her bed, and above this was a long shelf on which she kept her two battered suitcases, containing, one supposed, the few remaining things, the last possessions cherished and retained against long odds. For my mother was at the end of it and these were the last fragments of a lifetime – all she had to show for those years as a young woman, newly-wed, homemaker, mother, widow with property – for all those years preceding the day the jettisoning began.

Perhaps the life of the poor can be represented by a graph – a line that rises slowly like a scarp slope, reaches a peak, falls rapidly like a scarp face. And this line represents possessions and reaches the peak at sixty-five. After retirement, the pensioner begins to jettison – he or she, sells the table to buy a warm coat, unloads a chesterfield to pay for some coal. If she owns a house it becomes too large, for her children are abroad, and too expensive to heat, and she doesn't want to rent to strangers. So she closes off first one room, then another, then the whole of the 'upstairs.' She sells off the furniture, for the money comes in useful, and keeps only the smallest of those things which remind her of past times. The pensioner is lucky if she can keep her health and if there are enough of her own generation to visit her and whom she can get out to visit. She may, under these circumstances, finish her life in peace and dignity. But if she has owned no house then objects must be cast out at a much faster rate. My mother had sold our house twenty years before and spent the money. She'd got rid of the furniture bit by bit as she found it increasingly tiresome to move, and now her property consisted of a few old coats and dresses, woollen cardigans, photographs, and miscellaneous gewgaws. One of them is before me on my desk as I write, a cylindrical wooden jewel-box, decorated on the outside with hand-carved flowers and leaves. On the lid is a carving of a young couple dressed in Norwegian national costume. They seem to be about to be married, for the man is carrying a Bible. No, I'm wrong about that. If you look closely you see that it's a beer stein. At any rate the carving is executed with a naive playfulness, and the figures were painted in colours once bright, now faded to pastel shades.

There were photographs along the mantelpiece – several of myself, several of my sister and her son. There was a photo of Jocelyn and me as a married couple and the most recent was one taken in my last year of undergraduate work at the University of British Columbia, a 'commencement' photograph in which I wore the gown, hood, short back and sides, and supercilious smirk encouraged by photographers on these occasions. There was a cupboard filled with stuff I remembered from my childhood – photograph albums, *The Ringdove Story Book* she'd given my sister one early Christmas, letters in my nephew's childish scrawl. And in this same cupboard was her latest, more sinister possession – the plastic bags and bandages required for her colostomy. And the first thing I'd noticed coming into her room was the smell – it was very familiar for Jocelyn had sold aerosol sprays as part of her Fuller Brush deal – a sweet, herbal odour designed to cover the slight, but persistent, smell of faeces.

We greeted her affectionately, of course. I wasn't sure how much she knew about her condition despite the fact that this was the second thing she began to talk about. The first, and this seemed to me to be a sure sign she was getting better, was her landlady. We arranged the few old blankets against the crack between the floor and the door, sat down, and she started off.

'You saw her, didn't you, my dear? Oh yes, oh yes, you saw her all right, in spite of her little efforts to hide behind that door ... just wanted to get a look at you, that's all it is, just wants to know everybody's business ... the sly, rapacious bitch ... you'd think butter wouldn't melt in her mouth, wouldn't you? ... sweet little smile and a knife in the ribs, that's her ... that's her style ... don't let her take you in, my dear ... you're too good natured ... you don't know the world like I do ... it didn't take *me* long to get her measure, the crafty, ravenous, low-class slattern ... nice, well-polished hallway ... *but you should get a look at her kitchen* ... landladies ... they're all the same ... suck the life's blood out of you ... go behind your back ... like that woman did to me ... even went to the almoner, the *almoner*, if you please, of the *hospital* ... wanted to find out if she was going to be stuck with an invalid on her hands ... wanted to know if she'd have to carry me up and down the stairs ... '

'Maybe she just wanted to help,' I said.

'Help? Help? Not *her*, not Mrs. Swain ... not by a long shot ... artful as a wagon-load of monkeys, that one ... help? Help *me*? After she's gone behind my back and fixed the electric meter so's I have to sit crouched over it at night dropping one shilling in after the other? She gets a cut, you know ... ah, they're onto everything these old widows with a bit of property ... I'll tell you what else she did ... but keep your voice down ... she's not very far away, you can be sure of *that*, my dear ... she went to the Assistance Board and told them she was raising my rent ... fifteen shillings ... "What's all this?" I said to her. "What's all what," says she, bold as brass. "This extra fifteen bob," I said. "Well," she said, "why not?" She said, "It isn't you who pays," she said, and flounced out ... *she's a vampire* ... she's in the bathroom now, listening to every word we say. I've had enough of her, my dear ... I'm moving ... to a cheaper place on Freshfield Road ... at the end of the month.'

In a hoarse whisper she embarked on a discursive analysis of the way of the world and proffered wisdom we should all take through life with us – never leave letters lying around since 'people get to know your business that way,' never tell people anything because they'll listen sympathetically then use the information as 'evidence against you.'

I found this feud with the landlady, these snippets of wisdom, very encouraging. She seemed to be gaining each day in malice and weight. She switched, after winding up her tirade against the landlady, to a discussion, more reasoned in nature but no less acerbic in manner, of relatives. One aunt was jealous because a mutual friend of theirs had spent a lot of time visiting my mother in hospital ('and what did she expect to gain from *that*, my dear, that's what I'd like to know, though I suppose some would say it was nice of her to take the trouble'); another was superficially pleasant but basically two-faced; a third was a back-biter; a niece wasn't to be trusted. It wasn't long before we were back to Mrs. Swain.

'I went up to her and told her straight ... Mrs. Swain, I said, there are two sides to your nature ... one is very pleasant, very charming. The other is a devil incarnate ... you're nothing better than a common blackmailer. And what's more, I said, I'm *leaving*. And at the end of the month.'

The illness had been quite an ordeal for my mother. About a year before this she had been getting pains in her stomach, or what seemed like her stomach. She went to a doctor, an old doddering man about to retire, who told her there was nothing to worry about and gave her some pills. The pains got slightly worse. She vomited from time to time and started to lose weight. 'You've got a touch of colitis,' he said, and gave her some drops. Her sole thought was whether these pains, this loss of energy, would persist into the late summer when my sister was due to pay her a visit. The doctor gave her more drops and told her not to be a *malade imaginaire*. I asked her why she hadn't changed her doctor.

'You can't do that,' she said. 'For one thing they won't hear criticism of each other ... it gets their backs up ... they can make it hot for you in other ways ... they've got the whole of the government behind them ... there's nothing you can do about them ... they've got you completely at their mercy.'

Just before my sister arrived she began to pass blood. 'It's colitis,' the doctor said. 'Very typical. Nothing to worry about ... specialist? What do you mean, specialist? Go to a specialist if you want to, of course, I suppose it's your right. Go ahead ... see what *he* says.'

So he got her an appointment with a specialist. My mother saved it until after my sister had returned to Canada. She visited this office, was stripped by minions, and readied on a table. The specialist entered without a word, examined her wordlessly, shot a few brisk orders to the nurses, then told a nurse to tell her to come back the next day for a barium enema. The next day she was filled with a barium compound, ordered to walk over to another table where she was X-rayed. The specialist strode in. 'There's a growth in your rectum,' he said briskly. 'The whole lot's got to come out.' And with these cryptic words he marched from the room. A nurse ordered her to report to the hospital in a week's time while another nurse, somewhat more humane, explained that what the specialist meant was that he'd have to perform a colostomy. 'Is it cancer?' my mother asked, but at this the nurse immediately balked and said my mother must not ask questions and must, as a patient, learn to mind her own business.

During her story I was on my feet, pacing the room, uttering cries of horror. That she should have been treated first with such incompetence, then with such contempt then, finally, as a will-less object, to be knifed and manipulated like a piece of stone did not shock me so much as my mother's calm acceptance of it, the assumption that people are always like this and that nothing more is to be expected from them, that one is lucky if one escapes from an encounter with a fellow human being with one's pockets, reputation, life, still intact. What I found astonishing was her surprise that I should be angered by it; what terrified her was the thought that I should be tempted to get the ancient incompetent who'd treated her for colitis struck off the register, to approach her specialist and emend his behaviour. 'They can get you in other ways.' These grapplings with the medical profession were nothing more nor less than a demonstration of her world view's validity. Any show of my hand would merely make things worse for her. And how could I tell her that her doctor's incompetence was not only inexcusable but criminal. To have said so would be to have told her that the operation, her suffering, was not to prolong her life at all, and that the surgery had come too late. '*All's well that end's well*,' I said. '*What happened then?*'

Then she'd had the operation and very nearly died through it.

She drifted in and out of consciousness and only fully aware of the pain, discomfort, and one particular horror which made her shudder even now. This was what she called 'the drip,' the system of bottles and thin rubber tubes that fed into her arm. This was particularly bestial because the spigot kept falling out. It was during this stage that she received a visit from my in-laws who had driven down on Sunday. We were to hear more about this journey. It had begun when we had wired Jocelyn's parents that my mother was in the hospital and asked them to phone to find out how she was doing. We had forgotten that in those days not everybody in England had their own telephone. It was late November, no weather to be out in a frozen call-box grappling with the hopelessly inefficient British telephone system. Jocelyn's mother had to do it since Stan, her husband, was incapacitated with what *his* doctor had diagnosed as sciatica, but which turned out to be a critically slipped disc – *his* bout under the knife coincided with our arrival. Anyhow the news, when they'd got through to the hospital, after two hours in the call box and some thirty shillings or so later, was not encouraging. They felt they had to see her; they drove in wind, sleet, and hail, through traffic-blocked suburbs, icy streets, with Stan's sciatica tearing at him and to the tune of Sybil's nagging, screaming, fear-racked hysteria – evidently, from what I'd heard, both from my mother and from Jocelyn herself, a permanent condition of being as far as she was concerned – and what with all this they got to Brighton three or four minutes before visiting hours finished and the staff began booting people out. They found my mother with screens around her, blue in colour, liquids dripping into her veins, semi-conscious and unable to talk. 'Oh *no*,' Sybil bawled in exasperation, just before the nurse guided her to the door. My mother took this for an expression of anger, while Sybil later explained it as one of dismay.

'And afterwards,' my mother said, 'when I became stronger they sent me to a convalescent home at Hastings ... they were a dreadful bunch ... manners like pigs, most of them ... I couldn't even bear to watch some of them eat ... where they'd been brought up heaven only knows ... I had to sit next to one old man who crammed food into his mouth with a spoon, dribbling it out again at the corners ...

that's human nature, my dears, in the *raw* ... IN THE RAW ... that's where you see it, in places like that convalescent home ... and the nurses were dreadful, pert little baggages, most of them, sleeping with Tom, Dick, and Harry if the truth were known ... but in the medical profession, of course, they always know who to go to ... but they fed us well, I *will* say that for them ... '

'Did you make any friends there?'

'Friends? Among *that* lot. I should think *not* indeed ... they were *coarse* ... you know what I mean? ... *coarse* ... dregs of humanity, I should think. These National Health places are all the same ... anybody *decent* has the money to go private ... snobbish, la-di-da bunch they are too, my dears, I've worked in private nursing homes myself ... I could tell you a tale about those places.'

The supper she insisted on feeding us was cooked by now. She put a cloth on the little card table and set three places. My mother's cooking was very English ... meat pie, greens boiled to a pulp, and watery mashed potatoes ... all made edible, provided one were hungry enough, with a bottle of H.P. sauce. I got up, put a shilling in the meter, and a blanket over my shoulders. The room was damp and cold as a grave, but my mother didn't appear to notice it. English people, it is often said, are born chilled and it takes them a lifetime to thaw out. In the interim, of course, low temperatures don't seem to bother them. My own blood had been thinned by many years of central heating.

I sat toying with doleful pie and lugubrious Brussels sprout while the cold of the room ceased being merely noticeable and became malignant. My mother did not appear to be aware of it. She had embarked on a new aria – a tirade against someone I didn't know, apparently an old friend of hers. I could see that Jocelyn and I were in for an exhausting three months, though I understood perfectly well that our presence enabled my mother to release much of her hostility with salutary effect. I wondered whether it bothered me to play lance to her pustule and decided that it didn't.

When I next tuned in to my mother's voice it was to discover her reacting to something Jocelyn had said in defence of National Health. Jocelyn had worked in British hospitals and thought half the problem lay with vicious and bloody-minded patients unappreciative of the fact that they lived in a civilized country. 'We have just lived in the United States for a year,' Jocelyn said, 'where the sick are mercilessly robbed by doctors, hospital bursars, nursing home proprietors, etc., and what's more become, when fully recovered, uninsurable.' I had heard her defend, in another context, the institution of privatised medicine – one listens not so much to the words of such arguments, but to the music. Clearly my mother was beginning to irritate her.

It was like listening, once again, to the terrible rows between my mother and Jill, my sister. This is just how they would start – a feeling of mutual irritation, a flat contradiction, a hostile rejoinder. Then one remark would lead to another, adrenalin would start to flow, and soon there would be the most ghastly bust-up.

If anyone had cause, I thought, to detest my mother, it was Jill – though she would undoubtedly be too guilt-ridden to experience so negative an emotion. But her pregnancy was a case in point ... it went against the grain of everything my mother had tried to instil in her. At first Jill tried, as they say, to 'bring it off'. She took pills, hot baths, liberal doses of gin, motorcycle rides and bad advice. An abortion cost a lot of money in England and neither my sister nor her boy-friend could raise it. She decided to have the baby and the boy-friend offered to 'make an honest woman of her'. This she declined on the grounds that neither of them would, under normal circumstances, have chosen the other as a lifetime companion. There remained the business of keeping the facts from my mother, if for no other reason than that it would have confirmed the latter's view of human depravity. It would enable her to say, legitimately, 'I told you so.' Ever since babyhood Jill's ears had been filled with wisdom of the following sort: all men are sex monsters; sex is the only thing they think about; once a man has 'used your body' he is finished with you; the world is full of 'funny customers' (male) who'll rape you and afterwards bash in your head; that women are divided into the virtuous (very few) and dirty little sluts (the vast majority); that the sole point of a maidenhead is that it can be bartered for a wedding ring; that loss of one's virginity reduces one's chances of marriage to zero; that the world is full of old maids who have 'made fools of themselves' so it's best to keep one's ears open and one's wits about one; sell one's virginity to the highest bidder and, once it's sold, give in. Giving in (or sex) is distasteful, but one has to submit to it because your husband will neglect you and seek solace in other women. This means a ruined home and loss of security. The world is full of abandoned women, etc. Never trust other women, particularly sluts, since they'll lure your husband away from you. Her specific advice to my sister consisted of the following: you are too tall for most men, and read too much. You're at a natural disadvantage since you've got a good brain, and men are threatened by women with brains. You're too tall and you have a beaky nose. Men prefer snub noses and stupidity. Your other chief disadvantage is that you're a natural slut ... not, perhaps, out of bad morals, but out of good nature – eagerness to please combined with lack of wisdom.

My mother took it upon herself to correct these flaws of character by lectures, all conducted at high, semi-hysterical pitch, curtailments of freedom, constant vigilance, refusals to allow her to mix with boys and an automatic assumption, loudly and vigorously expressed, that on the few occasions she did so, my sister would have 'had sex.' This would develop out of Jill's easygoing lack of discrimination and the boy's rapacity – natural in all men. Her morality was a cross between Samuel Richardson's and the *News of the World*. One other highly important factor was the opinion of neighbours. What, for example, would the neighbours think *and go around saying* about a girl, a girl of fifteen, coming home alone after dark ... what would they say about *her* as *the mother in the case*? (She thought of life in terms of scabrous court scenes.) And if this boy were to see her home, why, this was even worse, for what would people (*being what they are*) think about a mother who lets her young daughter prowl around with men who were obviously out for what they could get? 'What are you trying to prove, anyway,' she'd say, 'don't you know the only thing a man would want from you what with your hook nose and good intelligence, is your body? And that once you've given in he'll throw you aside like a squeezed lemon?'

I used to watch all this – the scenes, fights, tests of will as my sister fought, throughout her childhood and adolescence, towards independence and a view of life emancipated from my mother's. At the age of eighteen she would occasionally come home, after a night out, an hour or so late. My mother, who normally went to bed directly after the nine o'clock news, would wait up in a state of terrible anxiety, making herself innumerable cups of tea.

'Where in the name of God is she? Oh, my God, what's happened to her? Perhaps she's been run over ... ten thirty, I said ... ten thirty at the latest ... *look at the time* ... after eleven and still no sign ... John, go down the road and look for her ... she's been raped and had her throat cut ... out in the bushes, that's where she is, doing God knows what ... '

It will be obvious to you, of course, that at the core of my mother's personality was a horror at the possibility that someone else might be experiencing pleasure: particularly sexual. When Jill got home my mother would instantly set about her:

'I've been so worried about you ... why do you do this to me? ... I thought you'd met with some terrible accident ... where have you been at *this* hour? ... who've you been with, that's more to the point ... oh my God as though I hadn't troubles enough what with paying the bills and keeping the home together ... and all you do is add to my troubles ... where have you been, hey? I demand to know ... you're no better than a common street-walker ... haven't you any pride? Let them make an absolute fool of you, don't you, you dirty slut? ... don't you realize whoever this man is he's back home *laughing* at you ... what happens if you get pregnant ... who'll want you then, I'd like to know ... *I* won't have anything more to do with you ... you'd be out on the streets, on your own ... how would you live, have you ever thought about that? ... because nobody would give you a job ... *nobody* ... nobody wants an unmarried mother ... social workers, that's what would happen, those social workers would be all over you ... prying ... wanting to know all about *me* ... busybodies, they are ... *spies* ... discover all your business and *use it in evidence against you ...* '

And so on into the night. My mother seemed to derive infinite pleasures from an aria like this ... her voice, loud normally, would rise to shrieking pitch; she'd stomp rapidly from room to room in her delivery, switching the kettle on, then switching it off, making and unmaking beds in her excitement, which on a word full of sibilants like 'spies' caused her bright blue eyes to flash, dart from side to side, and her lips to curl. My sister would try to shout back at first, but would gradually subside into tears and despair. People would go to bed, my mother might thresh for two minutes and sleep soundly, to be up again, full of piss and vinegar, as they say, at six a.m., which was her best time and everybody else's worst. She would wake my sister and stand at the foot of the bed while its occupant's eyes were still gummed half-closed:

'There'll be no repetition of last night's little episode, my lady ... we'll have the juvenile court on to you if it ever happens again ... you'll be in by half-past nine in future ... having *you* prowling about the streets with funny customers all hours of the night ... half past nine, do you hear? Now get up or you'll be late for work ... '

One may ask why people choose to put up with such treatment – why did Jill not pack her bags and take off? But to where? To a bed-sitting room huddled over a gas fire, at the mercy of landladies who, by and large, are just as problematic as my mother and demand to be paid for it, too. But there was another, profounder, reason, and that was her sense that my mother, despite her warped mind, her dramatic scenes, her authoritarianism, which applied to my sister and not to me (a man can take care of himself), had had a hard and pathetic life. The only man she cared for, a certain Harold Warner, had been killed in the First World War just as she was about to marry him ... on the rebound she married someone a good deal older than herself who turned out to be a drunkard, for whose job security she was forced to plead before unsympathetic employers. When he died she married my father who, she used to claim, kept her chronically short of money. At his death she was left with a small amount of insurance money – just enough for me to move us all to Norwood, away from old and unpleasant memories. She was unskilled and took a variety of dirty and underpaid jobs. My sister felt sorry for her and figured that life had dealt my mother a bust hand. So Jill's desire to live a life of freedom conflicted with a strong urge to be a comfort to my mother and to do her duty by her, a sense of which my mother had been careful to instil.

When I left for Norway, however, in 1949, Jill took the opportunity to leave home herself and to encourage my mother to sell and take a job as a housekeeper in pleasant surroundings in Buckinghamshire. It was my mother's Waterloo. From that point on she moved slowly towards the end, sloughing remnants of the 'home' she had tried to preserve for so long. It is not surprising, then, that my sister gravitated towards those men she thought would best exemplify all my mother's prejudices – bums, twisters, gamblers, lushes, on the one hand, together with innocent Irishmen and Jews on the other – all the people and all the races that my mother was so terrified of. Just before I left for Norway she started going with a man named Irish Jim who played the dogs. He was so Irish as to seem a stage imitation done by an incompetent and ham actor of Irish parentage and interests, but who was sophisticated enough to know the camp quality of Irishness and who could not at the same time resist it.

'Arragh, now, Mick the Miller, I'm telling yer, was a power of a dog, ah Mick was a grand dog, so he was, an this boyo a-runnin in the three-thirty at White City, now, he'd make Mick look like he was crawlin, an its all for the want of a few quid, I'm tellin yer, if it was a few quid I'd have in me hand, now, I'd be rich, so I would, an so would the feller that lent it to me.'

So my sister would go down to the bank and draw out her savings and lend it to Irish Jim, who'd promptly lose it on the dogs.

'Arragh, it's them *gangs*,' he'd say. 'What can a feller do against them gangs? Did you *see* him, now? Did you *see* him comin round that bend limpin as though he'd broken his foot? They'd *fixed* him surely. They'd got at the poor brute before the race, so they had, and tied his toes around with cotton, the murtherin spalpeens ... '

Once he got lucky and paid forty pounds for a diamond ring, which he attached to my sister's finger with many a ceremonious and endearing word. But three weeks later a hot tip prompted him to ask for 'a loan of that ring', which he pawned, using the money to play his tip. He lost, of course.

'Arragh, that's just me rotten luck,' he said. 'Anyway, darlin, I'll give yer the pawn ticket.'

And so he did.

Jill was drawn to him as surely and as irresistibly as a masochist is to the whip. If you believe, or if others have made you believe, that the world is full of creeps, shysters, spies, sadists, criminals, rapists, murderers, deceivers, lechers, panders, saboteurs, whoremasters, and so on, and if you see the average person as a Nazi surgeon in disguise, only too willing to carve you up without benefit of anaesthetic, then you will dismiss all evidence to demonstrate the contrary as a delusion and all apparent goodness in people as a snare. This was certainly my mother's attitude; it almost, through my mother's hard work as educator, became my sister's. But she possessed a faith in people, an innocence in dealing with them, which my mother was never able to destroy.

The cheap alarm clock ticked noisily on the mantelshelf. My mother was getting tired. We had finished the meal and were sitting over the two-bar, the cold creeping up the stairs and whining outside the door to be let in. She had talked about her operation, but I did not know how much she knew about her own condition. What were her chances of living longer? If she knew she had less than a year, did she want me to share this knowledge? Did she want us to reach some sort of emotional plateau where we could discuss her life, its meaning, and her children's feelings towards her? 'You've had a lousy time,' I said. 'But you've never had much luck, have you?'

'Oh, I don't know, dear,' she said. 'I can't complain. I've had a good innings and I'm in my seventieth year. Not many people of my generation have been so lucky. And I've had you children ... and a grandchild ... what more could I have wanted?'

'More grandchildren, I suppose,' I answered. 'It's a pity Jocelyn and I haven't got anything to offer you.'

'No,' she said, quite vehemently, 'no, it's not. You're far better off without them ... they're a terrible responsibility ... neither you nor Jocelyn are the type ... you both value your freedom too much ... besides, you're too used to not having them now ... no, my dears, be thankful you don't have them.'

And I took this to mean that my mother knew if we were to have children she'd never live to see them. She found such a thought intolerable and all she could pray for now, poor woman, was our sterility.

It was on a day of false spring that we hired a car and took my mother for a drive. It turned out to be her last glimpse of her native Sussex, for two weeks after we got her back to Brighton she told us she had to be readmitted into hospital.

'They're making me go back in. *That* place ... such a nuisance while you're here. You will come and visit me, won't you, dear? Of course, I know how *busy* you are ... so *busy* ... hardly the time, have you? Still, I know you'll find the time to visit me ... of course, they only allow you an hour a day ... and it's so far for you to come, isn't it? But just for an hour, dear, that won't kill you, will it? Not since you're going back to Canada so soon and you may not see me again ... it can't be helped, can it? If they tell you to go back in, *back you* go ... two little lumps, that's what they told me, two little lumps ... on the opening, dear.' (A mad little chuckle, a baring of the teeth.) 'Two little lumps, that's all it is ... *on the opening* ... '

These lumps were what are known as 'secondaries'. They manifested the fact that the cancer cells had escaped into her system when they did the major operation. The surgeon would remove them. Then they'd grow again – either on the colostomy opening or elsewhere. He would treat the new ones, but by that time it would be purely a question of prolonging her life for a matter of days. Perhaps they'd give her up, though, and let her die in peace. Let her waft into oblivion on a bier of drugs.

'Oh, God,' she said less guardedly. 'All I hope is that they don't give me the Drip.'

'It's just a minor affair,' we said. 'You won't get any Drip.'

'I couldn't stand that all over again,' she said. 'However,' she added, 'looking on the bright side, there's one consolation. I'll see all my friends on the staff. Thought the world of me, most of them did ... bitches and sluts, the lot of them, of course ... Irish, some of them, and *Jamaicans* ... '

'*Blacks*,' we said, feigning a shudder or two. 'What about Pakis?' we asked. 'And Yids?'

'Yids, dear, that's right, that's what your father used to call them. *Tin lids*, he used to say. No, there's no Jew there. Catch *them* working in a hospital ... getting *their* lily-white hands dirty. No Jew-boys there, thank God.'

'Then we must all of us count our blessings,' we said solemnly.

I drove down in another rented car and ferried her into hospital. The operation was what passes for successful and the next time I visited her I decided to stay in Brighton overnight to save the journey down the following day.

'Give me the key,' I said. 'I'll stay at your place.'

She glared at me from the bed and bared her teeth.

'Well,' she hissed, keeping her voice low and out of earshot from the rest of the crowded ward. 'I don't know what to do,' she said. 'I *suppose* it'll be all right. The landlady doesn't live on the premises ... but I'm so terrified you'll *smoke* ... '

'I won't smoke.'

'What happens if you lose the key?'

'I won't lose the key,' I said, trying not to snarl but at the same time thinking 'sod the key'.

'Well, it's fire I'm worried about. Fire. Whatever you do don't strike any matches ... make sure the electric kettle is switched off. Otherwise it'll boil away and blow a *fuse*.'

'I won't blow any fuses.'

'And for God's sake make sure the window's shut before you sleep ... if the wind gets up in the night it'll close with a bang.'

'I'll remember.'

'*I'm worried about that kettle*.'

'Don't worry about *anything*. Get some rest.'

I held her hand until she slept. Her breathing grew regular, though it remained shallow, and despite the paraphernalia of illness surrounding her, I sensed her acrimonious vitality. Under the mauve and slender lids her eyes, I felt, were watching me with my mother's own blend of terror, pride, concern, and detestation. My son, she was clearly thinking: professor, firebug, traveller, kettle-fuser, prodigal, scoundrel, married man, traitor, and window-banger.

Then I walked from the hospital up Freshfield Road. The days were growing longer and, though great flakes of soggy snow stretched down from a lowering sky, it was still light when I let myself into my mother's bed-sitter. It smelt of must, decay, and faintly of turds. Part of the latter smell inhered in the room itself and was a function of her disease, but most crept down fetidly from the upstairs toilet. It put me in mind of an epigraph from an old horror movie called *Cat People: As fog gathers in the valleys*, it read, *so evil stays in the low places of the world.*

'But it's the only one in the house,' my mother had complained. 'It's used by ten or twelve people. Dirty, filthy bunch they are too, my dear. Old men missing the bowl and *wetting the floor*; young chits who never pull the chain. *The things I've found there* ... my dear, I couldn't *begin* to tell you. It only gets cleaned once a week ... I've been up there a dozen times if I've been there once with one of my sprays ... trying to get rid of the smell ... *What on earth are you doing?* one of those dirty people said ... I'm spraying, I said ... spraying away the odour some of the filthy tenants leave behind them when they come in here, I said ... Oh, she said, I hope you're not referring to me, she said ... So I turned round and said, well, I said, if the cap fits, I said, you'll have to wear it, won't you? I said. That put *her* in her place, I can tell you that, my dear. And you know what that little hussy had the impertinence to say to me? Listen, she said, *why don't you drop dead, you old bag?* That's right ... that's exactly what she said ... why don't you drop dead, you old bag? I won't go before my time, I said, not to please you or anybody else, I said ... she flounced out after that, I can assure you.'

I stood for a moment in the barren room working out ways I could make it habitable. There was a heap of old, threadbare carpets and dishcloths lying in an oblique straight line which the door had pushed aside. I replaced them in their rightful position against the draft. I closed the heavy curtain and sat down in the easy chair by the two-bar. I switched the latter on. It glowed for a few minutes then darkened rapidly as the meter clicked off. I shoved in a shilling with haste.

The room grew colder, damper.

On the card table was a book from the Brighton Public Library. A.G. Street's *Farmer's Glory*. I tried to read it but, half an hour later, I pushed it aside. I could not concentrate on it. What had my mother found attractive about it? It was the expression of a temperament radically opposed to hers – positive, optimistic, life-affirming. To her the simple account of farming a stretch of country would be heroic ... a terrible battle waged against a long-drawn-out but inevitable failure. She would see Street as Beowulf to Nature's Grendel. But with Beowulf cast as loser. Street farmed a portion of Saskatchewan and I could almost hear my mother's voice: 'What about those wild *animals*, my dear, grizzlies and the like prowling round while you sleep? And those dreadful storms ... not sheet lightning, either, but *forked ... forked* lightning streaking all round you. And disease ... what if you were to become ill ... all those miles from a doctor? And prairie fires ... burnt to a cinder. And the neighbours? Ukrainians, I wouldn't mind betting. In a place like that you'd have to rely on them ... people like that. No, my dear, no ... it wouldn't do for me,' she'd say.

If there was any central theme to her life it was fear – fear of the dark, of heights, of thunder, of her neighbour's opinions, of employers, of other people 'getting to know your business'. More generally, fear of the social classes above hers, and below it, of foreigners, strangers, Catholics, Jews. These, together with nature, humankind, disease, and death, were some of the forces drawn up against her.

I put the book down and stared at the greasy wall above the suspect and fusible kettle. What if she were right, I thought. And not about trivia like thunder, heights, or the weather, but about people. Call hers a 'bad faith' model of the world. Is it so unreasonable? One would think, listening to her talk, that human beings were utterly depraved – like characters out of *Death on the Installment Plan*. Indeed, she was something like a Céline figure herself. But what if hers were an accurate description of human life? It is true that everywhere human beings are attuned to joy – they sense it, yearn for it, plan for it, but always, or nearly always, they find ways to frustrate themselves from achieving it. And if the phrase 'original sin' means anything then that is what it means.

I considered the old lady as sinner. She rejected the joyous aspects of life because fundamentally she did not believe in them. She was scared of neither hardship nor solitude, as though these were the very terms of human existence. I began to wonder what death meant to her – perhaps no more than a drifting back into a welcome unconsciousness. Did she see life like the pagan in the Anglo-Saxon story who saw it as a bird that appears in a lighted mead-hall; it flies in through one window, across the hall, then out another window into the moonless night? Or did she see it as certain types of Christian see it – as a vale of tears through which one labours upwards towards the light and an everlasting view? I could not imagine either of these concepts appealing to my mother except in a sort of combination. Life was not a vale of tears but an affliction – a series of irritations and discomforts, which the outer world tries its best to intensify, from which death as an emptiness, a total obliteration of being, is welcome enough. The slightest divergence from any routine must have been a terrible ordeal for her imagination. She was sustained by no belief except in the Powers of Evil and the forces of chance.

Her enemies were people, relatives, and ordinary physical objects such as a knife, a match, a shard of glass, six inches of water. She was embattled by the male sex, besieged by her fellow, predatory females; and her foes were her own animal terror and suspicion of her surroundings.

No, her view of life was that it was a narrow ship bouncing on yeasty seas and crashing waves, in shrieking winds and hail – that it was a journey through the darkness, against the cold, the wind, the raging sleet.

There was a newspaper she'd been reading, folded over at an incomplete crossword puzzle. I picked up a ballpoint pen ... she'd got stuck on a word of eight letters meaning 'kind of boat' ... ho-e-. I stared at it, mouth agape. It was too much for me – too *hard*.

I shoved the paper aside and found a pack of cards. My mother played a lot of solitaire. What was it like, I thought, to sit in this room over the two-bar, playing solitaire? I dealt the cards into the seven piles of Klondike patience ... black two on red three, turn ... red jack on black queen, turn ... finish ... turn over the stock, card by card.

Ten grim minutes later I reached the end of it. I stared at the cards in front of me. Five spades, three hearts, three diamonds ... and the ace of clubs.

I'd seen the two of clubs buried, buried well down in the stock. I picked up the pack again and began to shuffle. The room seemed even colder. I put a blanket round my shoulders – some thin scalpel of cold air had crept in through the window frames and had begun dissecting my neck. The two-bar clicked and blackened suddenly, like an ember plunged in water. There were vague noises, then a thudding sound from upstairs. I dealt the cards again, then got up to put a couple of shillings in the meter. They were the last. Nobody near here to change money into the rare, highly prized shillings *at this time of night* ... and when those are used up, I thought, I'll have to go to bed.

Some bastard flushed the toilet.

Let's make a cup of tea, I thought, staring at the electric and *verboten* kettle. It seemed from where I sat like a copper toy. Behind it was my staring wall – stained and greasy from the cooking ring and, possibly, by the deleterious action of being stared at by generations of indigent tenants. Two ancient layers of paper peeled at the top, by the ceiling. The kettle came with the room, so did the cooking ring, the curtains, and the bed.

In fact the only things that were hers were the card table, this chair of little ease, and the piles of near rubbish in the cupboard. I thought of our home in Battersea ... years ago ... before the war. An odd place. We had our own toilet, unusual on that street, but of course it was outside the house. Yet, inside, the place was furnished like a palace with a corner cupboard that had belonged to Lord

Nelson, fine hunting prints, a wooden plaque of the Iron Duke, a Chippendale or two. A curious, even incongruous, decor for a slum house. The explanation is that all this stuff had been given to my father, or stolen by him, in his capacity as French-polisher who specialized in country estates. And much of it had been left to him by *his* father, also a French-polisher, who had stolen it in *his* day. Where was this invaluable nest-egg now? Sold, flogged off, the lot of it, by my mother, and for a song, as soon as he was safely in the ground ... as though anything that recalled her married life was anathema. Thus this card table.

I opened the cupboard and rummaged around until I found the photograph album. Picture of my father encumbered by two kids, self and sister, one on each knee, Chanctonbury Ring in background: old man in pork-pie hat, open-neck shirt, no collar, *braces*; he was smiling cynically. He was crude, tough, and sadistic (just the man, of course, for my mother, for he represented everything that terrified her). Apart from his French-polishing he took an interest in slum youth clubs and worked in one in Battersea night after night, arriving home at midnight. On weekends, he would usually dig in the garden, avoiding my mother, and whistling to himself. Thinking, probably, about World War I. What do I owe him? I hope nothing. A compulsion to make jokes, maybe. The habit of singing gently in cockney while working round the house. His old songs, culled from music-hall and Edwardian ballad, are still on my lips as I paint a wall or sand a cupboard. I catch myself crooning:

It's a great big shime
an if she belongta me
I'd let er knaow oo's oo;
A-putting on a feller wot is six foot four
An er aonly five foot two.
They adn't bin married not a mumf nor more
When underneef the thumb gaoes *Jim* –
Isn't it a pity that the likes of *er*
Should put upon the likes o-o-o-f *im*?

Voice or no voice, jokes or no jokes, cruelty, war memories, ballads, toughness, the lot – all dead – all gone. He died in 1944 at the age of fifty, much, I suspect, to my mother's relief.

Photograph of self and sister when tots – little lamb, who made thee?

A sheaf of older photographs – sepia great-aunts, all of them bombazined and whaleboned and now defunct – the overfleshed skeletons you find in everybody's closet.

Lahst
  night
Dahn our alley came a toff.
Right
  old
Geezer wiv a nahsty cough,
Sees
  my
  missus tikes is catey off.
In a very gentlemanly way.

No more photographs. Time to hit the sack. But no, I was wrong. It was only eight-thirty.

Aha! She'd kept one of my books: *My Picture Book of Soldiers*. All right. Remembrance of things past. We appear to be into it tonight. I thumbed the pages nostalgically though even at the age of seven I was never much taken with the military life. By that age I had already envisioned my future as a malingerer. But here were illustrations of men in field caps and puttees polishing tanks left over from the battle of Cambrai. In 1937! No wonder, three years later, the British got kicked out of France. At the end of the book, on the flyleaf, was an appallingly talentless drawing done by myself. What looked like a man with the face of a fox, the ears of a cat, the tail of a skunk, stood upright, entwined with barbed wire.

It was not barbed wire. I remember drawing this picture and what it was supposed to represent. There used to be a programme on the BBC called 'Children's Hour', which ran a serial called 'Toy

Town'. It was M.C.'d by an invert named Uncle Mac who also played one of the characters in the serial: rather an irritating lamb who bleated in a Home Counties BBC regional dialect. (It was said of Uncle Mac, by the way, that his voice carried over the air one afternoon before the engineers had had a chance to fade him out and the message 'that should hold the little bastards for a while' entered the homes of millions of his juvenile fans.) I was expected to listen to this program, probably because the stuff was romantically supposed by my mother to appeal to a child. An uneasiness crept over me as I remembered that this drawing was meant to be Larry-the-Lamb, but it was an unhappy, put-upon lamb, for he was tied to a stake and was being flagellated by the dim androgynous figures in the background, intended, probably, as women. Possibly the image was generated by the contents of the book itself with its tale of military life which featured, as I must have known even then, discipline, court-martials, and Field Punishment Number One. All I know is that I had repressed this picture, and perhaps the fantasies leading to its creation, for at least a quarter of a century. I stared at my own art-work with mounting horror.

Says
    ai, gal
Ere's some noos that I've to tell,
Yer
    right
old
Uncle Fred a Camberwell
Lahst
    night,
Croaked is lahst wivvaht a light,
Leavin you is donkey and a cart.

The black bats of Freshfield Road began to cluster. I must have been about eleven and in the 'headmaster's class' at Cheam, Surrey, Church of England School for Boys. A small, frigid classroom with a tiny grate and gas lamps, lit by a flint at the end of a long pole, to illuminate, though dimly, the gloomy winter afternoons. Boys from other classes were sent in frequently to be caned by the headmaster – a tall, powerful man with icy grey eyes and a huge jaw. He was *cool*, for if he experienced any pleasure from these canings he hid it well. About twice a week a terrified child named Bowman would be sent in for a beating – a born loser, as they say. Most of us would undergo this punishment with a kind of bored resignation, but Bowman would resist, not with defiance, but with screams, blubberings, and attempts to escape, running around the room and hopping over desks ... the grim-jawed, tight-lipped head after him, quite slowly, confident of final victory, his great hand finally scooping Bowman by the collar. Then he laid the shrieking, threshing boy across the desk and whacked him savagely. The whole scene reminds me now of the rabbit flayed alive in Kosinski's *The Painted Bird*. It would take about twenty minutes, this process, from Bowman's entry to climax across the desk – the same period of time, perhaps, occupied by the faster sexual encounter that might take place during a busy day. Our pleasure as voyeurs was almost certainly sexual, of course, but mixed with delight in the breaking of classroom monotony. The Roman holiday ...

I stood up and paced the narrow room puffing at an illicit cigarette. Bowman and flagellated lambs! It was enough. The room seemed suddenly filled with my mother's presence.

'Stop it,' I said aloud. 'That's enough.'

'It's the way things are,' I could almost hear the presence answer.

I put on my greatcoat and stumbled out onto Freshfield Road to find the nearest pub. I would not, if I could find a half-decent hotel, stay the night in that haunted house.

With the aid of a double Scotch and a pint of beer at the barren pub down the road I attempted to drown out the messages from my mother's dark, negating soul.

High Worple

'ERE YOU ARE at last, then,' Jocelyn's mother said, at the door, her arms folded across her chest, cardigan drooped over her shoulders, back hunched and chin, with full complement of dewlap and jowl pointed forward half aggressively, half defensively. 'I thought you was never coming,' she said. 'Well, if you're coming in you'd better come in quick ... it's *bitter* out ... that man with you must be John, I suppose ... come in an *get this door shut* ... your father bought a whole bunch of noo weather stripping to go around this door, but its comin away already ... get's right up my nose, that does, the way they sell stuff nowadays ... ain't worff aving, the alf of it ... so that's im, is it? ... well, it's been five years, ain't it, five years since you got married ... since you said you got married, at any rate ... people round ere ad a lot to say about that ... well, they said, if she's married, they said, why ain't she over ere in England bringing im with er to see the family? ... garn they said, you're kidding us, that's what *you're* doin, they said ... well, they got a point, ain't they? ... per'aps *e'd* like to ave a go at that door now Daddy's in ospital ... corse, you *did* know e was in ospital ... *she* told you, I expect ... *is* mother ... notice you wasn't in any urry gettin ere, though, were you?'

We'd manoeuvred our way round her carping figure and took off some of our outer clothing and the newspapers so essential for keeping in the body heat. Jocelyn tried to explain that she herself had been down with a cold and that we'd decided to stay in Brighton until she felt better.

'*Ill* ... did *you* say you'd been *ill*? ... well, I carn't say I'm surprised to ere that, I *muss* say, wot with all that rich food you eat over there in Canada ... *starch*, thass wot does it ... don't you eat a lotta *starch* over there? ... well, take yer things off, then, if you're stayin, an we'll go into the front room ... I suppose you'll want a cuppa tea ... I ain't got a fire goin in the back ... carn't get no coal in, not now Daddy's in ospital ... I'm all on my own ere, you know, it's no good you thinkin I can manage because I carn't ... cor, you're a right one, you are, not comin ere straight away ... I suppose *e'd* like a wash, wouldn't e?'

I shook my head. We moved past her into the front room and switched on the electric fire. I could see right away we were up against a totally different proposition from my own mother. Mine was subtle; this one's attacks were purely frontal. Mine delivered her arias in a constant state of motion, or had done so when she was in her prime. This one was lethargic, sloth-like – her shapeless body, arms folded tight across it, moved only slightly as it followed you around the room. Eleven things about her, though, remained in perpetual agitation – one was her tongue and the other ten were her fingers. I said that her arms were folded – it would be more accurate to say that one was positioned on top of the other so that each set of five fingers had access to a biceps.

The sharp, brittle nails scratched at the arms, each hand moving horizontally towards a wrist. In this way she'd covered her entire arm surface and great red welts, botches, and lacerations were there to demonstrate the efficacy of her system.

I began to study her carefully.

If her body was sluggish, her voice was one of the most penetrating instruments I have ever heard. It was high pitched and strident and its tone like those you might expect to hear squeezed through the intransigent reeds of some ancient form of oboe dug up in an archaeological excavation. Her face was expressive, but it displayed only a limited set of emotions – fear, anger, disappointment, envy. Her mouth dropped at the corners and her sullen disposition had gouged two deep, blackhead-pitted lines from her nostrils to that amorphous region where her mouth merged with her chins. Only the most frustrated and painful life could have etched such a countenance, I thought. And I began to feel sorry for her.

'I suppose you want a cuppa tea,' she said, chin jutting. 'Well, less ave a look at you first ... yes ... you've been ill, all right ... you're pale ... you're *really* pale ... *cor you dunnarf look pale! ...*'

'All right, mother, for Christ's sake.'

'Wot you bin doin to yourself then? Workin too ard, I expect, tryin to save money fer this trip ... why dint you wait till you was ready, comin over ere like this ... wot's she workin for at all, anyway,' she screeched, turning her ravaged face in my direction. 'Ain't she ad enough? Why should she ave to work now you got a job?'

That suspicion that now dawned on her was too good a one to pass up.

'E as *got* a job, asn't e? I bet e asn't got is job no more ... e ad to give it up to come over ere, dint e? And ad to send you out to work to make ends meet ... after you workin all them years keepin im while e was a student ... I've always *said* it's not good for you to overdo it ... Well,' she said, 'less ave it, then ... e's outa work, ain't e?'

'Beg to report,' I said, 'I'm not. It's my semester free from teaching,' I explained.

'Go on,' she screeched back to Jocelyn, and her voice was like a damp finger rubbed over the lip of a Woolworth's tumbler. 'Does e expect me to believe that? Nobody as four mumfs off ... not off ... e's lost is job, ain't e ... tell the truth, now.'

'What's the good?' Jocelyn said. 'You wouldn't believe it anyway. Aren't you going to make us that cup of tea?'

'Ark at *er* ... *Lady muck* ... you oughta be ashamed a yourself ... not gettin ere any faster ... Daddy weren't *arff* disappointed ... *corse*, I don't know wot you're doin in England anyway, I'm sure, comin over ere in the middlea winter ... *why dint you come ere this summer?* We coulda gorn out wiv you then ... supposin Daddy ain't crippled fer life wot wiv that operation ... we could've gorn down to the coast.'

She shot me a look that excluded me from this pronoun. Jocelyn explained that we'd come to England because of my mother's cancer.

'Garn,' she said, 'gettin better, ain't she? ... that's what she told *me* ... mind, you carn't never tell wiv *er* ... lotsa people ave that operation and live fer years ... looked all right in ospital, she did, cepting she was asleep an we went all the way down there fer nothin ... fancy coming over *ere* juss fer that ... proper little worry-guts, *you* are ... carn't think why, neither, cos you wouldn't come all this way if it were me, an it's no good you sayin you would ... anybody would think it was one of *us* was ill ... look at yer father, in ospital wiv a disc operation ... an I bin avin these *pains* ...'

'Pains, Jocelyn said, 'what pains?'

'I get pains,' she said, 'I ain't sayin no more ... I reckon it's all a part of this *itch* ...'

'Then for Christ's sake stop *scratching*.'

'Really, Jossy, your *language* ... never talked like that before you went to Canada ... ain't done you no good at all, my lady, goin over there ... *in more ways than one* ... still, I suppose you want that cuppa tea ... come wiv me into the kitchen, Jossy, and we'll ave a chat while you elp me do the washin up.'

She led Jocelyn away much against the latter's will. I was in for trouble, I thought, and that's all one could say. Jocelyn's attitude towards her mother was a mixture of contempt, pity, and impatience. She was an only child and had been used, in her infancy, as an ally against her father. In this Sybil had had an easy task, for the old man stood for discipline and the doctrine that if you spare the rod you spoil the child. So he used Jocelyn as a kind of punchbag ... clouting her was simpler, though perhaps less pleasurable, than clouting the Mum. Jocelyn would only cry and run to her bed to hide; Sybil would scream the neighbours out of their easy chairs and into the street. She'd scream for the police. Since Jocelyn was an ally, however, Sybil saw that it was just as satisfactory kicking up the same fuss at his thumping Jocelyn as it was when he thumped *her*. It got so the poor bugger dared not thump *anybody* at all. He was too weedy to start a fight in a pub, and had to be on his best behaviour at work. He used to work out a lot of his ire against the world by playing soccer on Saturday afternoons, but Sybil put a stop to that soon after they were married.

There was a triptych of photographs on the mantelshelf – Sybil when young, a dark, attractive woman whose good looks were in those days only marred by bovine, suspicious eyes – there was one of Stan in RAF uniform ... forage cap, neat, well-pressed tunic ... he looked unsmiling and the third was Jocelyn in nurse's kit, taken in the days when, as her parents might have been deluded enough to think, she was still 'one of the family', before she had gone to the dogs by emigrating to Canada and marrying me. The room itself was in no way different from thousands of lower-middle-class English homes; two uncomfortable chairs facing the fire – high-backed to keep out the draughts that come whistling and swinging under English doors; highly polished gate-legged table, sideboard, dining chairs. Since this was the 'living room' it contained the radio, the telly, the newspaper, the dictionary, and the magazines. Down the hall a yard or so would be the 'parlour', totally unused except for 'special occasions' – those Sunday afternoons, in other words, when relatives came to inflict themselves for tea. I would expect to find therein a glass-fronted cupboard containing tiny coffee cups and plates. I was wrong about this, however, for Sybil and Stan had smashed all their wedding presents by the simple device of hurling them at each other during the early days of their marriage. They had moved around in the poor districts of London until, during the war, Stan's brother had found them their present house, which was situated near Rayner's Lane Underground Station in a curious district built up between the wars. As far as the eye could see there were red-brick, red-tiled terrace houses winding in streets that followed some ancient, Doomsday pattern of land usage – the kind of area where one hears old-timers say ah, that was all fields when I was a boy. Streets bore strange, archaic names like Spinnels, and High Worple. The men-folk here were in steady, respectable, and ill-paid jobs. Summer evenings you'd see them out weeding tiny gardens, tending roses, watching neighbours, and complaining over the fences about the coloured people. Sunday mornings they'd be out, polishing their cars or underneath them with wrenches.

'Aintcha got that timing right, Albert?'

'Nah. Runnin at two degree pahst top, still.'

These houses would all of them be dignified with an 'upstairs' – two tiny bedrooms each fitted with a dressing table on the back of which would be a triple mirror. You would see the backs of these mirrors, one after the other, in every top storey in the street.

Jocelyn had made a two-week excursion trip to High Worple five years before, just after we were married. There had been terrible scenes – an almost perpetual shindy; I was the villain who had altered Jocelyn so – the bum who was poncing off her wages as a physiotherapist, that's how her parents saw it. I'd never amount to anything; as soon as I was through college I'd kick her out – that was what happened to a cousin of hers. She was not as fussy about clothes as she used to be, and didn't plaster herself with as much make-up as was her wont ... 'What's the matter with you? Aint you proud of your appearance no more? *Look at your air*! That dunnarff get up my nose, that does, all that trainin you ad and now look at you, some kinda beatnik. God, your air's *terrible*, take this quid note an fer God's sake get yerself a perm ... come back to England lookin like that ... wot're people gointa think? Yore Uncle Erbert would die if e saw you lookin like that ... *look at your clothes* ... when did you lars buy yourself a noo dress? You were never like this when you lived ere ... you'd be better off in England ... away from *im* ... and wot's more you promised you'd come back after two years ... it's bin five ... fat lotta use *your* promises are ... it aint no disgrace to leave an usband if e don't work out ... why, there's a girl down the street who left *ern* ... it's no disgrace ... everybody knows why she left im ... time ter get out is now ... before you ave any kids.'

For ten minutes or so I had been vaguely conscious of the increasing volume of the voices in the next room. Suddenly Jocelyn's voice rose to a shout and she burst through the door.

'My mother,' she said, 'advises me to make sure I have a separate account in case things go from bad to worse.'

'Oo Jossy, you fibber,' she screeched, flying in at Jocelyn's heels, her eyes popping from her head and, in her agitation, she released her hands of the responsibility of scratching her itching arms so that they flew up to her head. '*Ow can you say such terrible things*,' she screamed. ' ... You never used to be like this ... *O wot's come over you*! ... I aint ever gointa fergive you, Jossy, fer sayin that ... I aint ever gointa fergive you.'

'Sit down,' I said, 'and keep cool.'

'Keep cool? Keep cool arter what she said to me? Oo's im to tell me ter keep cool?'

'I'm her husband,' I said. 'And she tells me everything. Just as I tell *her* everything. That's the way it is with us, and you'd better understand it. I neither know nor care what happened in your own married life to make you the way you are, but you'd better not assume that Jocelyn and I are unhappy together. As for banking accounts, what we have we share ... till death do us part. Got that? I don't care how things have been with you ... that's the way they are with us.'

'Jossy, I aint ever gointa fergive you,' Sybil wailed, beginning, at the same time, to sob. 'My own daughter turnin against me ... turnin against er own mother! ... oo ... ow, ow, ow, ow, ow!'

'Shut up,' Jocelyn snapped. 'Nobody's turned against you yet. But we will if you don't stop yelling at us.'

The wailing went on for some time.

'I meant it for the best,' she whimpered finally, beginning to come out of it a little. 'The best fer *you* ... you've really changed, Jossy, since you went over there ... I don know wot's got into you ... you've changed out of all recognition ... you aint my daughter no more, Jossy ... yor somebody else.'

'Let's get this cup of tea,' Jocelyn said. 'And after that we can discuss where we're going to stay.'

But it was some time before this subject got mentioned again.

'Well, I dunno ... you c'n stay ere, I suppose ... at least until Daddy gets outa ospital.'

'It'll give us a chance,' Jocelyn said, 'to look around for something more permanent.'

'If you think,' Sybil said eagerly, with a knowing, rather sinister smile and a vigorous shake of her chins, delighted to be discouraging, 'you're goin to find accommodation easily then yore wrong ... you gotta nother think comin ... don't you go around thinkin you'll find anythin in London, because you juss won't be able to ... I dunno that it's much good yore *lookin*, even ... corse, you c'n *look* ... nothin ter stop you *lookin* ... but if you wanna live in London, yore gonna ave ter pay through the *nose* ...'

'Perhaps Uncle Herbert will help,' Jocelyn said. 'He knows a lot of people.'

'Don't you go askin yore Uncle Erbert,' Sybil yelled. 'You don't wanna be beholden to *im* ... ave *im* sayin e got you a place ... nex thing I'll know they'll be droppin in ere fer cups a tea on Sunday afternoons ... juss about the distance Granny Thomas can manage ... no thank *you*,' she said. 'Don't you go around there without asking yer father first, an before you've bought yerself some new clothes.'

'Needs a lotta thinkin about,' she said.

'O well,' she said, 'I expect *e'll* be wantin to bring in some coal ... I'd better show im where it is.'

She stood up and I walked behind her, obediently, with the scuttle.

'Notice the way she can't relax,' Jocelyn said later that night in bed (it happened to be the same bed that she was born in). 'She can't settle to anything ... she moves slowly, but she's always *moving* ... pottering about from one thing to another ... it's as though she had a permanent, slow itch ... she can't rest and what's more she won't allow anyone else to rest ... that's why I could never get any reading done when I was a kid ... I'd no sooner pick up a book than she'd say ... *adn't you better start makin yerself some winter gloves?* ... or, *if you aint got nothing to do, Jossy, whyntcha clean out the back room?* It's a kind of mental itch ... nothing's ever right ... nothing will ever let her be ... life is just a series of petty torments and irritations to her.'

'She's pretty bad,' I said. 'But my mother's got the edge on her.'

'Come on, mine's far worse than yours. At least yours used to let you *read*.'

'She didn't let Jill read. But anyway, yours isn't *vicious*.'

'You haven't seen her at full blast yet.'

'Well, I'm not going to argue about it,' I said. 'I don't think you can compare them ... they're *different*.'

'I don't think I can stand it,' Jocelyn said. 'We're here for four months ... I think I'll go stark, raving off my head.'

'I feel sorry for them,' I said. 'We're all they've ever had and all they've got.'

'You're in one of your Jesus Christ moods ... I'm damned if I feel sorry for *mine*.'

'Dontchyou forget to switch that electric blanket orff,' came a voice from the next room. 'And I ope you aint gonna stay talking orl night ... Jossy, you get some sleep ... I don't like the sound a that cough a yorn ... to the doctor with you on Monday, my lady.'

'All right, Mother ... I was glad,' she whispered, 'that you gave her a little shit this afternoon. I can't do it ... she just gets me so mad I lose my reason ... I start to scream at her ... I know it's silly ... it just makes her worse, and so on, a vicious circle ...'

'How come she's so low?'

'Well, *I'm* low. So are you.'

'Now I've met your mother I think you're actually lower than me.'

'That's not true ... your mother's merely fake-refined ... she's far lower than anybody in my family.'

'It's a pity you never met my father,' I said. 'He was lower than all the rest of us put together.'

'She wants to believe that things are as bad between you and me as they are between her and my father ... she can't bear the thought that we might be even slightly happy ...'

'And remember,' Sybil screeched from the next room, 'that you ave to git down the doctor's early to git a *card* ... aint a bitta good waitin to see im if you aint got a *card* ...'

'They had a funny way of fighting,' Jocelyn said. 'As their voices got louder and louder she'd start stripping off her clothes ... right down to her tattered, revolting underwear, screaming bloody murder at him ... he'd start to walk out of the house and she'd cling to him, screaming; sometimes he'd drag her right down the street ... he'd be trying to stride out, she with bare arms clutched around his waist, dragging her feet, dressed only in her ghastly, ragged slip ...'

'Maybe that's the way she got her rocks off ...'

'I can't imagine her getting her rocks off, as you seem to want to put it. It's a disgusting thought.'

'The sex life of one's parents,' I said pontifically, 'is not a subject upon which one would normally wish to dwell.'

'Ere, you two, what time do you call this?'

'All right, Mother,' Jocelyn said wearily. 'Get some sleep. She's worried,' she whispered to me, 'that we might be talking about *her*.'

'An we're seein Daddy tomorrer, so no lyin in bed.'

'Good night. (Christ Almighty!)'

'G'nigh ... on second thoughts you better take that blanket orff altogether ahter that bed's warmed up a bit ...'

'OK, goodnight.'

'G'nigh.'

Sunday morning. Self, seated, dirty, sleep in eyes, flaked out in Sunday morning chair over electric fire reading copy of *Sunday Express*. In comes the Mum.

'Allo,' she said reluctantly.

Arms folded over chest, stooping, scratching, sucking in her breath.

'Brr..rr..rr ... in it *cold* ...'

'Sure is.'

Poised, restlessly, on threshold of room.

'I'd better put some coke on the stove,' she said. 'I spect you'll wanna shave.'

'No, thanks,' I said.

'Won't be wannin a *shave*?'

'Not for me, thanks.'

'Cor,' she said, and walked out. Voice in kitchen nominally addressed to Jocelyn but raised loud enough for me to hear.

'Dunarff get up my nose, that does ... fancy not wantin ter shave on a Sunday mornin! Whatever does e think e looks like?'

'Grotty,' I shouted. 'I look grotty.'

Sunday. Later in day. Dressing to go hospital visiting. Visiting the sick, I recalled, is one of the Seven Acts of Charity.

'Wot's that e's wearing?' I heard the Mum say in the kitchen. 'Big evvy thing like that ... aint e got no proper overcoat?'

'It's his Arctic parka,' Jocelyn said.

'Well, I aint goin to the ospital wiv im in *that* ... surely e's got somethin decent to wear? Whatever will Daddy think? And can't you get im to cut is air? ... an look at is trousers ... if them nurses see im like that they'll think your father comes from a family a Gypsies ... *Daddy's* the one gointa suffer for it, you know ... they won't go near im if they reckon is relatives 're riff-raff ... in any case I'm not avin im go outa *my* front door lookin like a rag-a-bone man ... we gotta *live* here, you know, arter you've gone back ... (an I suppose you *will* go back) you tell im to fix imself up a bit.'

'Here he is now,' Jocelyn said. 'You can tell him yourself.'

I stood by the door. 'Tell im wot?' she said.

'My mother says you look like a rag-and-bone man,' Jocelyn said.

'Oo Jossy, you do tell such lies ... that aint wot I said at all ...'

I put my *Observer* down and went upstairs to change my clothes. Better to pick only those bones liable to stick in one's throat, I thought.

One hour later. Preparing to blast off. The Mum in thick coat and hat like truncated busby, standing by to supervise car-grapple. We open garage doors and try to start car. Procedure made problematic by fact that, like all cars owned in area, it is immaculately kept and its paint-job beautifully preserved. Slightest scratch on shining, battleship-gray flanks would cause days of agony. Gap between garage walls and car flanks no more than an inch and a half on one side, and six on the driver's side. A driver, backing the car out, was forced to make a very tricky right angle turn out of the gate.

'*You'll* be driving, a corse, won't you, Jossy,' the Mum said. She had no intention of entrusting this precious object to me. Jocelyn turned the key and pressed the starter. The engine turned, but there was no joyous and triumphant firing of the mixture. Jocelyn tried again and again. The ignition light began to fade.

'Wot's the matter with it?' Jocelyn's mother screamed. 'I knew we shoulda gorn by bus ... *O my God wottever ave you done*? ... Yore poor father will ave a fit ...'

'For Christ's sake shut up,' Jocelyn yelled, suddenly losing her nerve. 'The battery's no good.'

'We'll push the cocksucker out,' I snapped, becoming rattled myself. 'Push it out and start the son-of-a-bitch downhill.'

'Don't you do nothin more to it now,' the Mum screeched hysterically. 'I'm goin down the road to phone the A.A. ... you leave it juss where it is ... you get a scratch on that car and there'll be ell ter pay ...'

While she was gone, Jocelyn and I heaved the little car out of the garage with difficulty and pushed it down the gentle slope of High Worple. Chaps came running out of their cells to help push.

'Its yer *choke*,' one of them said. '*Choke's gone*.'

In fact the cam that ought to nudge the choke lever up and down had slipped out of alignment. We got it started and turned back.

'We'd better go look for Dracula's Daughter,' I said.

We found her standing by a phone box watching us.

'I called them an told them not to bother,' she said. 'Jossy, I thought *you* was gonna drive. Your Father'd go mad if e though a stranger was drivin is car.'

We changed places and drove off in a flurry, as they say, of green shit and yellow feathers.

In most British hospitals visitors are discouraged. A patient is allowed two at a time for one hour per afternoon, if that. This hospital was situated in a curiously bleak portion of Highgate and was an old, pre-Nightingale establishment filled with relatives in their Sunday best and bearing flowers. The entire place crawled with activity. While waiting for Jocelyn to come out of the ward to let me in I explored a corridor and found what I was looking for – a tiled kitchen with a huge machine consisting of a boiler and a bank of long, stainless steel tubes. I recognized it straight away, of course; there was one at my school. I gazed at it with perverse nostalgia. It is a machine for making dead-man's-leg. Flour, suet, and water are poured into these tubes and the steam turned on. The mixture swells within the tube, toughens, and grows slippery. It is slid onto a table as a long, thwacky roll of shiny greyish-white. Kitchen minions slice it into sections. It is very rubbery – vulcanized – and the inexpert feeder risks skidding it off his plate when he touches it with a fork. It is purported to be very nourishing ... it 'sticks to the ribs'. As a variation, a cook may thin down some treacle with water in a bucket and ladle the mixture on top. This is regarded as luxurious, however, and your serious dead-man's-leg eater prefers to take it straight. The machine is versatile, for it can be used to turn out 'jam roll', 'plum duff', 'ginger pud', and other delicacies.

Jocelyn relieved me at my vigil and I joined the Mum at Stan's bedside.

He lay lean and uncomfortable in a newly made bed. He had the face of a disconsolate collie. The Mum sat by his side pouring poison into his ear.

'Cor,' he said, 'I'm glad ter meet you.'

'Sorry,' I said, 'it's under these circumstances.'

Conversation languished.

'How're they treating you?' I asked at length.

'Oo, they're pretty fair in ere, you know ... some of these nursin trainees're very elpful ... particularly them blacks ... I was real surprised at that ... you would'n think these blacks were good for anythin, would yer, but some a them're top-notch ... surprising ... never mind you can't tell whether they washed or not ...

'Corse,' he said, 'can't do nothin for myself yet ... but the doctor says I'll be up in a week.'

'You were lucky,' I said, more tactfully, 'that you had a surgeon who knew what he was doing.' But I was thinking: Poor sod, that's all you needed. Some kack-handed butcher with a U-accent and a Parkinson's tremor in his hands. Hospital beds make people look meek and good-natured, but you could tell, easily enough, that old Stan had been a bastard in his day. You could tell that by the thinness of his face and by the way dyspepsia and disillusion had carved deep chasms around his tight lips. In the days of the Depression he was an unemployed carpenter without much hope of a job. He joined the Air Force and began working on air-frames. This was steady job enough for Sybil, though it was with reluctance that she married him. Like my own mother, she'd heard too many stories about men and sex to enjoy either. Sex was not to her, as the old joke has it, what the English upper-classes have their coal delivered in – this was more a case of 'if you don't give in a coupla times a week he'll find some slut who will'. But Stan was a steady chap who owned a motor bike and dressed himself up in a nice blue serge suit and a forage cap. In the services, of course, the men learn to look after their own clothes ... no trouble there. Cooking may be a snag

... dead-man's-leg and toad-in-the-hole with its variations[1] were easy to make, however ... and there'd be no lunches. Sunday dinner'd be the biggest bleeding drawback ... in lower-middle-class England this is the big meal of the week – a ritual, a ceremony that few people enjoy and that fewer understand. It goes like this: woman gets up early ... she has to get the breakfast, troop upstairs with cups of tea, light the stove, and shove in the roast beef. Then she's got the roast potatoes to do, the Yorkshire to mix, and the greens (which need such long, hard, salty boiling) to supervise. She has to put the treacle tart on early enough for it to achieve the approved stucco consistency. The kitchen gets hot and the woman irritable. Her hair becomes uncontrollable and starts wisping over her face. The husband, meanwhile, stays in the sack ... he is the breadwinner and this is the only chance the poor sod gets for a lie-in ... he reads his *News of the World* and smokes fags ... wife takes him up a bit of haddock about nine-thirty. He gets up at half past eleven or so and 'comes downstairs'. The more emancipated husband goes to the pub and returns at one to eat this enormous meal. Afterwards the adults in the family begin to zedd off in order that their digestions, pitching and yawing, may attempt to cope with the latest intake. The children watch this gape-mouthed zedding with dismay and boredom ... is that what life's about? Is this what 'day off' means? Wait until you're our age, the elders say, you'll be glad of a day of rest ... Jesus! ... but wait ... worse is yet to follow! At four o'clock everybody gets dressed up to visit a relative for salmon paste and watercress sandwiches. It's very important that one's clothes are one's best ... there is the neighbourhood opinion to consider, apart from the sensibilities of the relatives. In my day this typical

1 Recipe for CHOP TOAD (a variation of toad-in-the-hole). Fry two mutton chops in fat 'rendered down' from a chunk of fatty mutton. Allow to cool and grow stale. Keep out of refrigerator and place in fly-blown larder for six days at room temperature. Mix up some batter, smear it thickly over chops and cook the son-of-a-bitch in an oven until the outside is crisp and the inside grows soggy around the chop. Serve lukewarm with cabbage well-boiled in brine. Bangers may be used instead of chops.

family might go for a walk in the park but now, of course, they watch the telly. It all sounds bland, harmless stuff, of course, a ritual that has pretty well supplanted religion. (Few go to church in this milieu ... they have very little to thank God for, very little cause to offer praise.) But it is joyless and oppressive and its chief danger is the sense of blasphemy that accompanies dissent from it. It was, in 1966, on the wane among the more active and emancipated young people, but we ourselves were expected to participate in it as you shall hear. In any case, Sundays were out as far as taking Jocelyn's parents for a car ride were concerned ... there was always 'dinner' to be cooked and the 'lie-in' to be propitiated.

'Wodyou ave fer dinner, Stan,' she asked, fussing with an already immaculate pillow.

'Ooo, bitta roas' lamb, spuds, an cabbage.'

'Roas' *lamb*? This time a year? Ooo, I wouldna thought they'd give you roas' lamb ... no noo potatoes nor mint sauce?'

'Wrong time a year fer noo spuds ... wod *you* have.'

She told him.

We drove back through a cold drizzling rain, towards Pinner. The streets were dingy, empty of people, lined with tightly closed shops. This was swinging London: a dead and joyless Sunday world.

I sat in the back of the car experiencing the deepest depression since the day I left England thirteen years before. Self-pity spouted up within me like a busted water main, and my mind began to crawl with images from childhood and adolescence; a school building built in the 1870s with small windows and thick walls and tiny rooms marooned in an asphalt playground separated by railings from the bordering street, and I, a child of ten, sitting on the school steps watching for signs of life in that street – after all, a main road; a bus passes, women in trousers and their hair in curlers carrying shopping bags to the butcher's shop where they would queue, for this was wartime, for the meat ration ... a man floats by on a bicycle, and after that, nothing. My ears ring with a kind of droning silence.

Here am I, now, driving back to Stan and Sybil's place, my mind alive with recollections of London parks – verdant pastures imprisoned in strips of asphalt and concrete and wound about with cars and trucks and buses, their windshield wipers ticking against the drizzle. My mind shifted to the dreary streets of Norwood where I lived after the war – a land filled with the decaying mid-Victorian houses built in yellow brick of a horrible dinginess, sitting unpainted and rotting in gardens of weeds and thick-leaved, flowerless shrubs and privet hedges glistening in the rain.

I remembered the viaduct along Falcon Road near Clapham Junction and the large concrete caves beneath it filled with the smell of decaying cabbage, then a few twists and turns of the road later and you came to the old town of Battersea where my father's youth club, Caius College Mission, stood with its tiny, barren windows and its parquet floor smelling of sweat and mildew.

Later in my life we moved from Battersea to a suburb some twelve miles south. I saw, as clearly as though they had materialized from the past, two city-wallahs dressed in their pin-striped trousers, bowler hats, black bum-freezer coats and tightly furled umbrellas, whooping outside the house across the street from which a third city wallah would emerge as though from a cell, and up the hill they would bound, towards the station and a day in the city. Faces loomed behind windows – bleak, pale, hostile. Streets deadened by Sunday boredom and a curious Sunday heaviness, a desultory texture ... the Sunday *desult* ... almost tangible, like a gas-blanket hung over the entrance to a dug-out, would fall over the world like a shroud ... the *desult*, the *desult ... let's get that desult hung up*! I saw faces distorted with boredom and disgust ... and adults, the grown-ups, in parlours bored and whispery over well-balanced cups of tea, bitching constantly like Sybil, or retreating into passive aggression, like Stan.

Or what price the seaside, water like knives, into which one was not allowed to enter; deck chairs on the beach, rentable; a man in a peaked cap comes round, a glittering machine like a pencil sharpener around his waist ... he'd issue you a ticket, as on the busses; a ticket for a deck chair going nowhere.

Galvanized iron sheds, washing on lines, and high fences

smelling of creosote and *desult* on dusty, suburban afternoons.

What wind, what wind, would ever blow through this rubbish and bring it to life?

We were coming now into High Worple and for no reason at all the oppression that had overwhelmed me began to lift and some of my *alegría*, the birthright of us all, came drifting back. But Jocelyn seemed meditative and inaccessible – more sombre than I had seen her in a long time. She could not say what was wrong, except that the afternoon had appalled her, nor did I press for details. For one thing, of course, I didn't have to, and for another I was very much in awe, in those days, of the darker, negative emotional states. They struck me not as distortions but as somehow more appropriate to the human reality. A solemn humour seemed to me to be more true, more *profound*, than my own customary cheerfulness which seemed, in comparison, shallow and thoughtless.

At any rate, I knew better than to try communicating my recaptured good spirits. We went out for a quiet drink at a pub, returned, and after some muzzy telly-watching, went to bed, each a little isolated from the other by contrasting moods.

I was awakened by a terrible moaning – a series of deep, rhythmical moans almost sexual at first, but intensifying into loud and terrified cries for help. Jocelyn lay on her back, her head rolling from side to side and on her face an expression of unutterable torment. I pulled her to me and tried vainly to comfort her.

But it was at least twenty minutes before she could speak. The light was grey with a north London dawn and I could see through the window part of a sky filled with dark, scudding clouds. Rain pattered against glass.

Fervently I hoped we hadn't woken Sybil.

'Just a dream,' Jocelyn whispered, eventually.

'That's all it was,' I agree, believing at the time she wasn't being ironic at my expense. 'Just a dream.'

There was another long silence. But I felt her body very slowly begin to relax against mine. Then she told me about it – a dream, I thought, like any other; nothing much to it and what there was seemed to a non-dreamer like myself without much emotional content. But at any rate she dreamed she was in a room, like this bedroom, only there was nothing in it, only her. A room with blank walls and no furniture, just Jocelyn sitting on the bare floor of it. And a window in one wall: a window she wasn't supposed to look out of. But she could see a snail creeping up on the glass ... one of those little snails you see moving up flower stems in the garden. Green and yellow shell. Just stuck there on the glass. She gazed at the snail but knew she wasn't supposed to look past it, towards the outside.

'Supposed?' I said. 'Sounds like you'd been given orders.'

'I just knew it,' she said. 'I wasn't supposed to be in the room ... and that's why I found it so sad ... *I'm not supposed to be here at all ...*'

'In the room? What do you mean? I don't understand.'

'*Here*. I'm not supposed to be here ... *anywhere*. It's not my home. I wish you could understand that ... there isn't anywhere for me to go ...'

She was crying again, but more quietly. I was no longer scared of waking Sybil. For the first time I had an inkling of what Jocelyn was talking about. I felt a wave of hopelessness go through me, then I began to shiver with the cold. I lifted the blanket over our shoulders more and huddled against her. I pulled my free arm in to me as though against the approach of something unknown and terrible.

She didn't want to go too close to the window because that would mean looking out of it and she already knew and feared what was on the other side ... just nothing ... nothing, stretching into the distance where it became both blank and dark ... so there she was, alone, in this forbidden room, watching the snail and knowing what lay beyond it. And thinking nothing. Feeling her aloneness and the emptiness stretching into the dark.

'There's nothing to think about,' Jocelyn said.

'Nothing at all?'

'There wasn't anything in the dream and there isn't anything now. There never is.'

'I don't understand.'

'I know you don't.'

Now it had grown quite light. I was becoming aware of sounds starting a new day: a coper's and a grappler's day. A floor creaked as Sybil hefted her body from the bed to the slippers on the carpet. Cars had started in the distance; horses; hooves sounded in the road outside. Hooves! I could hardly believe my ears – something from my childhood – rag-and-bone men and brewer's drays. 'Listen,' I said. I disengaged myself from Jocelyn and looked out, into High Worple. A white cart named United Dairies in big blue letters stood at the corner of Spinnels. A man in a white coat and peaked cap, straight out of Hitchcock's *The 39 Steps*, carried a crate of milk bottles to a house across the street.

'Come and look,' I said. 'There's something out here; it may not be much, but it's something.'

We stood there watching the milkman on his rounds until the coldness of the room drove us back to bed. She drifted into a gentle sleep in my arms and I remember thinking: she's going to be all right now, my poor Jocelyn. She's going to be all right.

The Best Years of Your Life

AS I WRITE this I am thinking about gardens and my head teems with images of elms, ponds, ha-has, and cultivated wildernesses that surround the great English mansions and of places like Kew patterned out with carefully nurtured rare shrubs exotically leaved and coloured and sleek with outrageous foreign flowers. And I think of the wild gardens on the edge of cliffs sprouting arbutus trees, winter jasmine, and silao bushes whose leaves and dark blue berries are shiny in the West Coast rain. As I look through the window beyond this typewriter I see the North Shore Mountains (decapitated today by low cloud) and, framing them, the thin branches of February trees. Below the trees is a wet and mossy lawn and an untidy cluster of hydrangea shrubs whose solid blossoms of last summer have withered to brown skeletons: yet it is also snowdrop time and I see hosts of these little white flowers clustered around the base of an apple tree and amongst them the thrusting green spikes of crocus.

But mostly I am thinking about a garden of my childhood. It was close to a village called Yately, in southern England. It surrounded a brick, thatch-roofed cottage and lay wild and open to the sunlight – a tumult of antirrhinum, delphinium, wallflowers, and stocks. Blue flowers, rich, velvety red flowers, mauves, yellows – and the marvellous scent of them rising up like voices in praise: the whole magical place alive with carnation and iris and all those boisterous plants blooming, in my surely inaccurate mental picture of it, all at the same time. And I am nine years of age, walking through this paradise of colour and smell to where the rabbit hutches were kept – a dark, sweet-smelling straw cavern filled with sly eyes cocked suspiciously, and long silken ears I could see when the light was right. There was a chicken shed, walking past which I would hold my nose, and another hutch where they kept the ferret – a shy, silky animal packed with a violent and demonic energy. Beyond this garden was a tall privet hedge heady, when it rained, with its own rank smell, and behind the hedge a ditch with frogs and bulrushes, then a field.

My father ran a boys' club in Battersea, and Yately was where its summer camp was held, two fields down. My sister and I were farmed out at that cottage, which possessed a mossy water butt with smooth, dark, rain-water and whose owners were named, by some stroke of punning cosmic genius, Mr. and Mrs. Tubb.

And as I remember the Tubbs' garden at Yately I see a picture of it so detailed and densely real I feel I could reach out and clasp it to me – as though it were a landscape I could enter again at will. I see it now as clearly as I see myself and Jocelyn lying in that room at High Worple. And I am a visitor there, lost in wonder at this couple, at their closeness, at the intensity of their love for one another, at the texture of wallpaper, coverlet, electric blanket, painted window sill, and of window glass – fogged, damp, and so permanently cold that our names written on it by my forefinger that morning we saw the milkman stayed there for the duration of our visit. This picture has acquired the reality of a physical object for me. It is as real as those small, personal things I associate with Jocelyn that I come across even now and over which hangs a deep silence – a hair grip at the bottom of a suitcase, a forgotten photograph, a set of knitting needles at the back of a drawer. Over each there hovers a balloon, like those you see in cartoon strips, but a balloon without words.

But it was in that field, behind the garden at Yately, that I first encountered what it was like to carry around in my imagination a world of landscapes both lost and *there*. Amidst this buttercup-dotted grass I stood one day, struck suddenly with a sense of self-hood – what am I? Who is this? I am ME, I, this moving, abstracting, wafting, infinitely fluid creature, part of that field and yet not; a thing apart, with a driving, powerful quality of being ... clench my fists and I can spring flying into the air and across to the trees. Disintegrate and re-enter myself, *become* myself – like Peter in the condemned cell whose angel told him that his bonds, his gaolers, his imprisoning walls were constructs of his imagination only.

I didn't, of course, think about St. Peter at the age of nine, nor did I have the language to describe, even as inadequately as this, my experience. What I remember most is a feeling of being spellbound, thunderstruck at my hand stretched out before me: at the recognition that this odd thing was not only mine but *me*. At that instant my mind was filled with great, reaching befuddlement as though something magical and extraordinary were there about to be defined and, by just reaching in the right direction I would not only discover it but some other infinite secret that lay behind it. And that this secret had to do with the word 'ago' – long ago. I muttered the word and called it out, and my thoughts reeled in front of it. What does it mean to say that something's past? Where is it? Where's it gone? It still exists, in some weird way, like the light of a snuffed candle that wings its way across the universe forever. I knew with a kind of long, swooning happiness that nothing dies, that the moment, the *ago* moment, is still somehow there, *here*, and it is I, this infinitely fluid thing, that moves – neither spatially, nor in time, but in some other mode carrying that ago-moment with me. What does it mean, this phrase, what did it mean then – *eternal life*? That is what my nine-year-old mind was trying to cope with.

Jocelyn told me once that she too carried around with her an image of childhood bliss. She is playing in a field full of long grass with a cousin of hers – they're lying together, rolling about in this field under an azure summer sky as though it were too long a day ever to end. She said that her cousin was so warm, cuddlesome, pliable, and filled with puppy-fat and laughter that she couldn't believe any other experience was as real and that if this was what life was then she hoped, as a tot of three years or so, that it would never change into anything else nor that it would ever stop.

Oddly I have a photograph of her and this cousin; Jocelyn had long, lustrous hair, then parted in the middle: her grin is huge and delighted and her arms are around the little boy. Both are clearly squealing with pleasure. But the 'real' world for her was not this but the slum in Fulham and the violence that Stan and Sybil did to one another and which she knew about at the back of her mind even when cuddling her small friend – the stench of blocked drains, the sourness of stale food and uncollected garbage, the malevolence of a household where the caring for things and people was secondary to the struggle for domination between her parents – a battle that Stan, in those days, appeared to be winning.

We knew that if we lived closer to Pinner than to Brighton my mother would complain. On the other hand we flinched from the uproar that one mile south of the dead centre of a line drawn directly between the two sets of parents would cause. So we rented the top of a semi-detached house in Streatham closer to Pinner, but near a main-line station on the railway to the south, and as soon as I could I took a train to Brighton.

The big town was cold, that morning, but invigorating. I wore my Arctic parka, two pairs of trousers, a pair of skiing socks, and several layers of newspaper. I collected my mother and took her for a walk down to the sea-front and onto the pier. The streets were icy and she walked very slowly, like a mountain climber, carefully securing one foot-hold before she ventured on the next. Crossing the road became a delicate business – she did not trust, and was wise not to, the pedestrian crossings, for tiny cars would dart out from nowhere and swing their front wheels at your ankles. This kind of driving had caused my mother's illness – she had been run over by what she called a mad-jack in a sports car. She had not, ostensibly, been badly hurt – merely shaken up, and had it not been for her fear of the law, medicos, and authority, she could've shaken the mad-jack's insurance company down for much more than she eventually got. But, as she put it, 'if you give them trouble they'll make it hot for you in other ways.' Nevertheless, the cancer had grown inward from the base of her spine, the point where the car had hit her.

She was no longer the vigorous woman I had remembered, up at six, at the foot of one's bed by quarter past with orders for the day, admonishments for the day before, philosophy for all times, out grappling with employers and other enemies by eight-thirty, home at five to 'do the house', cook the supper, and pick a fight with the landlady. Tiny, bird-like steps, now, frequent stops for rests and cups of tea in tea-shops, a gentle, slightly self-mocking manner, quiet, husky voice. I made mild fun of her slowness and pauses. We went on the pier and she watched me lovingly as I recaptured my childhood with those extraordinary slot machines dating back to the Victorian age ... place a penny in the slot and you can watch clock-work puppets enact the execution of Mary, Queen of Scots.

'What do you do all day?' I asked, winning threepence at poker-ball.

'Oh, my dear, not very much these days ... it's just so nice to rest after all those years of work ... I go to the library once a week or so ... do the crossword in the *Evening News* ... take a nap in the afternoon and listen to the wireless ... Thursday afternoons I go to tea with my friend Betty ... I'd like to invite her over to Eastern Road, but it's not really the type of place you can ask people to visit you ... I used to go for walks before I was taken ill ... and I expect I will again, when the summer comes ... I'm getting my energy back, gradually ... putting on a bit of weight ... you can live for years, you know, after this operation ... though if anything were to happen, I wouldn't complain ... I've had a good innings ... I'm in my seventieth year, you know, and not many of the people I've known have lived to say that ... Vi and Lil died in their late fifties, my brother

John died at twenty-nine, and Edwin at thirty-five ... Granny was the only one in our family to live to be old ... she was a marvellous woman, in every way ... she could see through *anybody* ... *nobody* took *her* in ... she was over ninety when she died ... and she lived on her own, to the very end, a burden to no one. That's how I should like to be ... of course, I'm better already ... you can't have a lump like that without it affecting you ... Mrs. Mills, the sister said, you have a *very big lump* ... that's just the way she put it.'

'Did you ask them what it was?'

'Oo, my dear, you can't ask them questions like that ... did they tell *you* anything?' She turned a beady, half-fearful eye towards me.

'No,' I lied. 'Only what they said to you ... that you had a *lump*.

'We're looking forward to exploring London,' I said, changing the subject. 'After all these years. Jocelyn's excited about the shops ... you miss that kind of thing in Vancouver.'

'Don't you let her spend all your money,' she advised, her eyes beginning to flash angrily. 'You spend something on *yourself*. You need clothes, for one thing ... I noticed she isn't keen on keeping your clothes in repair ... for instance I see there's a button off that thing you're wearing ... I'll sew one on for you when we get back ... she isn't keen on doing things like that, is she? When I met her that day in London she told me she wasn't interested in housework ... well, my dear, I said to her, none of us are, I said. But we've got to get used to it, haven't we? I said. *I* had to, in *my* day ... she changed the subject quickly enough ... she could see I was cross ... Don't you let her get away with anything ... your father would've had a fit ... Here, mend these, he used to say, throwing his underwear at me ... and mend them I had to, interested or not. Don't you let her get hold of too much of your money ... I bet she'd be a proper little spendthrift if she had the chance ... I never had the chance ... right up until he died I never knew how much your father earned ... he used to give me thirty bob a week to do the housekeeping ... that's all you're going to get, he'd say ... it was like getting blood out of a stone. Don't spoil her ... be guided by me ... *you'll store up trouble for yourself if you're not careful ...*

'If you want to know what a woman's going to be like,' she said, 'take a look at her mother ... mind you, I'm not saying Jocelyn's altogether like hers.'

'God forfend.'

'Sybil's not too bad when you get to know her,' she said charitably. 'She's eaten up with jealousy, that's her trouble ... eaten up with it ... she's *jealous of her own daughter* ... you can see it a mile off.'

This flat in Streatham was by English standards of the day fairly comfortable. It was up a flight of stairs and commanded a view of street, bus stop, and tall late Victorian houses paraded in front with their concrete gardens on which, by night, small cars would sit condomed with plastic sheets against the weather. Buses, nominally due every ten minutes, travelled up and down the street, but it was a commonplace event that there would be neither hide nor hair of a bus for forty minutes and then a stately procession of about five would show up, as though they felt safer travelling in convoy. At least, as I found myself explaining to an irate fellow passenger, they let you take your pick.

The flat contained a living room, bedroom, pleasant enough kitchen, and the essential 'airing cupboard' – a storage place for one's washed, dried, ironed, but still damp and getting damper clothes. No English refrigerator chuckled and gurgled coyly in the wings of the kitchen – instead there was a marble slab in the larder which, the landlord claimed, did almost as well. Walls and windows streamed with condensation – books and papers began to rot and mildew almost instantly as they do in the tropics, but water dripping down the walls could be caught before it reached the floor by means of absorbent pads designed for that purpose, which were available in hardware stores. In those days, the sixties, central heating in Britain was still a rarity and thought to be enfeebling. Double glazing was almost unknown, most plumbing external to the house so that pipes froze in winter and, in freezing, expanded and cracked to gush water in the thaw. We were preserved from this particular fate. There was no shower, but the bath was fitted with two taps and the hardware store could sell you a rubber gadget that looked rather like a double-arsed enema syringe. You could affix this to the taps so that a single jet of water, its temperature adjusted to the bather's taste, would issue from a single shower-head.

I had forgotten how cold it could get here in the winter; how the cold surrounds and blankets you like a second skin since in those days no public building was heated and no bus. People froze their blood during the day and would light big fires at night, provided they could afford the coal, and roast in front of them catching chilblains in the process. Men and women crept out of doors huddled in coats and newspapers, their bodies bent forward against the biting North Sea Winds, accepting their fates, public transport, no disposable income, and their cold, wet homes with what they themselves describe as wry humour but which came across to me more like neurotic passivity.

Each morning I would attempt to write. I would park my portable typewriter on the table by the front window, adjust my sweaters, and turn on the two-bar heating element, which would, in an hour, block the view out onto the street with condensation. I wrote copiously about England, Wales, mountain climbing, about my own misadventures ranging in locale from Marseilles to the Arctic, from Scandinavia to Northern Ontario. I wrote about the DEW-Line. For some reason or another I wanted to write about my own life, particularly my negative experiences, and found myself, as I do now, enjoying it. Gone was the urge that had driven me for some years, and that was to return, to write fiction. Instead I became, as though under my mother's influence, absorbed in dark visions and events and in trying to find a pattern in them. I'd returned, in fact, to an earlier mode of writing, which had disgusted a good friend of mine – look, why don't you write about a rose? he asked. Most days Jocelyn seemed happy enough to wait for me to finish my self-imposed stint. We would eat lunch, then we would make forays into the city and act like tourists. We did what visitors to London do and for which London is most loved by those not born and bred in the place. We visited, in other words, bookshops, pubs, the Tower, old restaurants, the Temple Gardens, and Hyde Park and the theatres. These are experiences closed, for the most part, by their price to working-class residents except on very rare occasions. Very soon it became obvious to me that we did not have enough money flowing in to entertain ourselves in the manner of rich tourists. My pay cheque, deposited in Canada twice a month, was about double the pay the average Britisher received 'in 'and' but it was not enough.

We relinquished our plans one by one – Austria for a week's skiing, Scotland for a week in the Cairngorms – it was as much as we could afford to get to Cornwall, a place that held memories for us both. Coupled with this was the expense of commuting – from Streatham to Pinner at least once a week, and the same for Brighton. It seemed obvious that I ought to augment my salary with a job.

Accordingly I applied at County Hall, an enormous building done in Penitentiary Gothic, near Waterloo Station, for a job as a supply teacher.

It was an unadorned and cavernous place warrened with small, inaccessible rooms in which every radiator was used as a ledge for the empty tea-cups and dirty saucers endemic in British office life. Among other things, the place acted as a nerve centre for the South London educational system and it was to County Hall that people applied for teaching jobs and there that those same teachers, speaking out of their turns, might someday be called to give an account of themselves.

A man gave me forms and told me I'd be telephoned. The forms were difficult and demanded lists of jobs (and proofs of jobs) for the last ten years, description of degrees, letters of recommendation, etc., and they invoked other bodies such as a pensions authority located at the delightfully named Honeypot Lane, and a tax collector in Liverpool. I wondered if They would connect me with the reckless youth who had told them to desecrate his father's grave, then thought this required too much efficiency. Each office, though, needed contacting and each generated its own sub-set of forms. I filled these out, patiently, over a period of about a week. Then waited to be called.

As soon as Stan was out of hospital and mobile enough to drive his car, we thought it might be tactful to invite him and Sybil to

Streatham along with my mother whose energy, in a patch of deceptively mild weather, had begun to creep back. We'll feed them, we thought, the whole pack ... give them a meal they could remember with affection. We roasted some pork marinaded in white wine and served it with chestnut sauce; simmered broccoli sauted with shallots in a tiny quantity of chicken broth with a dash of soy sauce, and another of sherry. We gave them roast potatoes as a concession to their English customs, but forced them to eat a fresh fruit salad spiked with rum to follow. We gave them a pleasant though by no means uncommon German wine to drink.

'Woss this, then?'

'Chestnut sauce.'

'Chessnut sauce? ... Did *you* say *chess*nut sauce? ... Well, I never erd a that, I *muss* say ...'

'Juss cos you aint erd of it before, Sybil, don't mean ter say it don't exist ...'

'*I* think they've gone to a lot of trouble,' my mother said, 'to make us a delicious meal. And *I* think it's delicious ...'

'Oh, it's *nice* ... I aint sayin it aint *nice* ... but you gotta admit this could be any meat ... thass the trouble wiv all these fancy things ... you can't taste the *meat* ... it's idden in all them *spices* ... thass what I've always said.'

'That's what you've always said, Sybil?'

'Thass wot's she's always said, John,' Stan answered. He told me once that the only way to hack it was to cultivate a sense of humour.

'Well, it's delicious,' my mother repeated, her eyes sparkling and her voice ascending a tone or two. 'You're a very good cook, my dear.' This remark was ambiguous since both Jocelyn and I had worked on this meal.

'She takes a damn sight more trouble than I woulda taken, any'ow,' Sybil said, cashing in on my mother's statement and choosing to interpret it, falsely, as praise of her daughter. 'Plain olesome food's good enough fer me,' she said, giggling slightly, wattles vibrato.

'Cor, I dunno ow I'm gonner move arter all that.'

'Your back all right?'

'Yers ... it's all right ... you got anuver cushion, ave yer?'

'Here.'

We cleared the table. Over coffee we showed them a bunch of snapshots.

'Here's one taken by a friend of ours in Sausalito.'

'Cor ... look at is *air* ... you look juss like a girl, dunnee, Stan?'

'Though I'm a man,' I said, 'there's a girl inside me that's trying to get out ... I've been thinking about having that operation.'

'What do you mean,' my mother said aggressively, 'there's nothing wrong with *your* masculinity.'

'I never said there was, *I'm* sure,' Sybil simpered.

'Here's one of Jill and David's father.'

There was a pause while Sybil checked this out. David, of course, is my sister's son born, as they say, on the wrong side of the blanket. Sybil had met Jill and the two of them had tangled. It was to Jill that Sybil had first confided her notion that I was keeping Jocelyn a prisoner in Canada against her will and that if it were not for me and my malign influence Jocelyn would be back in England, living down the street, being a comfort to Sybil in her old age. Jill had rejected this concept with some scorn and had thus caused bad blood between the two of them.

'Thass David's *father* ... *really?* ... *David's* father? ... cor ... I wonder what she sees in *im?*'

'He's very handsome,' my mother said, hackles rising.

'Andsome is as andsome does, if you ask me ... Innee *dark*, though ... e's really *dark* ... I think there's something Jewish about him.'

People blenched. There was a sultry pause. This used to be and maybe still is a deadly insult in lower-middle-class England.

'Jewish,' my mother shrieked. '*Jewish?*'

'Hush,' I said.

'Well, Sybil, I think there's something Jewish about *you* ...'

'His name's O'Finkle,' I said, 'and he's an Irish Jew.'

'Cor ... some people dunnarff take you up fast ...'

'Some people shouldn't going round casting snacks ...'

'Castin snacks? Oo was castin snacks, then? I'm sure *I* weren't castin no snacks.'

'You've only got to look at David,' my mother said after a pause, 'to see there's no Jewish blood ... like a little snowball, he was ... blond all over ... lovely blond skin,' she said, her eyes glittering sexily, 'and lovely little limbs ... I used to kiss them all over,' she said. 'Couldn't *help* myself, just like his Uncle John's when *he* was a baby ... lovely blond limbs, dimpled all over ...'

'Jesus,' Jocelyn said later, 'your mother's got a warped mind. Fancy coming out with all that stuff about the lovely limbs ... my parents were as embarrassed as I've ever seen them.'

'It got up their noses,' I said. 'I could tell that, all right.'

'I bet you were the only man she ever really fancied,' Jocelyn said. 'Sick though that sounds.'

'Why would she fancy men of any kind? She's shit scared of them.'

I repeated an anecdote my sister told me. She claimed it was her first memory of our mother. She was telling me, Jill said, never to pull up my knickers in front of a man, or pull up my skirt, and when I was older she would give me a little book to read. I was about four and I remember to this day the look on her face and her wagging index finger. I was standing in a tin basin at the time, on the kitchen floor, having my back scrubbed with what felt like pumice stone ...

'What a mind,' Jocelyn said. 'Why was she so terrified that Jill would wind up an unwed mum? It's almost as though she willed it on her.'

I explained that my grandmother brought up her five children completely without male help. I'd never been told the exact circumstances. 'She had a hard row to harrow ... but she did it, and that,' I said, 'explains my mother's adulation of the old girl and all her values.'

'It explains nothing,' Jocelyn said. 'Why did she see men as demons and women as sluttish and long-suffering victims? Why has she got so black a view of human nature? And why does she fancy *you* above and beyond the style in which mothers always fancy their sons.'

I could find no answer. Perhaps a full explanation lay in the nature of my mother's experience of life, experiences both dismal and unrewarding. But it was only when we were about to leave England that she revealed any evidence of a more concrete nature.

We tried feeding relatives only once more ... Jocelyn's lot ... over from Staines. Uncle Herbert and Aunt Mavis, Granny Thomas, Cyril and Gertie (two cousins from Bournemouth), and Stan and Sybil. They arrived in a car packed with their bodies and some slide projector apparatus. Herbert was a careful, stout, rather sedate man who was purported to have one lung. Gran was a very old lady with a large, beaming face into one side of which was plugged a deaf-aid. Mavis had had a stroke and had to watch what she ate, and Stan, of course, had to be careful what he sat down on. Sybil, unsatisfied with her itch, which by now she had exploited in such a way that great patches of skin were reduced to scarlet flakes, had cultivated a 'bowel complaint'. Cyril seemed in good health barring a smoker's cough and a wall eye, but Gertie, a tiny bustling woman of about sixty, was going bald and shook from time to time with a faint, but perceptible, Parkinson's tremor. All were stiffly suited and sat with rear ends balanced on the edge of their chairs, and plates balanced on their knees.

'Would you like a beer, Herbert,' I asked, 'or a cup of tea?'

'Oo, I think we'd all like a cuppa tea, wouldn't we, Erbert,' Sybil said. 'Im an is beer.'

'Yes, a nice cuppa tea, ey, Gran? Ow about a nice cuppa tea?' he bawled.

'Yes,' she said, in a tiny voice, 'I'd like a cuppa tea.' She nodded and beamed at her son who turned to Jocelyn. 'There! Gran'll ave a cuppa tea, Jossy. Ow about you, Cyril?'

'Oh, yers, a cuppa tea'll do me.'

We brewed and poured tea and issued thin lobster paste sandwiches, a dash of watercress, and some heavy cakes. The company sat chomping and balancing uneasily.

'Watcha think of Viet Nam, Herbert?' I asked.

'Nasty business, that,' Cyril said.

'Don't nobody start talking politics,' Sybil said. 'We ad enough a that last time.'

This, I found out, was a reference to certain events one Christmas seven or eight years ago which was to me obscure.

'Watcha think of the crime wave, Stan?' I said, trying again.

'Look at is *air*,' Sybil said. 'It aint *me* that likes it like that ... it *do* look a mess ... why don't you ave it cut?'

'You all right, Gran?'

'I'm all right, Erbert.'

'It's all these young kids ... look at the money they got! We ad ter work our guts aht, in my day, jus ter make ends meet ... we ad ter kiss the boss's feet juss ter keep our jobs ... two minutes late, boy, an aht you went.'

'Yer dead right, Stan, yer dead right.'

'No discipline, thass what does it ...'

'Still it aint no good *my* tellin im ... ow they let im get away wiv it beats *me* ...'

'Where yer going for yer olidays this year, Erbert? You decided yet?'

'Dunno, yet, Gertie. Not much money about this year ...'

'They wanta good *whippin* the arff a them ... spare the rod and spoil the child, thass *my* motto ...'

I began to wish that Stan could have the opportunity of trying out his dictum on the class I'd got.

Three weeks after my journey to County Hall I was facing my first class. These children wore blazers and gray flannel trousers. The school itself was a secondary modern – which meant that its inmates would leave at fifteen and sail forth into the world – as baker's boys, apprentices, day labourers, or more likely, it occurred to me, as spivs, pick-pockets, smash-and-grab, and B&E artists. These were the boys who had failed their eleven-plus examinations. The striking thing was that nearly a third of them were either West Indian, or black African, or Indian coffee-coloured. Third World immigration to Britain had occurred after my own time there and

North American experience said to me that black children spoke with deep south, Aunt Jemima accents. These kids spoke broad cockney of the most glottal sort:

'Oy, sir, are you gonna tike us?'

'Oy, look at im, e finks e's gonna tike us ...'

'You go'a be a lot bigger than *you* are ter tike us, sir, we're warnin yer ...'

'Oo, sir, you teachin on supply? Wotcha get, five nicker a bleed'n shot?'

'Wot was the nime a that stoopid bleeder we ad last time, on supply?'

'Green ...'

'Yeah, thass right, Green ... cor, e wun *arff* a stoopid prick ...'

'Ere, sir, you know wot e done? E was standin right where you are wiv is bleed'n arms stretched aht tryin to stop us from fuckin off outa that bleed'n door ahter the bell rang ... "stop", e was yellin, "stop ... stop".'

'Stop, boys,' somebody bleated in imitation of the unfortunate Green. There was a chorus of laughter and cat calls.

'If you show us plenny a films,' one kid yelled, '*we* won't fuck yer ahabt, sir.'

'All right,' I said, feeling my voice rise a notch and go ineffective. 'It's chemistry today ... elements, mixtures, and compounds. Give me an example of an element.'

Silence. Somebody began to titter.

'Mixture, then,' I said. 'Give me an example of a *mixture*.'

'Shit,' someone sneered.

'Yeah, sir, *shit* ... ow abaht shit? ... *Shit's* a mixture.'

Roars of laughter. They were right of course. If anything is a mixture, shit is. Should I write this on the board under one of the three categories I'd printed there? I turned, and was immediately assailed with apple cores, sticks of chalk, a sodden sandwich. An empty but by no means light satchel struck me on the back of my neck. '*Got* im,' somebody yelled. I turned and faced them. 'Yah,' they sneered.

'Cut it out, you little sods,' I yelled. There was a respectful silence. 'Next person who moves, or makes a noise,' I said, 'I'll take him outside and beat the living shit out of him.'

I turned again to the blackboard and immediately a chorus of hollow groans broke out. I swung around. Silence. Turn again. Groan. Swing to face the class. Silence and respect. One child was on his knees, pretending to pray to me. Perhaps because the nature and destiny of my predecessor, Green, was still in my mind, or perhaps because this group of boys was the antithesis of Stan and Sybil in ethics and philosophy, I found myself warming to these lay-abouts, spivs, drones, and juvenile delinquents. 'Long may they thrive!' I found myself whispering. Long may they insult authority! Long may they take the piss out of whatever jerk that's shoved in front of them with orders to push them around. That's all very well, I thought, but how am I to survive here? An idea came to me.

'If you want to muck about,' I said. 'We'll muck about.'

I got a broom out of the closet in the classroom and swept down on them like a bayonet drill instructor ... In! Out! On guard! It was great stuff. They fought back with a will. Before the bell rang I'd knocked some kid's tooth out. I visualized lawsuits, irate parents, terrible scenes at County Hall.

'I'm sorry about your tooth,' I said to the victim.

'Ah, thass all right, sir,' he said amicably.

I discovered another way to amuse them. Show them films. We'd darken the room, put the screen up, and run off the films sent by the Ministry of Education. There was one about sheep-raising, for example, with a sequence dealing with castration they particularly enjoyed; and another wherein a shepherd de-maggots a sheep's arse ... close-up of the sheep's woolly, beshitten ring and the shepherd's fingers, probing around it. Close-up of arse-maggot.

Some liked to draw. 'Get yer books out,' I'd yell, 'and copy the fuckin diagram on page 3.'

Books would be thrown about, water spouted from laboratory taps, cries of Oi, sir, some bastard's nicked my bleed'n pen. It was good in its way and I liked and sympathized with the students, but I'd had enough after about a week. I made a little money and lost only a section of my jacket to a small boy with a razor blade who sliced it neatly while my back was turned.

‘Spare the rod and spoil the child,’ Stan said. ‘Thass *my* motter ... nuthin like a good idin ...’

‘Yer right, Stan, yer dead right ... thass wot some a these young blokes c’d do wiv ...’

‘All this part a London,’ Mavis was saying, ‘as gorn dahn and dahn ... them blacks’ve just about taken it over ... arff a dozen families in one ouse ... live like pigs, they do ... everywhere you go you see a black face, nowadays ...’

‘Ah, London aint what it was ... all them noo buildins goin up ... all these council flats ... I wish *I* could get my ands on one ... bunch a scruffs livin in them, workin at two jobs wiv the missus out to work an all ... cheap rent ...’

‘They’re the ones makin the money ...’

‘Corse es got a good job now,’ Sybil was boasting, ‘but e aint always ad a job. Jossy ad to work the ole first two years they were married while e went to college ... I cried my eyes out, I did, when I eard about *that* ... girl a *mine* workin ter support er usband ... whatever would people think?’

‘It all worked out fer the best, though, init Sybil?’

‘Well ... yeah ... I suppose you *could* say that ...’

‘Nah, London aint wot it was, I don’t mind tellin yer ...’

During one of my walks around the city I found myself strolling across Blackfriars Bridge from the South Bank to Charing Cross. The South Bank looked much less decayed than it used to, for the bomb damage had not been cleared up in my day. I stared down at the brownish, oily Thames and recalled the last time I crossed this bridge, in 1952, on a glorious spring morning, my army discharge in my pocket. I’d come up from Aldershot, changed into civvies at Waterloo, stuffed my army gear, which I was supposed to keep for two weeks’ camp with the reserve each year, into a kit-bag, then, from Blackfriars Bridge, hurled it with a terrible curse into the river, narrowly missing a passing tug. It made a loud, satisfactory splash. I watched its ripples for some moments until I remembered that England is full of the type of murderer who likes to decapitate his victims, put the torsos on trains, and wrap the heads in bags for distribution into the river. I moved away quickly, for I might have been spotted by some bogey. I walked briskly across the bridge, up past Charing Cross into Trafalgar Square, and thence into Hyde Park where I took out a skiff onto the Serpentine. The sky was flecked with tiny, fast-moving little clouds and the trees were out in fresh new leaves.

There seemed then no time frame and no urgency: no one road before me but a network of them, some dusty and rutted, others clean and well-maintained, criss-crossing and leading nowhere. No duty, no oughts, no imperatives, only an intoxicating sense of the world's complexity and joyousness, and a pulsing, singing feeling in the blood as though a great arch stretched itself across in the sky on which shone the words BE NOT ANXIOUS.

And for a long moment I saw Stan and Sybil, Gertie and Cyril, and my own mother as men and women to be held not in contempt or under the aspect of satire, but in a state of brotherly tolerance. For what lay at the root of their personalities was fear, anxiety, the same as it did mine. They were frightened of change, of strangers, of foreigners, of poverty, of death. Fear of these things explained their suspiciousness, their need to control and manipulate, just as anxiety about my own future, my sense of impending catastrophe controlled my jumpiness, my travel lust, my high-pitched gabbling speech. I must irritate the hell out of these people just as they irritated the hell out of me. Do not be anxious, I wanted suddenly to shout. Give it up! It doesn't matter! It's under control! Hand it over!

It has taken me many years to trust the state of being I found myself in that afternoon, to trust that delectable, heyday euphoria. It always seemed to be followed by some disaster or other as though men and women ought to expect punishment by the Reality Principle for feeling blithe. And the experience itself seemed to me philosophically wrong: if all is universal delight, I thought, then the army is too, and so is cancer, and so is Buchenwald. Be cautious of happiness – this seemed to me a sound approach to the world. And the Gospel injunction – *be not anxious* – was something I knew about only in my head; a little piece of fake knowledge dissolving into false consolation at the next catastrophe.

It did not occur to me then that euphoria may be our natural condition.

When I was seventeen or so I ran for the first time into Franz Kafka's work, which has fascinated and haunted me ever since. There is a story about an explorer visiting an island penal colony and being shown an execution device consisting of a bed and above it a rack of needles. The prisoner is strapped to the bed and a tape with a punched message is fed to the system of needles which tattoos words on his back. Not only on his back, but *all the way through him* as though he were a stick of Brighton rock. This process lasts several hours: the needles jabber back, forth, and sideways, writing their message while the prisoner is ingeniously kept alive. Almost at the end of the ordeal, the explorer is told, a change comes over the victim; he becomes passive and euphoric as though he had suddenly and for the first time understood what the needles were telling him – as though he'd finally 'got the message.' These messages are individualized, so to speak, appropriate to only one victim – such as the words BE JUST appearing on the latest prisoner's body. Perhaps Kafka is saying that to understand something, the entire body must be involved, as though God is trying to print a message on the whole being of each of us: a message that exists for each one of us alone.

Sometimes I feel that BE NOT ANXIOUS are the words designed specifically for me alone – that they are trying to force their way beneath my skin.

The Symbols at your Door

HERE I AM NOW, in 1983, at an Anglican summer camp at a place called Sorrento on Shuswap Lake in the interior of British Columbia and we sang a song last night that twirls around my head and won't leave me. '*I'll sing you green-oh*,' goes the song, '*one is one and all alone and ever more shall be so*.' Two for the lily-white boys; three,

three the rivals; four for the Gospel makers; five for the symbols at your door and six for the six proud walkers. A nonsense song, a series of gnomic utterances, a caster of weird spells. I don't know about these lily-white boys, but doubt if I'm one of them. Nor do I know who the proud walkers are except they form a club so named in the fiction of a thriller writer named Francis Beeding remembered, now, I think, only by old-timers like myself. But I do know about the symbols at your door because they consist of the ordinary world read in a particular kind of way. For instance, there is a beach here where you can swim: bright, glittering water and an almost violent sun. Walking back (proudly) to the camp you cross a boardwalk over a swamp then enter a thick patch of woodland where the path goes steeply uphill. Then, about two hundred yards later, you emerge from the woods out onto the brow of a cliff – a field lies before you, a kitchen garden, then cropped lawns and flower beds. The main building, believe it or not, is called Nova Vita – new life. Scattered trees create a dappled, cool, and gracious landscape. From that water you emerge as from a birth and your journey takes you through darkness to a sort of paradise beyond.

This is a symbol, then, a symbol at the door and your own set of symbols will be like this, but perhaps not as obvious and sometimes, in the lives of a few, certain images, certain patterns will recur.

The lamb of Freshfield Road, for instance. It's been with me, in its many guises all my life. It is a symbol at my door, something that is there all the time, which I have ignored or misinterpreted, and which is the key to my own deeper self, just as the symbols at *your* door, made up of everyday things like lambs, woods, and beaches, are the key to *you*. I think I have become more deeply aware of these everyday things, of their inner meanings, over the last year or so – since Jocelyn's death – and I think it is the process of grief that has made me more conscious of them.

Grief is a Kingdom one enters at irregular intervals and at different depths and, I believe, against one's will, as though some dark arm from that world grabs you by the neck at whim and pulls you in. In this Kingdom the laws are different and the scenery is strange. I fall, for instance, but slowly, as though against nature, very slowly into a spiralling blackness, a pit inconceivably remote and black where no light enters or escapes. A kind of swoon during which the real world of forests, sky, mountains, sunlight, children, angels, laughter and human relationships vanishes and, in the depths of despair, I forget it ever has existed – nothing is real except this black hole – this unutterable darkness. And I will never escape it, never: it is who I am, and where I am for ever, and my grief is totally without consolation – there is no ease, no remedy, nor will there ever be. I come back from this pit – of course – to a world of love, and health, and order, but what I have experienced stays in my memory as a pale shadow of what it is like to be apart, forever separated from those things that make me human and where God is absent, for I call out to God from this black hole but nothing answers and I do not believe He is there.

I think that when we grieve and enter this dark Kingdom we experience a taste of Hell. And it is, in some extraordinary way, good for us – as though we need this journey into the otherwise unimaginable void to make us whole. Nobody would ever choose to make such a voyage, we are fortunate that the tragic events in our lives force us there. Being there, on and off over the last year has slowed me down, reduced my ambition, and increased my delight in the everyday events and landscapes of my life. Through grief we learn to be aware of the slow, steady pulse of the world and of the space and time systems beyond it. Above all we have the time and the slowness to study the symbols placed at our doors and discover the inner meaning of them. Time to understand this garden, a beach, a machine that writes upon your back, a beaten lamb.

'Well,' said Sybil, 'I don't know,' she said, 'I don't know, I'm sure, wot we're going to do after you've gorn back. I don't know why you don't stay over ere, really I don't, what with im out of a job.'

'How many more times,' I said, 'do I have to tell you I'm on a paid research semester? That I haven't lost my job?'

'Nah,' she said. 'Oo are you kidding? If you was to do that over ere your job would be gorn by the time you wanted it back. I don't believe you'll ave that job ... goes right against the grain of things, that does.'

'God, Mother, you are so completely stupid sometimes.'

'You ain't lived as long as I ave ...'

'I can't wait,' I said, 'to get the hell out of here.' I got up and went to the window, which opened out, in its minimalist way, onto High Worple. I'd certainly had enough, and Jocelyn and I had begun to count our remaining weeks and days in England, much as one does in prison or the army. I thought of friends and colleagues and the work that was waiting for me to do and I felt a surge of delight and longing. What were we doing here among these venomous, empty prattlers?

'Ark at *im* talk? Oo does e think e is, I wonder? Jossy, ow you going to live over there? I ope you aven't given up *your* job, what with all the money you've been spendin over ere ... spendin money like water, you ave ...'

'That's not your business ...'

'You're my daughter,' Sybil said. 'Corse it's my business.'

'Ere,' Stan coughed, rather feebly, from the depth of the morning paper. 'Less not ave no arguments.'

'Neither of you have any right to tell me how to spend my own money,' Jocelyn said, 'even though you've done just that in the past.'

'Done wot, might I ask?'

'I remember,' Jocelyn said, and her voice rose a notch and became a fraction louder so that I turned with a feeling of trepidation from my view of the spring rain splashing down the gutters in the front. 'I remember when Daddy beat me up for taking my own money.'

'*Woss* this?' Stan said. '*Woss* this?'

'I was at school and they used to have a tuck shop,' Jocelyn said loudly, her voice trembling with tears. 'A tuck shop where we could buy cakes and doughnuts ... and they were a penny each and you'd only let me have threepence a week so Thursday and Friday I had to do without ... and all my friends used to go to the shop at break ... and buy a doughnut, or a cake ... and they'd ask me to go with them

... and I'd have to say I didn't want to ... that I wasn't hungry ... I ... I ... got to a point one day when I didn't want to do that any more ... to feel any more left out ... any more left out than I felt already ... and at home ... what with you and Daddy ... and so I broke into my piggy bank where I'd been saving the penny a week you gave me for that ... I broke it open and took a penny out for this doughnut ... and you came in and caught me and told Daddy and he came in with a strap and put me over his knee and beat me ... he beat me until I thought he'd never stop ...'

'Wot?' Stan said. 'I don't remember any of this.'

'He did ... he did ... he beat me, I remember his face all red and him shouting ... thief! he was shouting ... thief ... dirty little thief ... and all the time hitting me ... I thought he'd kill me ... and IT WAS MY MONEY ... all the time it was my money ... I'd saved it ... and it was mine ... and you called me a thief.'

Jocelyn wailed with a grief I had not heard before and began to sob as though, and now I know this feeling, as though she could never be consoled. But it is only now that I can cry with her: at her innocence, her longing for acceptance, at the savage injustice levelled at a lonely and trusting child.

II. It would be absurd to say that our time in England had fled quickly; individual days seemed pathetically short; yet taken together they formed a lagging of three months – long as any prison term. My mother kept an accurate account of time on our behalf ... we hadn't been in England a week before she started telling us how little time we had left. This was in character as I remembered it, for any outing during my childhood was coloured by her fear that we'd miss the bus or train home. Towards the end she spoke of little else but our imminent departure. It must have puzzled her considerably that They were keeping her in hospital for such a long time for so minor an operation. Since my visits to her were confined to hospital visiting hours she pleaded with her doctors to let her out. Finally they did so, for they knew it made no difference.

'She'll grow weaker,' one of the interns told me. 'Until she won't be able to do anything herself at all ... then we'll have to get her into a nursing home ... if we can find a vacancy, that is ... such a pity, though, isn't it? She's looking forward so much to getting out of hospital and recovering in the sunshine.'

So my mother came back to Freshfield Road in some sort of hospital vehicle and we visited her just after she returned. Her face had grown sunken and drawn, and the flesh around the temples had vanished and the stretched skin there had grown mottled – a yellowish brown. They'd given her drugs to keep down the almost incessant pain.

I cursed the butcher of a surgeon who had inflicted upon her that pointless, graunching operation back in the winter.

Since we could not take her for walks any more, nor to tea-shops, nor round the Lanes, we stayed in her room with our coats on and talked about the past. During this period she expressed her almost constant anxiety about Jill's projected visit to her in the summer, about whether her health would be sufficiently recovered by then. And I noticed something else about her ... one very curious change ... she was trying very hard to be charitable to her enemies.

'Looking back on it now,' she said, 'I can see I was much too demanding in Montreal ... I suppose I could have made more of an effort to get on with your friends ... even that little vixen, Aviva, downstairs ... proper little monkey *she* was ... as for *that man* ... vile though he was, I knew it wasn't altogether his fault ... mother drunk most of the time ... and that business you and he were involved in ... that he messed up ... it must've been a terrible shock to him.'

'What business?'

'That business with the prospector.'

Since I'd ceased confiding in my mother at the age of sixteen or so, I'd not realized that she knew anything whatsoever about Arthur Turner. There was no reason why she shouldn't, except it would have made things awkward at the time ... she would have made my sister's life a misery until I'd promised to have nothing to do with him.

'That business with the prospector,' I said. 'Was no fault of Jerome's. He pursued the bugger up and down England for several months. Persistence ...'

'I don't believe it,' my mother said. 'And in any case, that's not what counts ... its *politeness* that counts,' she said, her eyes beginning to flash. '*Politeness* ... plain, ordinary, common or garden civility.'

She thought about it, then forgave him in her fashion. 'It's all over with,' she said. 'Thank God I'll never clap eyes on him again.'

As at High Worple I stood and walked to the windows. The sky had darkened but the wind had dropped and it seemed a shade warmer. I could hear the voices of children playing in the street. A man strode past on his way to the pub, puffing at his Woodbine. Six p.m. Opening time. Not much more of *this* ... spring was here, not the false spring that reverted to winter a month or so back, but a genuine, unhesitating, upward swing of the sun. Summer was on its way. Time to travel again ... to get out.

I sensed an uneasy gap in the conversation behind me and turned from the window in order to bridge it. My mother was staring at me almost in horror.

'I'm going to tell you about it,' she said. 'I want to tell you about that Hayman business ... you've a right to know ...'

'Forget it,' I said uneasily. 'I don't need to hear it.'

Jocelyn frowned at me. 'If she wants to talk about it,' she said, 'let her. What's the matter with you?'

'It's a long story,' my mother said. 'And it's no one's fault ... it was a *miscarriage of justice* ... that's just what one of your father's friends called it ... no one's fault, that is, that's still alive.

'I was married before,' she continued, 'you know that, of course ... I was eighteen when I met him ... and he was a good deal older than me. I didn't know the world then ... I was green, didn't know what people are really like. I know now, and it didn't take me long to find out.

'The only man I've ever really loved got killed in the war. I met this other one in Folkestone, just after Harold was gassed in France. That's right, my dear, gassed ... that's how he died ... in Flanders. There were plenty of other women in the same boat ... but knowing that didn't help ... so I married Jack Hayman ... big and handsome man ... I thought I was in love with him. We got married and rented a place in Folkestone ... we settled in ... he had a job in a printing shop.'

My mother seemed much calmer now. For the first time she began to talk to us as though we weren't children, and she sounded more real – for perhaps half an hour she spoke without malice, scolding, twisting, or manipulating.

'We hadn't been married more than a month,' she said, 'when I found out he was an alcoholic. Usually he stayed home in the evenings, at least for the first few months ... but one night he came in late from work, staggered in through the door and passed out in an easy chair ... white as a ghost, he was, face all pinched, shivering and gasping. Every now and then he let out these terrible cries. I was scared out of my wits ... I thought he was dying. It wasn't until I got close to him that I realised what it was I could smell as soon as he walked in through the door ... when he came to a bit I gave him some strong tea to sober him up ... just so's he could get to bed. But the next day it happened again.

'I'm not going into details, my dears. You can imagine the rest. As he grew worse and worse we ran out of money and he lost his job – his personality was changing ... he'd go into such terrible frenzies when he'd punch out at anything that stood in his way, me included. He got another job and lost it within a week. We moved out of Folkestone to London, but nothing helped him ... it went on like that for over five years.

'Finally I left him,' she said, somewhat defiantly. 'What else was there to do? Your grandmother knows the way the world turns ... you get out of that, she said to me. Get out and let him go to hell. Well, your grandmother should know ... she'd had the five of us children ... all brought up in the workhouse ...'

'What's this?' I said. 'What's this? Workhouse? I didn't know about any workhouse.'

'I told you that,' she said. 'Years ago. Our father was a businessman in Brighton who was already married to a woman who went mad ... no divorce in those days, my dear, and you couldn't just live with a woman openly ... not if you wanted to keep your standing. And he was quite poor ... so it was the workhouse for us ... all of us born to an unmarried woman ... but that's another story ...'

'Wait,' I said. 'What with you, and Aunt Vi, and Aunt Lil ... John and Edwin ... you mean to say you all lived in the workhouse ...'

'For ten years,' she said, 'on and off ...'

'All bastards,' I said. 'What with you lot and David ... our family's as full of bastards as a Shakespeare play. I didn't know any of this ...'

'Anyway, I left him,' she continued. 'And I can't tell you what a relief it was. It was like being born all over again ... I worked in London ... sewing for Bourne and Hollingsworth ... and lived in digs ... I lost touch with Jack completely.

'Then when I met your father I began to live with him ... there was no question of us getting married ... but I took his name and neither of us thought much more about it. In fact we were very happy ... your father was doing well ... his relatives ... all the Battersea crowd ... were nice enough to me ... at first ... and to my face ... it wasn't until your father and I had been together for a year that I got to know them from their other side ... it went on like that until I got pregnant ...

'Well, I'm not ashamed of anything ... I don't care what anybody thinks ... I wasn't ever going to go back to Jack Hayman ... I don't care what the rules of the Game are ... and your father was very good to me in those days ... but when I got pregnant it was a different matter ... they told me that the way I was built together with the way the baby was lying I'd probably have to have a Caesarean ... and that I'd have to go to hospital ...

'It's not like it is over there in Canada ... people have their babies at home in England ... in those days they did ... hospital was a rare thing ... but I didn't give it much thought ... when the time came to go into hospital I trooped through the door with my suitcase and sat down in the admitting office ... they asked me my name and like a fool I told them – Mrs. Mills ... that was the end of it, my dears, for the next thing they asked me for was my wedding licence ...'

'They asked for *what?*'

'Hospitals,' she said bitterly, 'wouldn't accept a pregnant woman in those days unless she had a marriage certificate ... if she hadn't got one, out she'd have to go ... out onto the street. Well, I didn't have a marriage licence in the name of Mills ... I've never felt so ashamed ... I turned tail and ran out of there ... with those chits of nurses giggling at me behind my back. So I went to another hospital under the name of Hayman ... that was all right ... I could prove I was still married to *him* ...

'Well, there wasn't anything I could do about it ... that's what hospitals were like ... so the name of Hayman went on Jill's birth certificate ... I regret only the inconvenience it caused her ... it was a *miscarriage of justice*, that's what it was ... if he'd've died and I was married again, no one would have had anything to say ... but he was dead to me ...

'You live respectably,' she said, 'trying to make your own life, and they treat you as thought you were a slut.

'But Jack showed up again ... he found out where we were living and he tried to get money out of your father ... he was living in a room in the worst slum I've ever seen ... your father went round there, several times, and tried to make him leave us alone ... we asked him to consent to a divorce ... he just laughed at us and told us to go to hell ... luckily for everybody he died of pneumonia just a couple of years after you were born.'

'So my name's Hayman, too,' I said.

'No, dear, you were born at home ... and in any case as soon as he was safely in the ground your father and I got married. I never told Jill about any of this and I hope you never do. I can't bear the thought of her despising me ...'

'You should know Jill better than that.'

'You don't understand,' she said. 'Girls are different ... they have quite a different attitude towards their mothers than boys ... and particularly when she was younger ... she was so loving ... respected me so much ... her whole world would've collapsed ... and then when she was older I could never find the right moment ... she was so critical ... and perhaps I pushed her too much ... I was so terrified she would get herself into the sort of mess I'd got into ... and Granny ... one mistake ... and your life's gone ... I was so worried about her.

'No,' she said, 'if there'd been any justice I could have divorced him ... but he never went with other women and the laws were different then ... it was a miscarriage of justice, that is what it was ... a miscarriage of justice ... it was that generation ... the whole generation ... they'd play cat and mouse with you ... kick you when you were down ... that whole generation, my parents, and their parents ... rotten and hypocritical to the core ... nowadays some dirty little tart can have one baby after another each from a different man and no questions asked ... and the Government'll pay for it ... *through the nose* ... they've gone to the other extreme, nowadays, if you ask me.'

A piggy bank and a workhouse. Perhaps a bastard. Or half a dozen of them, I thought, stretching back into the past, row after row of them ... all scrabbling, grappling, and coping. Claiming their inheritance. Whatever that was. It certainly explained my mother's persecution of Jill and, though the old lady had sworn me to silence on the grounds that Jill would not visit her in the summer should she know the truth, it was clear to me that I must tell her – as soon as I got back to Montreal. It was the only clue we'd ever had that made sense of my mother's behaviour.

III. One of the ways I remember my father is as a man of catchphrases. 'What's the time?' someone might ask him. Slowly he would pull out his pocket watch, consult, and, '*It's three o'clock*,' he'd answer. '*And still no word from Nancy*.' This used to baffle and delight me. It seemed to plunge me into the world of Romance and Enigma, contiguous with my own and just as real, entered only through the language of the absurd. Who is this Nancy? I remember thinking. Some prodigal daughter, perhaps, or a straying wife, or a cook gone to the market to buy a chicken and never hide nor hair seen of her again. A figure out of Victorian melodrama. I would not have dreamed of checking her identity with my father for fear of receiving some banal reply. There were few questions that would get a straight answer. 'How much does it cost?' I might ask him. 'Money,' he'd say. 'Money and fair words.' Once, when quite young and innocent, I asked him if there was, in fact, a place called Brighton.

'Why,' he said, delighted to find a sucker. 'It's over the bridge. "Over the bridge! Over the bridge! Over the bridge to Brighton!" "But, porter, I've got a tin chest!" "I don't care whether you've got a copper bottom, it's *over the bridge to Brighton*!"' This was done in gruff Cockney for the porter, and falsetto upper class for the encumbered lady. That contiguous world was outside reason and logic, but somehow it was a *better* world, containing as it did event-particle and high drama.

Catch-phrases are part of English folk comedy, the music hall tradition. I think immediately of the Tommy Handley radio show called ITMA, a morale booster during the war, which was composed almost entirely of them ... *can I do you now, sir? ... it's being so cheerful that keeps me going ... don't forget the diver* ... repeated week after week in endless permutations and they'd be taken up by school-child, matron, black-market spiv with his slouch hat, retired colonel, face beaming with apoplexy, bus conductor, munitions workers, etc., in a great, linking, democratic delight in the absurd. Truly a people's war.

My father must have known what English cement ultimately binds the classes together. 'Goodbye,' he'd say to a Cambridge don at Caius College, which sponsored the Battersea youth club. 'Goodbye, *and thank your mother for the rabbits*.' Or he'd tell Sir William Elderton, another sponsor, an insurance magnate, that it was *over the bridge to Brighton*. *Still no word from Nancy*, he'd advise the Vicar of Battersea, if it were getting late and somebody wanted to know the time. People seemed to like him for these routines with which he must have found it easy to gain their confidence. Not only that, he spoke two languages: glottal cockney to the men he worked with and to strangers of London origin, while to his friends, and he had many, in the middle and upper classes he would, unless he saw fit to entertain them with ethnic wit, speak a slightly more received version of English. He was always, however, recognizable as a Londoner, but a Londoner well read, knowledgeable, and able to move around among all condition of people with an ease many of us envied. Part of this ease came from his profession (which, while I think of it, has its own lovely jargon: you Body In, you Fatten Up, you Rub your Work with a Pounce Bag). It moved him in exalted circles where he would regale his audiences with splinters from his alter ego: theories on Fielding, the sonnets of Shakespeare, and the politics of his day (then the Conservative Party variety, which stood for a tacit support of Hitler against the Soviet Union, an exaggerated respect for the social programmes of Mussolini, and a sneaking sympathy for Oswald Mosley and the British Union of Fascists).

Lines, routines, catch-phrases, war memories and ballads, the lot – all dead – all gone. The Grim Reaper came for him on Boxing Day, 1944, whilst he was playing an ill-advised game of soccer. There he stood, between two goal posts, slightly overweight, hoarse from smoking too much, a little breathless from lungs somewhat damaged by World War I gas attacks, feet gnarled and phlebitic from the trench warfare of that futile combat, hung over from what black market liquor he'd been able to scrounge for his last Christmas party the night before, unexercised and full of rage – at my mother, his lack of success, his lost opportunities, his growing entrapment. He kicked the ball a couple of times, so I heard, then clutched his chest and keeled over as the Reaper kicked him back. Down there at Freshfield Road where a cavalier attitude towards death seems the most advisable, I recall a song he used to sing that strikes me as appropriate:

> Gaily the troubadour waltzed around the water-butt
> Singing: 'Oh, my truelove, come, oh come to me.'
> Suddenly a brickbat hit him on the coconut
> And never again will he sing his melody.

I wasn't there, of course. The unequal battle between him and the Reaper took place on Clapham Common and in the form of a match between the Home Guard, in which my father was a part-time warrior, and a detachment of army cadets. The weather was extraordinary over that Christmas, for a snowstorm had covered the land, melted, then frozen rapidly again so that branches of trees, twigs, wires, grass-blades, hydrangea stems, gutters, pylons, fences, and pipes were set in ice like transparent aspic. We wandered in it, amazed. Then a knock on the door as we sat down to lunch, used to the old man's absences, and not caring to wait for him. I answered it: a young, pink policeman with the beginnings of a moustache greyed with frozen breath. He asked for my mother and I knew, with an intense feeling of horror and despair, what was up and I knew the world would never be the same again. The copper urged my mother to go to the hospital and there was a long period of waiting in anguish whilst she went to verify. For her, this was the beginning of a new and exciting era – a kind of heyday.

IV. I am thinking now of Gogol and his story 'The Nose'. It's about a man who wakes up one morning to find his nose has vanished from his face. He searches for it everywhere, even puts an advertisement in the paper, then runs into it on the street: it is dressed in the uniform of a senior member of the Russian diplomatic corps. At the story's end the nose returns to him and all is well. Gogol himself had a long nose; it was said to be so long, so sensitively tipped, that he would strike his own chin with it. There are, in his stories, many references to noses – the lengths of them, the pimples to which they are prone, the hairs that in certain cases sprout from them. The subject *nose* recurs throughout Gogol's work like a comic continuo against which he constructs his main themes. As he lay dying, starving himself to death, the doctors round his bedside attempted to cure his melancholia by applying the classical remedy of leeches. 'And where,' you may well ask, 'did they apply these leeches?' To the most visible, the most sensitive part of him, the focus of his own waking attention and his nightmares and the core, it might be said, of his creative personality. And so he died, shouting with horror, a cluster of these vile animals sucking at his nose.

I tell you this not to make your flesh creep, but to illustrate the fact that there are symbols in our lives powerful enough to bring about their own actualization. So it is with the image of the lamb – the Beaten Lamb of Freshfield Road. It is a symbol at my door that suddenly became tangible, whose origin I was at last able to trace.

What follows is an account of this pursuit – the tracking down of my own personal emblem – and I will begin with an event that occurred a year or so after Jocelyn and I returned to England.

We were lying in bed, snug and mellow, thinking positively about our future together. We loved one another, had been married seven years, and had weathered, or so it seemed, not only that bad visit to our homeland, but something I thought at the time far more terrible.

'It's just as well,' she said. 'I don't think we were cut out to be parents.'

'Too set in our ways.'

'Too old, maybe.'

'After all, we're thirty-seven.'

'Thirty-seven!'

'A bit too old to start being parents.'

'That's what I think.'

'I think so, too,'

'Yes ... it's a pity, though,'

'It's a pity ... but we're getting a little long in the tooth.'

At this period we were living in an apartment in the Kitsilano district of Vancouver. Wood panels, fireplace, stained-glass door. Our cat, a beautiful, soft-eyed Persian tabby cat called Dulcinea had, just before Jocelyn went into hospital, given birth to three kittens – blind, ears-infolded, tottering, sucking, nuzzle, and fluff. We could hear them in the back of the cupboard their mother had chosen for them, scrabbling and mewing feebly. It was very peaceful and, at times, like this, we could recapture the dearness of our early time together: the first snowfall in Montreal, the cabin we rented one winter at Val Morin, in the Laurentian mountains, the sweet inns of that country with their blazing log fires, the ski hills, almost deserted in those days, and the little restaurant where we would eat supper once or twice a week. We could relive that feeling and also the closeness and inwardness of our student days in Vancouver.

'We'd make lousy parents,' Jocelyn said.

'Oh, I don't know. But I think it's just as well.'

'If she'd lived ... we'd've devoted our lives to rearing a hopeless cripple ... condemned to constant surgery ... strapped to splints and special beds ... always in pain ... I've seen so much of that.'

(Jocelyn had spent some time as an orthopedic nurse at the Great Ormond Street Children's Hospital.)

'I could do it, I suppose, if I were younger,' said Jocelyn.

'Yes.'

'Younger, and less selfish.'

'I don't know about that.'

'I do. *You're* selfish ... and stubborn. And I'm too neurotic.'

'Uh-uh,' I said, thinking *here it comes*. Her voice had grown that sudden harsh edge.

'I think what with one thing and another it all happened for the best.'

'It's not often I like the phrase,' I said. 'But I think it's true of us.'

'God, I never, *ever*, want to go through all that agony again.'

'I'm sorry I didn't take it seriously. But then neither did the doctor.'

'*What did* HE *know?*'

'Precious little, as it turned out.'

'That's the story of my life ... nobody listens to me ... *nobody thinks I'm important*.'

'Jocelyn, for Christ's sake, that isn't true. It's that you seem to over-react to everyday things so that when something really goes wrong nobody quite believes you. It's like the boy who cried wolf.'

'*Cried wolf* ... that's what you all think of me.'

'I'm sorry that I didn't take you seriously ... what more can I say?'

'You can't even apologize properly.'

To this there seemed no appropriate reply. We both, in our isolations, drifted off to sleep.

This baby we spoke of arrived five weeks prematurely and it was true that Jocelyn had complained of a great deal of pain. Many of us thought she complained needlessly about what was after all a commonplace experience and this, I have to say, was not a male-medical-establishment view but that of our women friends, from whom the men in her life took their cue. The baby, a girl, was born with multiple deformities: one leg twisted, an arm shorter than the other, an oesophagus unconnected to the stomach. She was trisomic – a chromosome deformity – and she lived a scant twenty-four hours in an intensive care unit. There was nothing to be done: the pediatrician thought that heroic measures, as he called them, were inappropriate, and we agreed. Most babies of this sort don't get born at all. Jocelyn, during this period, was distraught with grief and horror. Not only was this the end of our fantasies of parenthood, but her experience with sick children made her aware of the pain in store for this daughter should she survive and, more than that, the pain and agony for us. So when the baby died we felt a tremendous relief as though, sentenced to years of torment, we had been reprieved. Yet behind that euphoria lay grief – like an amorphous, treacherous animal, awaiting his time. That day, though, I walked home from the hospital with a light enough heart. The ordeal seemed over.

Next morning, quite early, an efficient female voice from the hospital's laboratory told me on the phone that she and her colleagues wanted to do research work on my daughter's body to investigate this abnormality. I agreed without hesitation. 'Ah,' she said, 'but you have to sign a form, a document giving us your permission.' I said I'd drop down there on my way to visiting Jocelyn, and did so. Jocelyn was in good shape that day – we talked gaily about the future and made twenty or thirty plans. Nightmares had been raised and then, by this fortuitous death, dispelled. (It was not until a long while afterwards that I allowed myself to face the pathos of our daughter's short, doomed life, nor could I at that time think of her as anything other than the cause of her mother's pain. Thus I evaded the fact that the pregnancy, the birth, had been a total disaster, and neither of us could acknowledge it. So I missed the chance of sitting with Jocelyn, holding her in my arms, rocking her back and forth, and howling out my anguish. Had I been able to do this, our lives would've been very different.)

So I said nothing about the research project; in my stupidity I felt that she might be too tender to speak of such matters, thus I protected her. One consequence of this paternalistic act followed immediately. The same woman phoned me next day and asked me to come down and sign a paper.

'*I've already done it*,' I said.

'What you signed for,' she said, 'was an arm. Now we would like to work on an eye. *Will you come and sign for an eye?*'

It is a measure of my own lack of consciousness during this period that I did as I was told. I must have thought it a nuisance but that I should go through with it for the sake of science.

Next day, early, the woman asked me to sign for a hand. Cursing the inconvenience of it, but nothing more, I did so.

I heard nothing for a week. Then the voice asked me to dispose of the body. This time I finally reacted. 'You've been cutting that baby up,' I protested, 'and now you're asking me to take away the remains.'

'Yes,' she said, her own voice rising, '*and that's the law*.'

I felt both powerless and victimized. But I went to the funeral home near the hospital and told the functionary, a fat, horn-rimmed, dark-suited little man from whose discreet manner the aggression of a Bible salesman struggled to escape, that I did not want to see the baby, that I had not seen her while she lay in intensive care, for that (to my present regret) was something I felt I couldn't face. The salesman said he would arrange it, take care of things, bury her somewhere and I need have nothing to do with it.

'It'll cost you thirty dollars, Mr. Mills,' he said, 'and I'm afraid we must ask for the money in advance. And in cash, if you please. Sometimes in cases like this we're left holding the ...'

'Yes, yes,' I said. 'I'll bring you cash tomorrow.'

A short time afterwards I started writing a novel. I'd written two before – based, as first novels usually are, on my own immediate experience. One was about a young man travelling and working in Europe, the second about a young immigrant to Canada working in the Ontario bush. Neither was published; neither, indeed, deserves to be published, though there are good things in both, particularly the latter. In the past I have raided these manuscripts and cannibalized them. *The Land of Is*, though, my third attempt, was based on my own experience only in the sense that I used for it a locale with which I was familiar – Vancouver – and on sexual fantasies, not necessarily my own, but which I knew about from my reading or from conversations with friends and men and women in pubs. I intended it, quite cynically, as a pornographic novel whose purpose was to make me rich. I studied the classic works in the genre – *Justine*, for instance, and *The Story of O* – and found myself bored by their grandiosity, pretentiousness, and lack of wit. I turned with some relief to the case histories of Krafft-Ebing, but these seemed even duller, or rather, since the cases themselves are very often hilarious what dulls is their compiler's absence of the comic spirit. When I began work on *The Land of Is*, then, I realized two things: first, pornographers are both serious and humourless, and secondly, though I may be without much humour myself, I possess more than they. The novel began to turn into a satire of my pornographic models, then to a satire of other things as well. It was published and received good reviews. It made me no money, but it remains a highly original (I believe) satirical novel and above all, a *funny* book.

There is one section, though, that is not funny at all. A character named Scheisshausen, an officer in the German army, is captured during World War II by Yugoslav partisans who torture him by suspending him over a slow fire while some systematically hack parts off him, others plug appropriate orifices of his body with unspeakable objects. It is a harrowing passage and many readers found it out of kilter with the tone of the rest. 'What's it doing there?' my friends asked. 'What's it all about? *It sticks out*,' they said, '*like a syphilitic sore*.'

The image bothered me, too. I remember the feeling of great pleasure experienced during the writing of it, but no more nor less than in working on the rest. I wrote the novel in about six weeks and knew, for the most part, that sense familiar to everybody who writes regularly, of being taken over, of becoming an amanuensis. The writer becomes a delighted observer or his or her own facility, as though it were that of a beloved friend. (Of course, when writers approach their desks in the expectation that the same thing is about to happen, they discover they cannot take their temporary gifts for granted.) So the writing of *Is* was a joyous experience for me, and the Scheisshausen episode emerged with the same ease and feeling of rightness as the rest of it. It was only later, when I puzzled over the book myself, the Muse, so to speak, fled, that I realized that the passage was more than likely a nightmare based on the systematic butchering and flaying of my own child.

For some reason I was shocked by this revelation, even though the hospital scissions and luxations seemed obvious sources for the Scheisshausen image. I'm used, as an English teacher, to deciphering a text and I ought to have recognized its provenance long before. What shocked me, though, was that I had not realized the extent to which my daughter's death and subsequent mutilation had so firmly reached into the entrails of my psyche. Conventional wisdom suggested that was a natural consequence of an unhealthy turning inward. It was true that I was not able to talk to Jocelyn about what happened with the research team until long after the event and long after I'd written *The Land of Is*, and my friends of the time were not able to deal with any discussion of the business. Indeed, they recoiled in horror and insisted I be taken 'out of myself' with discussions of an intellectual and impersonal nature: the latest film with writing on it, for instance, or the novels of Anthony Powell, or the poetry of Charles Olson, or some other distraction. And I did not challenge these friends, for it seemed obvious that this was how civilized relations were maintained and this was what civilized people did – keep their griefs and nightmares strictly private and under control and instead speak of whatever enthusiasm they can drum up about the structure of wit in the films of Jean-Luc Godard, or the distinctions to be made between *langue* and *parole*, or between signifier and sign, or other mind-fucking, garbage-pullulating pastimes of a similar nature. Thus it was that I explained away part of my own book: an event in my own life had created it – it had appeared in my writings strategically altered and distanced, and I was pleased because it was a way of demonstrating to myself that I hadn't, because of my profession, become too literary. I hadn't, after all, been influenced in my work on this novel by the writings of Thomas Nashe, whose delightful prose poems I had been 'teaching' that year.

v. But our abortive attempt at parenthood was only one passage, dark though it was, in the eight years following my mother's death. We were much caught up in work, travel, and projects. I became a novelist and teacher, Jocelyn a designer – first of dresses, then of landscapes, then of the interior of houses. Her energy in each of these activities, all of which she chose to perceive as meaningless, lasted just long enough to create a success she found puzzling and unacceptable. The decision against having our own children was an easy, though perhaps uncourageous, one to take and we were tempted to adopt children only once – in Mexico where we were almost seduced by the mysterious, solemn-eyed children of the Oaxaca country we lived in, and we drove back to Canada just in time. During those years Jocelyn moved in and out of depressions of increasing intensity which left me anguished, bemused, and guilty. Nevertheless, I believe those years were good ones.

In 1974 we thought we had acquired the detachment to take a holiday in England and enjoy the place free from the joyless and strait-jacketing obligations concerning relatives. Accordingly we trusted to a kind fate to prevent us running into one of them on the street: fate smiled and, during the few weeks we were there, hiking around the Cotswolds, the Brecon Beacons, the Yorkshire coast, we recaptured some of the closeness of our golden age when, as we used to think of it, we were young together. I arrived in England first for a week alone : to hike strenuously along the South Downs, haunt of my youth, and to visit old friends.

I started off in Eastbourne, walked up onto Beachy Head and across the Seven Sisters – green turf, chalk cliffs, air like cocaine, into Jevington and Alfriston, to Lewes and an ancient inn. The next day to the Devil's Dyke above Brighton, and the path along the hill top that runs parallel to the magical road that winds through Poynings, Fulking, Edgburton.

It was a Saturday afternoon, the beginning of May, cool and clear, few people about on the footpaths, hawthorn in blossom, tall trees and shrubs of it tossed about by the breeze from the hillcrest, chestnut trees nodding in valleys, cow-parsley and buttercup bordered the deep lanes through the chalky soil, and gorse blazed on the lea slopes. From up here I saw three miniature cricket matches far below, on the green of each village with its Anglo-Saxon name – of Edgburton, Fulking, Poynings – those little settlements along the spring-line. White, sedate figures engrossed in their silent games and beyond them the Weald, dark with oak and ash and noisy, as you walk through it, with lambs and cattle and I knew that each field, each wood, each cottage, retained its life only by a profound and deepening struggle between those who wished to preserve them and the highway builders, housing estate sharks, town and village councils frantic for tax revenue who wished to bulldoze them, and cover them with asphalt and concrete shopping malls. Sadness at the temporariness of the landscape before me made me aware of unfinished business of my own and I walked, on impulse, down a path that led to a place I knew where I could catch a bus to Brighton.

An hour later I was there, on the sea front, among a mere sprinkling of raw cockney accents down for the day under the hot spring sun and cool sea air, among the aromas of fried fish, whelk stalls, rotting seaweed and drying nets, and my own griefs and feelings of guilt. Flights of steps lead every hundred yards or so onto the famous beach, a long, wide, steeply shelving stretch of shingle. The sea here curls onto the land and pulls back, rattling its stones. I felt myself slip back in time eight years and visualized helping my mother across the street by the aquarium, making sure she didn't slip on the patches of thin ice, pottering along the sea front with the wind against us and turning, with relief, onto the pier with its slot machines and pin-ball games. I felt her presence at my side and I began to live again, this time more fully, that morning I helped her down from the double-decker bus that pulls up outside the station. Slowly, for she could do little more than shuffle, we walked to the counter where I bought a ticket to London. There was a moment, blessedly short, when we stood at the platform entrance.

'Well,' I said. 'Take care of yourself. You'll be feeling better soon ... as soon as the summer comes.'

'Yes.'

'And Jill's coming over.'

'Yes ... oh, I do so hope I can hang on for that ...'

'*Of course you will.* Well, I'd ...'

'You'd better ...'

'Yes, I'd better be getting on the train.'

'*Goodbye, John.*'

'Goodbye. I'll try to get back next year.

'John ... *I hope you have a happy life* ... you and Jocelyn.'

'We'll do our best. I'm glad we've had this time together.'

She nodded and began to cry. I hugged her as though to reassure her, and jumped onto the train just as the guard's whistle began to blow.

I sank back onto the cushions with an awareness that we had seen one another for the last time, that I knew it, that she knew it, that I had evaded the moment, and that all I could feel was a tremendous relief.

I remembered that vividly, and my stay at Freshfield Road, the bleakness, the poverty, the copper kettle and the window I didn't bang. I remembered the photographs – *My Picture Book of Soldiers* – and the tormented Larry-the-Lamb. It struck me with the force of an epiphany that the torture scene in my novel not only had to do with my daughter, but also with my mother. The novel's episode somehow described perfectly her experience under the knife, and my own horror at it exorcised in the image of a German soldier being systematically taken apart as though he were a mechanical object.

This concatenation of images, bewildering yet so obvious, released something in me and I began to grieve. Walking along the beach, deserted but for me and a few well-scattered early sunbathers, the tears streaming from my eyes, I was able to grieve for my child, after all those years, and for the first time for my mother – for the torments in her life, and for her lonely death.

VI. And so, it seemed, the matter rested.

During the next few years, as my marriage began to deteriorate, it became increasingly clear that this journey to England was, for Jocelyn, a kind of psychic turning point. It had put her in touch with her own isolation, her parents' attitude of combined hostility and will to dominate. She never, on this visit to the land of her tormented childhood, nor on an even more disastrous one in 1976, ten years later, succeeded in effecting a reconciliation with them. So her life became darker and more perplexed, and my own, as I fought with her depressions and my growing inability to cope with them, more fragmented and painful. Both of us knew that our relationship had grown mutually destructive and we separated in the spring of 1981. But all this, together with Jocelyn's death by suicide, is part of a different story and one I doubt my ability ever to tell.

But a few months before our separation, Jocelyn became a patient at a branch of the University hospital called Day House where a version of psychotherapy was practised: the patients attended by day, worked together on projects, fed themselves and cleaned up, wrote their autobiographies and, in groups, discussed their own and other people's past and present behaviours. One evening a week they would each bring a guest who would sit in their circle and join in. On the first of these I attended I was asked to speak a few words about Jocelyn and me and, to my very great surprise, I found myself describing the death and mutilation of our child with all the original, though in those days well concealed, emotion so strongly present that I had to leave the room.

So I knew it was time to grapple once more with this part of my life, for its power to affect me both deeply and savagely had not diminished in fourteen years. I talked about it to friends of sufficient emotional stamina, to a psychiatrist, to priests, but nothing I said or heard seemed to engage the problem, nor did my feeling of agitation diminish. Yet as Jocelyn and I began to reach our decision to separate and new people came into my life I made contact, through a long chain of coincidence, with someone able to help me.

I have no wish to say much about the technique I was introduced to except that it is practised by a variety of therapists, even those of the utmost intellectual respectability. It involves a sort of self-hypnotism whereby you lie on your back, relaxed, breathing rhythmically, and letting your mind race until it begins to focus on whatever problem you wish to confront. You need someone by your side to make sure your breathing remains regular and that you don't fall asleep. Catch your breath in immediately after exhaling and immediately begin to inhale. Your body may start to tingle; you may go into a panic thinking thoughts like *here am I, fifty, old enough to know better than to fool around with hyperventilating New Age therapies of doubtful origin and this tingling is the coronary that hits men about this time of their lives and here you are adrenalizing yourself into a heart attack.* But the tingling, suffusing your whole body like St. Elmo's fire, passes and leaves you with a peaceful, mellow emptiness.

I am in the garden, for instance, at Yately and I see my father's friends, Mr. and Mrs. Tubb – big, amiable, slow people – and the antirrhinum, stock, and cornflowers. Rabbits munch softly in their hutches ... I am alone, though, walking slowly past the cottage, past a little stream, past fruit trees and gardens hidden behind valerian-covered walls ... past a pond bordered by the soft brown spikes of bulrushes ... and I'm in Yately village ... almost, in those days, an archetypal place ... eighteenth and early nineteenth century cottages, a Victorian villa or two ... a village green and a pub – called the Dog and Partridge ... a greengrocer named Tice whose shop was a drowsy, sweet-smelling place filled with obsolete bottles and decorative biscuit tins and where a white-smocked assistant would belabour a pound of butter with wooden paddles to shape it, then mark it with a seal. Then, off the road, there was a splash of small farms and dairies, and council houses and a tiny school where, that first year of the war, I became a pupil. And so my mind went back into memory ... into that era and texture I share only now with Jill so that when we die the unique *Yateliness* of things – a feel of light and shade, greenness, blackberry bushes and wild, wet-smelling privet hedges, and the deep silences where you hear the flapping of a crow's wing two fields away, and the other field where my father's boys' club had its summer camp ... a long black army hut, a sprinkling of tents ... a marquee ... all that will have gone forever.

And here it was that the Battersea boys congregated for two or three weeks in the summers, carrying on, in raucous, good-humoured dialect, the feuds and brotherhoods of the streets, as though totally unaffected by the dramatic change in scenery they had just experienced.

That last summer of the war ... flying bombs like daggers drawing straight, inexorable cuts across the reddish gold evening skies. And then the rains came and the fields became waterlogged like paddy fields in the monsoons ... mothers arrived to escape the bombardment leaving fathers at home to risk their lives in the streets of the city and their sexual beings with the swarms of single girls, working as auxiliary soldiers, bus conductors, munitions workers, and the influx of young women from the provinces taking up their lives in the city as *vivandières* to the Americans. Thus the intrigues and quarrels began.

Down to this refugee camp came my mother.

Already convinced of her superiority to these slum-dwelling women, settled most comfortably in a stance towards life which perceived feuds and passions of the most violent sort as not only normal but as convenient ways of keeping the adrenalin flow regular, the phagocytes in the bloodstream active and hungry, she moved into the Yately milieu with the ease of a foot sinking into a well-oiled boot.

My father moved about these people like a good regimental sergeant major, here keeping good order and military discipline, there jollying along – *thank your mother for the rabbits – it's two o'clock and still no word from Nancy* – the fallen in spirits. He was, as I look back on it, impressive in his diplomacy. A young man from Battersea, who had brought his mistress to the camp and thus angered and made jealous the horny sex-starved youths who were more rightfully there, was taken to one side and a few quiet words were said. Later, after my father's death, this man sought out my mother and arrived, weeping, on the doorstep. He had lost not only a hero, but, as he put it, a 'saint'.

I did not perceive my father as a saint at that time or, indeed, later. But certainly his stature increased during that year and I saw him as a gigantic, powerful figure. In retrospect, it's likely that the stresses and balancing acts of this period brought closer the heart attack that was to kill him. It was difficult to believe that, since he died at forty-nine, I might not, and for many years afterwards I found his repressive presence at work in my life.

Over the bridge to Brighton! But I've got a tin chest!...

I see him quite clearly – bald, about the height I am now, craggy of face, choleric by a disposition that had to be, here in Yately, held in check. *What's it cost? Money and fair words!* I see him as a much younger man, before I knew him; brown-haired and good-looking, gay in manner and much sought after by women. A man who'd experienced excitement in the World War I he remembered with so much nostalgia – wounded and gassed, invalided out, he had worked his passage on a freighter to Australia and joined the Australian army. I see him as a child, Bertie Mills, wearing glasses and studious looking: and there's a school prize, a book, and in it the words of his headmaster 'the best boy this school ever had'.

Then I remembered with a searing clarity that his birth had been troubled: his mother's pelvis was narrow and he had to be brought into the world by forceps – he was extracted from the womb, so the story in our family went, thrown on one side with the doctor shouting, 'Save the mother! Save the mother!' but both survived. I saw that event, some thirty-five years before my own birth, as clearly as though I had been present and I felt the terror, the injustice, the violence of it as though I had been my father at the moment of his birth and I cried out in pain. Then, as the person sitting by my head moved towards me I recalled, again with the utmost vividness, that I too had been a forceps delivery and that this was what linked me to my father – ripped out of that secure, whole place into a fragmented world by a glittering, cold, metal instrument in style and general appearance like those that severed my mother and my own child – that what I had seen was the human being, quivering and vulnerable flesh, screaming out in pain, lacerated, marred, and sutured by machines, that this was my

German officer, tortured over a fire in the Balkans, and this was the picture I had drawn of the lamb, strapped to a tripod, whipped, beaten, and carved by mechanical Furies.

Departures

DEPARTURES ... YES ... one springtime, many years ago, a Monday after the war. I looked out to sea from the Floyen, the hill above Bergen in Norway, towards the purple, twilit islands at the mouth of the fiord. The journey I had made, across Sweden to the Norwegian ports to work on the herring fleet, had been both successful and a failure. The money I earned at sea on the small fishing boats that plied from Narvik, Svolvaer, and Aalesund had vanished on dry land. I thought that I was looking for, in my words of the time, 'a place where a man could be free and want nothing'. It hadn't happened, but the journey had been there to make and I was glad I'd made it.

Water trickled over rocks. I thought of my friend Sam Hartstein on the other side of the frontier, still working in the winter sports hotel and up to his eyes in waitresses. There was a thaw due in Jämptland, though ... I imagined that even now Sam was making plans.

Two young men, takers of the evening air, disembarked leisurely from the funicular railway. I had run down its track every morning at six o'clock to catch the first tram out to Langevick where I had a job in a steel factory. Two more days of it, only two more days and the last of the fare money would be in my pockets. Hit North Shields, draw some cash from the Assistance Board, hitch-hike to Chester where I was expected. I began making plans.

The first morning the army lay behind me I awoke with the sun brilliant in the panes of the lattice window ... there was the clip-clopping of a horse's hooves on the roadway and the scrape of wagon-wheels ... a hawk circled over the dark, newly ploughed earth.

And now this ... just before Jocelyn and I were due to sail back to

Canada we took a boat out onto the Serpentine, in Hyde Park. Both of us felt blissful – loving and at peace. The sky was utterly cloudless and the wind, our implacable enemy throughout the winter, had dropped and mellowed.

All shall be well, all manner of thing shall be well. That's Juliana of Norwich speaking. Depends on what you mean by 'well'. Well with Jerome, for instance. He'd been at McGill some years now, doing mathematics. Soon he would get his master's degree. I wasn't to know then, of course, but Jerome failed to get his Ph.D. Instead he succeeded in forging his transcripts and got hired as an instructor at some university in Illinois. Then he discovered that the pay scale was too meagre for his needs, so he worked at another university, ninety miles down the road, and functioned quite cheerfully at his moonlighting trade until discovered. He was fired from both institutions and disappeared into the construction industry and, since 1972, nobody has heard from him.

All shall be well ... all manner of thing with Jocelyn and me. I'd gone back to school, at the age of thirty-one, studied for four years then, contrary to Sybil's expectations, got a job. I'd been teaching for five months before this England journey. Finally I had discovered something I could do easily and something I enjoyed. O all shall be well, I thought. We'd rear children, animals, flower gardens.

All shall be well with Jocelyn. There was no reason at all for her to work any more – unless, of course, she wanted to. I have never wanted anybody associated with me to suffer in the Land of Jobs. She could go to school ... travel ... find another career. The world was opening up for her, too ...

All shall be well with England. Though it hadn't changed as much as I'd hoped, and the classes our parents belonged to were just as much characterized by fear, rage, and negativity as ever, the young people we met seemed admirably restless and energetic.

Nobody could've predicted the advent of Margaret Thatcher,

nor the Falkland Islands adventure, nor the Los Angelization of Southern Britain.

All shall be well with Canada. It was, in 1966, before the changes in Quebec and the *zollverein* with the U.S., the country of the future, a land where a man or woman could live freely and want nothing. A place of enterprise and youth.

I am writing the last words of 'Unicorn Evils' in my office at the University of Giessen in Germany where I am a visiting professor. I wrote the first of them when Jocelyn and I got back from England twenty-five years ago. My stint in Giessen is almost over and I am getting ready to move out. The future seems at least as problematic for me personally as it did in the past. And not just for me: outside my window a parade of students passes – they are carrying signs which read *No Blood for Oil*, and *Stop the War in the Gulf.* In the downtown area two lines of silent people carrying candles make a vigil along the Seltersweg. I would not have predicted any of this either.

But then, in the spring of 1965, the wind across the artificial lake in the middle of London blew warm against our cheeks, coming in from the sea and over the South Downs. The primroses bloomed on the banks and, above the budding trees, we could see the old, grey-white buildings of the city basking in the sun.

John Mills was born in London, England in 1930 to working-class parents. He spent the London years of his youth trying to avoid service in the British Army; eventually he ended up in Canada. After a job as a radar technician in a desolate northern station, he started hanging out with a group of Montreal bohemians that included Irving Layton. He floated through a series of odd jobs, finally marrying, earning his doctorate and taking a position as an English professor at the newly-opened Simon Fraser University. Mills has lived in Vancouver since 1965.

His essays have appeared in *Bad Trips*, *The Macmillan Anthology*, *Best Canadian Essays 1989*, and *The Georgia Straight*. He has published four novels, *The Land of Is*, *The October Men*, *Skevington's Daughter*, and *Runner in the Dark*.